DRUG FREE HEALING 11 : Medical Science Supporting Scriptures

SAFE WITH OUR LORD JESUS CHRIST, MY LOVING BROTHER

DRUG FREE HEALING 11 : Medical Science Supporting Scriptures

DRUG FREE HEALING 11 : Medical Science Supporting Scriptures

To
My sisters Wynta Williams Huggins, Bridget Williams, and Patricia Konan; my brothers Cyril Bobby Boynes, and Nestor Konan; my doctors, Jon E. Hemstreet, Orlando Rangel, Mike Stangherlin, and Stacy Walker; my partners, Messenger Cindy Rodriguez, and Georgia Alicia Shaunce-Ziegenbein; my best friend, Eberechi Anozie.15. Eberechi , the fourth of five siblings , was three years old when he heard from his parents while they were seated for dinner that I was a homeless man, very ill and dying . At once, Ebere refused to eat or let his siblings, and parents, Lovelyn and Onyema, settle down to their meals until his mother gave him the satisfaction by driving to pick me up from where I was a squatter to the family meals table where I was served a portion from the family meal.

PLEASE NOTE THIS

The purpose of this book is not to advocate a rejection of medications, but to draw attention to other means by which God heals our ailments, and to show how healing that occurs in a drug-free environment which once was limited to churches and faith healers is now becoming part of the medical establishment's treatment protocol. This book offers me an opportunity to look back on my recovery from a dying experience as an ailing homeless man so that I can now boldly proclaim from the highest heights new scientific data suggesting, "faith in God can prolong life." I have a wonderful physician myself in the person of Dr. Orlando Rangel, at 4160 N. Armenia Ave. Tampa, Florida. Even he recognizes my dependence on God Jehovah as my ultimate healer. Dr. Rangel is open to his patients freely exercising their "faith factor" as I do in my first line of defense against potential health crisis. For I firmly believe the scriptures hold the secret to good health and long life even as they assure us of our eternal salvation through faith in Christ Jesus.

In Ezekiel 47:12, the scripture tells us that : "There will grow all kinds of trees for food...and their leaves for healing." This does not mean Jehovah God is opposed to his children using medications, or consulting physicians about their ailments. In the Deuterocanonical Holy Bible , the book of Sirach states: "Honor physicians for their services, for the LORD created them; for their gift of healing comes from the Most High...The LORD created medicines...and the sensible will not despise." (Sirach 38:1-4)

DRUG FREE HEALING:

MEDICAL SCIENCE SUPPORTING SCRIPTURES

Messenger K. Hezekiah Scipio

DRUG FREE HEALING 11 : Medical Science Supporting Scriptures

Copyright © 2015 Messenger K.Hezekiah Scipio

BIBLICAL HEALTH CENTER INC NONPROFIT
501(c) 3 Tax Exempted Under Internal Revenue Code
**P.O.BOX 291964,
TEMPLE TERRACE, FL.33687**
Email: biblicalhealthcenter@gmail.com
www.biblicalhealthcenter.org

DRUG FREE HEALING 11 : Medical Science Supporting Scriptures

Table of Contents

Acknowledgment	11
My Doctor Writes	13
My Story	15
The Pain	21
Zig Zags	24
The Mind Of Jehovah	29
Why We Are Sick	31
Healing	33
Fasting and Prayer	41
Long Life and Salvation	63
Trees For Healing and Food	67
Chapter One: Beginning in Garden	73
Chapter Two; Fig, Good Fig, Bad Fig	76
Chapter Three: Cypress, symbolism and properties	79
Chapter Four: Olive, its symbolism, dietary benefits	90
Chapter Five: Grape	101
Chapter Six: Oak	113
Chapter Seven: Bread Flour: Products of Wheat	118
Chapter Eight: Lentils	127
Chapter Nine: Mandrakes	143
Chapter Ten: Sheaves of Grain	154
Chapter Eleven: Honey	165
Chapter Twelve: Balm	174

Chapter Thirteen: Resin – Boswelia	178
Chapter Fourteen: Myrrh	185
Chapter Fifteen: Pistachio	197
Chapter Sixteen: Almonds	208
Chapter Seventeen: Barley	216
Chapter Eighteen: Flax	229
Chapter Nineteen: Hyssops	239
Chapter Twenty: Palm Tree	247
Chapter Twenty- One: Coriander	267
Chapter Twenty-Two: Cucumber	275
Chapter Twenty-Three: Onion,	283
Chapter Twenty-Four: Leeks	288
Chapter Twenty-Five: Garlic	289
Chapter Twenty-Six: Cinnamon helps stop Type 2 Diabetes & recipes	297
Treating Loneliness Seven	307
Chapter Twenty-Eight : Believing	311
Chapter Twenty-Nine : Loving	314
Chapter Thirty : Hymn Singing	319
Chapter Thirty One : Scripture Studying	322
Chapter Thirty Two : Keep on Meditating	336
Chapter Thirty Three : Forgiving	345
Chapter Thirty Four :Connecting With Jehovah God	350
References	363
Index	367
Glossary	369

DRUG FREE HEALING 11 : Medical Science Supporting Scriptures

www.biblicalhealthcenter.org

www.biblicalmassage.com

www.godsplantthatheal.org

Email :   biblicalhealthcenter@gmail.com

THANKS FOR YOUR TAX DEDUCTIBLE DONATIONS

Please log on www.biblicalhealthcenter.org to order directly any copy of our books or products, and thank you for your generous tax deductible donation.

Biblical Health Center Inc. Nonprofit ,Christ-centered organization is tax exempted under 501 (c) 3 of the Internal Revenue Code. All donations of gifts, transfers, or bequests are tax deductible under sections 170, 2055, and 2106 of the Code.

Biblical Health Center is committed to proclaiming adherence to John 3:16, Matthew 22:36-40, Joshua 1: 8, Hebrews10:25, and Philippians 4:6-8 as key to the promise of Psalm 91:14-16, and as Divine formula for stress reduction and alleviation of loneliness.

Biblical Health Center Inc.
P.O. Box 291964
Tampa, Fl. 33687

Acknowledgment

I believe God is still at work assigning his angels to specific missions in the lives of each one of us. I do believe these angels come to us not as winged beings, the products of artistic expressions, appearing and disappearing at will, but as ordinary folks – men, women, and children to, with divine calling to minister to us for our good, and that by us, others too may enjoy the grace of God that comes through Christ Jesus.

I also believe that these angels in the guise of ordinary people may themselves often be unaware, and we too, to whom they are assigned may fail to recognize them at the time of their divine appointment, that they are emissaries of the Most High God under an unction to perform extraordinary acts. These acts may take the form of just a simple smile when it is most needed, a pat on the back, a prayer, sharing the scriptures, a word of encouragement or consolation, kindness offered, generosity accorded, friendship extended, or love given.

Sometimes we view these angels-in-disguise unfavorably because they may scold us, rebuke us, reproach us, or chastise us for our thoughtless actions. But they remain the same people who will eagerly help us, guide us, instructs us, counsel us, inspire us, feed us, or dress our physical, emotional and spiritual wounds. Whatever their gifting, their goal ultimately is to lift us up from the abyss of gloom and despair to the heights of hope to bask in the glowing rays of God's grace.

I thank God for the angels he has placed on my path. Each one's imprint on my life is a significant contribution to this book. I count among the many messengers God sent my way, my brother, Cyril Bobby Boynes who is now in union with our Lord Jesus Christ, incredible sisters and motivators , Wynta Huggins, Bridget William, Lovelyn Anozie , and Pastor Patricia Byrd Konan. My brothers Pastor Nestor Konan , and Pastor Onyema Anozie. My friend and daughter, Leander John Baptist, and my own insufferable cousin, Shine Attitsogbui.

I am deeply indebted to Dr. Jon Hemstreet, my primary care provider for being such a wonderful and caring personal physician to me, and my current primary care physician, Dr. Orlando Rangel, and his staff.

I thank God also for Mary Roberts, Students' Primary Advisor at Siena Heights University, College of Professional Studies, Adrian, Michigan, Professors Anthony Farina, Gail A. Ryder, James Sam , Laurie Kosek, Richard Deighton, and Dr. Parvindar Mehta.

I am also thankful for Tracy Jones of the National Certification Board for Therapeutic Massage and Bodywork., and my chiropractor friend, Dr. Mike Stangherlin. And finally, to my fellow class mates for their unstoppable encouragement, I am grateful to Georgia Alicia Shaunce-Ziegenbein, Michael Mull, Marisa Moore, Charneal Kitchen, and Kim Parks. These are all Jehovah God's Angels He sent my way to fulfill His own purpose. I will always be thankful.

My Doctor Writes

I remember well the first time I met Messenger K. Hezekiah Scipio-Akpabla. He had been discharged from the hospital and presented to my office very ill. His symptoms involved almost every system in his body. Because of his multi-organ involvement, his prognosis was quite poor although no definite diagnosis could be established in the hospital. Mr. Scipio and I discussed the next treatment steps we should take including additional testing, medications, and specialist consultation. Despite these further evaluations and more testing, his diagnosis remained elusive, and his condition did not improve. Mr. Scipio stated on one follow-up visit that he wanted to be withdrawn from some of his medications and that he would pursue natural healing methods. Initially, I was not in favor of this approach, but eventually we agreed to keep him only on essential medications and monitor his progress with natural remedies. Remarkably, with time, Mr.

Scipio's condition improved to the point where his vital signs and laboratory values returned to normal.

I was honored and surprised when Messenger K. Hezekiah Scipio-Akpabla asked me to write the foreword to his book. I am trained in western allopathic medicine and do not have expertise in natural remedies. In fact, I am sometimes skeptical of these treatments and was not enthusiastic, in the case of Mr. Scipio, to exchange his western medicine for natural ones. But his improvement has been a wonderful lesson for me in the power of natural substances to heal. Mr. Scipio has taught me other valuable lessons as well, and his book is more than a natural remedy primer. In its pages, you will meet a man with powerful faith; his faith was not shaken. I also learned from Mr. Scipio-Akpabla the power of positive thinking. No matter how badly he felt, he always had a wonderful attitude and a kind word for me. I was always humbled by his kindness in the face of physical pain and suffering. In conclusion, this book offers lessons in natural remedies. But in the person of Messenger K Hezekiah Scipio-Akpabla we have a teacher for our Spirits. I am very lucky to have had the opportunity to learn from such a person. I encourage you to learn from his knowledge of healing herbs, but also from the example of faith and kindness traits so rare and needed in our troubled times. **Jon E. Hemstreet, MD,** Tampa General Hospital, 34th Street Family Center, Tampa, Florida. October 2007

DRUG FREE HEALING 11 : Medical Science Supporting Scriptures

My Story

Healing by faith in Jehovah God through his Son Jesus Christ, once activity confined to churches and "faith healers," is becoming part of the medical establishment's prescription for illnesses. According to Harvard professor of health and spirituality, Anne Harrington, and researcher for the National Center for Complementary and Integrative Health, "increasing public interest in the effect of spirituality on health, has spurred 70 of America's 125 leading medical schools to open research centers where medical students also study spirituality's health connections" Scipio, Messenger , K Hezekiah, 2015, New Scientific Data Suggest Faith In God Can Prolong Life, p. 27)..

Scientists found that , the Faith Factor can:

> Break the anxiety cycle and relieve the anxiety-related symptoms of nausea, vomiting, diarrhea, constipation, and short-temperedness.
> Combat attacks of hyperventilation.
> Alleviate the pains of headache, backache, and other pains, such as angina pectoris.
> Effectively treat many types of hypertension and heartbeat irregularities.

Alleviate insomnia.
Be utilized in the treatment of cancer
Prevent the harmful effect of stress
(Herbert Benson, M.D ,1983,Beyond The Relaxation Response, p.121)

The knowledge that one's "faith factor" can actually be a person's healing factor became evident to me experientially after every medical treatment failed to make a positive impact on my declining health, and my prognosis was becoming extremely poor. That was from 15 years down to 8 years ago, I am still alive by the will of God, and looking forward to celebrating my 120th birthday in just 44 years . Pew Research has suggested that by 2050, Americans will live to 120 years. This is not news because the last time I checked for Yahweh Almighty God's term limit for humankind's life expectancy, it has not changed since Genesis 6:3 "Then the Jehovah God said, 'I will not allow people to live forever; they are mortal. From now on, they will live no longer than 120 years.

I began this book 12 years ago and published the first part in 2007 under the title, "God's Amazing Bible Plants Healed Me." I had moved from New York City to Tampa, Florida seriously ill, and the medicines that my doctors had prescribed were not working. I had no family. I had no employment, and I was homeless. So all I could do was to have a conversation with

Yahweh Almighty God through his Son Yeshua. I asked for his wisdom that I might discern the plants in the bible that according to Ezekiel 47:12 are "for food …and healing." I asked him to show me by the power of his Holy Spirit, the plants to use, and to reveal how I would use the plants for my healing.

I prayed that, if the purposes for my recovery were to fulfill his own Jehovah's own design, then on my recovery, I would also go on and proclaim the knowledge he imparted and the gospel of Christ Jesus. I was not bargaining with God; instead, I just wanted to place myself at his will and say that if he wanted me to be with Jesus Yeshua, I was ready.

On my recovery, Jehovah God gave me a job to do as a security guard; I was assigned to Everest University campus on Hillsborough Avenue, which was less than six blocks away from Tampa campus of Moody Bible Institute where I was also a student.

One day in the summer of 2008, while students at Everest University, were holding a "cook out " party under the trees by the parking lot where I was posted to watch the cars that were parked, I was encountering an extraordinary experience. In 2008 Obamacare was not in effect, and many poor and middle class people could not afford the high cost of health care. So while the students were playing music, and eating, and enjoying themselves under the trees, I was hearing a different kind of music; I was hearing gospel music - of praises and worship. I saw all sorts of healthcare professionals going in and out of cubicles attending to the sick free of charge. I saw and heard a preacher preaching the gospel of Christ Jesus. I saw a combination of a Pentecostal Revival meeting and a health fair.

I thought it was a sign of my calling to go to Health Ministry in order to become God's instrument of compassion and love to the needy and uninsured. Our Lord Yeshua Jesus commanded his followers, according to Mark 16:15-18, to go , "preach, teach the gospel...and lay hands on the sick, and they shall recover". I concluded , that because I was 70 years of age , I did not have enough time on my side to go and study to become a doctor; the closest for me to being a doctor and be able to lay hands on the sick for them to recover, was to be massage therapist. I resolved to go to college and study Massage Therapy.

I was very disappointed, however, that during my studies most of the subjects of studies concentrated on massage techniques and modalities rooted in Eastern religious principles. And since idolatry and syncretism are anathema to biblical Christianity, I set out to investigate whether the Judeo-Christian establishment before or during the time of Jesus practiced any healing technique that could be identified with massage therapy, and whether I could find any evidence that massage and aromatherapy as components of biblical holistic healing.

I published my findings in a book, Biblical Massage and Holy Spirit Touch, in 2010, while I was in the middle of my final graduating and board certification examination. I had vowed that on graduation, I would open my own clinic where the ambiance would reflect a place of worship, and therapy would combine the gospel message, prayers, gospel songs of praises and worship, with biblical meditation and biblical massage. I would name the therapy, "Biblical Massage" in order to give God all the glory.

Following my graduation, and Board Certification in Therapeutic Massage and Bodywork, I took in addition to my day time professional work, a night time job at the campus of the University of South Florida, as a foot patrol to raise the capital for my clinic. I opened a nonprofit clinic, Biblical Health Center Inc. ., on August 31 2013. It was a clinic where I played cds of gospel messages interchanged with gospel music and hymns of praises and worship, while the client received massage therapy that started with prayer.

The Florida State Department of Health official, who inspected the Clinic to determine my Establishment License eligibility, was very impressed. She remarked, "This is a first!" She suggested I offered an apprenticeship program as well and followed through by sending me an email containing guidelines for offering apprenticeship.

On February 23, 2014, however, I received a letter from the owner of the building housing my clinic stating that the building was sold to Dollar General Store, and that I had to vacate before March 3, 2014 .

I was so devastated and disenchanted I thought I had fooled myself into thinking God had called me to his ministry of mercy and compassion. The motivations I had had before instantly disappeared. I was beginning to age rapidly at 74 years, and for the first time, I qualified my age with an adjective – old. I felt as if God had finished with me. I was ready to die because if God did not call me to his ministry, then I had no more purpose to life. I would live every day as my last. I gave away almost everything I had. I gave away my bed. I slept on $20.00 airbed so it would be easy on those clearing the apartment when I died. Then on June 23, I had a telephone call from Siena Heights University Primary Academic Advisor, Mary Roberts informing me Siena Heights University at Adrian, Michigan, was granting me an admission to pursue a degree in Applied Science in Healthcare, and that the decision followed a degree transfer arrangement with the National Certification Board of Therapeutic Massage and Bodywork..

Oh, That Pain!

I came to Tampa from New York 15 years ago to die, but Jehovah God said, "No, not yet, " when the medical thinking was that I would not survive. I was so sick that my doctors expected me to die. When I arrived in the City of Tampa, I did not know anyone there , and I remained unemployed because the ailment would not allow me to work , and without work, I had no money; without any money in reserve to pay my rent, I became homeless.

I went in and out of hospitals and clinics many more times, than I had ever been during the rest of my entire life. . On one such visit, my forever reassuring primary care physician, Dr. Jon E. Hemstreet at Tampa General Hospital had this to say to me:, "You seem to have a mysterious problem…And a case of anemia too…We'll have to investigate where you're losing blood from…and determine the prognosis."

To say "a mysterious problem" was an understatement. They were mysterious problems.

Plural. Period. I was under a barrage of illnesses of unknown origin. The diagnoses included atrial fibrillation, mucus laryngitis, dyspnea - shortness of breath – sleep apnea , joint pain, neck pain, wrist pain, pain in my left shoulder, pain in my left and right sides.

I could not lie on my left or on my right side without feeling excruciating pain. I hurt so badly. My cholesterol level was high. My blood pressure poll vaulted. I am left handed. I could not move up my left arm to an angle forty-five degrees from my side, let alone, lift it over my head without feeling overwhelming burning pain.

Sometimes, my left arm felt as though it was going to fall off from its socket. It took me fifteen to twenty minutes to walk one short block. At bedtime, I could not sleep through the night. I sat up in the seat more often than not out of fear of choking should I lie down. If I lay down, my body hurt. If I lay on my backside and somehow sank off into sleep, I choked. My esophagus, felt as if there was a loose skin tissue present which flapped determinedly aiming at blocking my airway. My heart would then react; it would pound repeatedly like the thudding of a thousand racing feet. I would cough incessantly. In the daytime, I felt drowsy all day long. If I went to the library, I was ready to sleep in no time. If I was riding on a bus, I felt so drowsy I could drop asleep within five minutes of a thirty-minute ride.

DRUG FREE HEALING 11 : Medical Science Supporting Scriptures

In church, I struggled to stay awake. My blood pressure systolic/diastolic levels zoomed to 195/110mm Hg. My blood test results said I had an "abnormal serum protein." I did not know what it meant then. I do not know what it means now. I don't want to know. If the serum didn't contain red or white blood cells as serums do, and it wasn't going to clot as it should do too, I did not want to bother to find out what it wasn't doing that it was supposed to do. I had blood tests quite very often. I even had tests to check for HIV, HPV, and diabetes among the many laboratory tests. All came back negative. I had fasting and non-fasting blood tests almost every six weeks. I had whatever tests in health care parlance that ends in "ogram" or "oscopy." I had all of them, or many of them!

I ate very little. I suffered a chronic loss of appetite. I slept on two occasions at Tampa General Hospital for a Sleep Study, and was diagnosed with sleep apnea. Once, I fainted from hunger, sheer exhaustion and dehydration. You might say all those conditions came with the territory of aging, and to "Get a life, Old man!" I beg to disagree because Almighty God is still on his throne. Jesus our Lord is still alive, and because He lives, I have no fear for tomorrow. I am singing, rejoicing in the Lord! I'm singing psalms of praises. In fact, I'm singing Psalm 103 all the way:

"Bless the Lord, O my soul, and all that is within me bless his holy name.

Bless the Lord, O my soul, and do not forget all his benefits—
who forgives all your iniquity, who heals all your diseases,
who redeems your life from the Pit,
who crowns you with steadfast love and mercy,
who satisfies you with good as long as you live,
so that your youth is renewed like the eagles…"

Zigs and Zags

If you had told me to get a life a year before, I would not be offended because I had thought the same excessively, but it lasted only for the duration I had ignored the Holy Bible, and let its open pages remain on my desk unread day after day. I had thought so too during the length of time I made no time for prayers, and deluded myself into thinking prayers rather than saying prayers. I had thought exactly that way when I was continuously full of myself, and was not humble enough to go before my Lord Jesus , ask him to save me from my sins, and reveal the Father , Jehovah Almighty God's plans for my life.

When we are in the throes of despair and hopelessness, we tend to grasp on any loose straw for rescue. We listen to any loose lip for advice instead of seek wisdom from above. It was Dr. Chip Ingram, pastor of "Living On The Edge Radio Ministry" based in Atlanta, Georgia, who said: "Geometrically, the shortest distance from point to point is a straight line, but in God's economy, it may be a zigzag. "

My life of sickness in the last several years was full of zigs and zags! Sometimes, it did not seem the medicines were any good for me. At other times, the prescription painkillers did a great job. However, over a time, where a 50-milligrams' daily dosage was considered sufficient for me, the enemy of pain became resistant, and called for an increased dosage. Only if I knew Jehovah God had his own super painkillers in bible plants, and they are without side effect!

Flexeril, a muscle relaxant known by the generic name of "Cyclobenzaprine", was a powerful response to my pain. I was able then to sleep through the night on taking it. However, I also felt drowsy in the daytime. I dozed off even if I did nothing at all but stood up and stared. I was all day in lala land once I came under the drug's influence. Ultram, which goes by the generic name of Tramadol, was to me a terrific weapon against my chronic pain. I thought Tramadol was the mother of all euphoria inducing drugs. It took away my pain, at least, temporarily.

For the first ten days that I took the medication, the pain appeared to subside -- driven to the ropes until its effects wore off. But it came back doing Muhammed Ali's "rope-a-dope" hits with my nervous system: lunging counter attacks with vicious ferocity.

While on Tramadol, I developed symptoms of anxiety, irritability, itching, headache, lightheartedness, to list just a few. The problem with painkillers is that you do not know which might be at war against another medication. Better stay away from pain killers.

Some painkillers and cardiovascular drugs are mortal enemies. Remember, I was diagnosed with atrial fibrillation. It is enough to say atrial fibrillation is some type of a heart defect causing excessive pressure on the left aortic valve as the blood flow forces its way through my narrowing atrial passageway. This condition put me at risk of unpleasant consequences if it remained untreated.

Check with your healthcare official for details if you experience similar symptoms. I do not want to scare you. I do not think there is anybody deliberately raising a scare either.

If you were in my place, and were taking medications such as Zocor, Triglide, and Gemfibrozil, you would be bothered by media reports claiming that some painkillers increase the risk of stroke or heart attack for users. If the source of such claims was the FDA (Food and Drug Administration), the Agency that regulates drugs use in the US you should believe, and flee from pain killers.

Knowing what I knew about the increased risk of mixing some types of painkillers with cardiovascular

DRUG FREE HEALING 11 : Medical Science Supporting Scriptures

or hypertensive drugs, I was in no mood of taking any more medications without first asking Almighty God Jehovah what he thought about my taking any more drugs. By the way, if you have not yet accepted Jesus Christ as your personal Savior, be advised to read the bible. Believe in the Lord Jesus Christ, and Jehovah God the Father will forgive your sins. That is God's irrevocable promise! If you have a bible with you, open John chapter 3 verses 16, 17 and 18. Here is the Word of God: "For God so loved the world that he gave his only Son, so that everyone who believes in him may not perish but may have eternal life…Indeed, God did not send the Son into the world to condemn the world, but in order that the world might be saved through him. Those who believe in him are not condemned; but those who do not believe are condemned already, because they have not believed in the name of the only Son of God…"

No matter how sinful we are, or what ignoble crimes either you or I have committed in the past, let us now come boldly to Jesus. He tells us to "go and sin no more". Accept him as your personal Savior. He will forgive your sins as he has forgiven mine. With the forgiveness of our sins, comes our spiritual healing.

If anyone tries to discourage you from going to the Lord, please listen to my story while I identify with the blind man that Jesus cured who went out ignoring threats of censorship by powerful interests, and proclaimed what Jesus did for him: "One thing I know, that, whereas I was blind, now I see." (John 9:1-7, 25) He told the opposition. I too do not know how my healing came about. One thing I know, however; whereas I was deadly ill, and dead in my sins, now I am healed. I am healed in body and spirit.

The Mind of Jehovah God

While we are seeking Almighty God's mind about our ailments, and his prescription for them, for, ultimately, Jehovah God is our Healer, we must all know that until Jesus comes again, we will all die eventually. We will all die because we exchanged perfection for imperfection, immortality for mortality, goodness for evil. The scriptures tell us that in the beginning when Almighty God created heaven and earth, and humankind, He made all things good. We were made perfect, and were to enjoy eternal life here on earth, but our ancestors Adam and Eve accepted the lies of Satan, the Deceiver, and disobeyed God Almighty to let sin enter us. Genesis chapters 1, 2 and 3 tell the full story. With sin, we opened also into our lives the floodgates for death, sickness and disease, envy, slander, God-hating, gossiping, haughtiness, boastfulness, craftiness, corruption, faithlessness, ruthlessness, covetousness, wickedness.

The scripture says; we have "...exchanged the truth about God for a lie, and worshipped and served the creature rather than the Creator, who is blessed forever. Amen. Women exchanged natural intercourse for unnatural, and in the same way also, men, giving up natural intercourse with women, were consumed with passion for one another...And since they did not see fit to acknowledge God, God gave them up to a debased mind and to the things that should not be done...They know God's decree, that those who practice such things deserve to die..." (Romans chapter 1 verses 18-32)

We would have lived forever but for our sin through Adam and Eve, our fore parents. However, in spite of our fall, Jehovah Almighty God mercifully made a way for our salvation through the sacrificial death of His Son our Lord Jesus Christ.

Knowing we are mortals with corruptible bodies prone to sickness and diseases, Almighty God also made available for us many means of respite. God Almighty chose different ways to prolong our lives, for the healing of our infirmities to end suffering, none of which is superior to the other.

DRUG FREE HEALING 11 : Medical Science Supporting Scriptures

Why We Are Sick

Prayer – not just any prayer, but the prayer of faith, trusting God and being submissive to his absolute will – is an essential component of what we must do to be healed. We learn this in James 5: 13-15: "Is any among you suffering? They should pray…Are any among you sick? They should call for the elders of the church and have them pray over them, anointing them with oil in the name of the Lord. The prayer of faith will save the sick, and the Lord will raise them up; and anyone who has committed sins will be forgiven."

Some illnesses lead to death. Some do not lead to death. Rather, they happen "for God's glory, so that the Son of God may be glorified." (John 9: 3, & 11:4) Some sicknesses come on us because of bad choices, or decisions we made in the past. Some we suffer because we put on false pretenses and appearances. Outwardly, we show off our religious fervor by our consistent church attendances, paying our tithes regularly, giving cheerfully. We are ceaselessly marking the bible at every noteworthy verse, talking Christianese, and acting as if we were the holiest among the hollies. Yet secretly, we indulge in ignominious sins, which we find ourselves too proud to confess. We become sick because of the games we play in our relationships with the Lord. The bible warns:

"Whoever…eats of the bread or drinks the cup of the Lord in an unworthy manner will be answerable for the body and blood of the Lord. Examine yourselves, and only then eat of the bread and drink of the cup. For all who eat and drink without discerning the body, eat and drink judgment against themselves. For this reason many of you are weak and ill, and some have died…" (1 Cor.11:27-32)

DRUG FREE HEALING 11 : Medical Science Supporting Scriptures

Healing

The bible urges us to confess our "sins to one another,"(James 5:16) so that we may be healed. "The prayer of the righteous is powerful and effective." (James 5:16) Examples of such effectual fervent prayers are evidenced in Elijah's restoration from death of the son of the widow of Zarepath as told in 1 Kings Chapter 17 from verse 1 to 23. This is what the scripture says: (Elijah) " cried out to the LORD, "O Lord my God, have you brought calamity even upon the widow with whom I am staying, by killing her son?" Then he stretched himself upon the child three times, and cried out to the LORD, "O LORD my God let this child's life come into him again." The LORD listened to the voice of Elijah; the life of the child came into him again, and he revived."

Here is another example narrated by Dr. Luke in Acts 20 reading from verse 7 "...On the first day of the week, when we met to break bread, Paul was holding a discussion with them; since he intended to leave the next day, he continued speaking until midnight. There were many lamps in the room upstairs where we were meeting. A young man named Eutychus, who was sitting in on the window, began to sink off into a deep sleep while Paul talked still longer. Overcome by sleep, he fell to the ground three floors below and was picked up dead. But Paul went down, and bending over him took him in his arms, and said, "Do not be alarmed, for his life is in him…Meanwhile they had taken the boy away alive and were not a little comforted"

Sometimes, we are healed when we cry out to God. He hears our prayers, and answers our prayers in accordance with His will. When He hears us, it is not because "we named and claimed," but because He is doing what He has said He would do. "Almighty God himself has commanded us in Jeremiah 33:3; "…Call to me and I will answer you, and I will tell you great and hidden things that you have not known." He also said; "I know the plans I have for you…plans for welfare and not for evil, to give you a future and hope. Then you will call upon me and come pray to me, and I will hear you" (Jer. 29: 11-12)

Sometimes, we fall sick not because of anything evil and sinful we may have done, but because the result will be to the glory of God. Our Lord Jesus Christ said of Lazarus' sickness;

"This illness does not lead to death; rather it is for God's glory, so that the Son of God may be glorified through it." The Gospel of John chapter 11 reports this, as we read from verse 17.

" When Jesus arrived, he found that Lazarus had already been in the tomb for four days. Now Bethany was near Jerusalem, only about two miles away. And many of the Jews had come to Martha and Mary to comfort them about their brother. When Martha heard that Jesus was coming, she went to meet him; but Mary sat at home. Martha said to Jesus,"Lord, if you had been here, my brother would not have died. (But) even now I know that whatever you ask of God, God will give you."

Jesus said to her, "Your brother will rise." Martha said to him, "I know he will rise, in the resurrection on the last day." Jesus told her, "I am the resurrection and the life; whoever believes in me, even if he dies, will live, and everyone who lives and believes in me will never die. Do you believe this?"

She said to him, "Yes, Lord. I have come to believe that you are the Messiah, the Son of God, the one who is coming into the world." When she had said this, she went and called her sister Mary secretly, saying, "The teacher is here and is asking for you."

As soon as she heard this, she rose quickly and went to him. For Jesus had not yet come into the village, but was still where Martha had met him. So when the Jews who were with her in the house comforting her saw Mary get up quickly and go out, they followed her, presuming that she was going to the tomb to weep there. When Mary came to where Jesus was and saw him, she fell at his feet and said to him,"Lord, if you had been here, my brother would not have died." When Jesus saw her weeping and the Jews who had come with her weeping, he became perturbed and deeply troubled, and said, "Where have you laid him?" They said to him, "Sir, come and see." And Jesus wept.

So the Jews said, "See how he loved him." But some of them said, "Could not the one who opened the eyes of the blind man have done something so that this man would not have died?" So Jesus, perturbed again, came to the tomb. It was a cave, and a stone lay across it. Jesus said,"Take away the stone." Martha, the dead man's sister, said to him, "Lord, by now there will be a stench; he has been dead for four days." Jesus said to her, "Did I not tell you that if you believe you will see the glory of God?" So they took away the stone. And Jesus raised his eyes and said, "Father, I thank you for hearing me. I know that you always hear me; but because of the crowd here I have said this, that they may believe that you sent me." And when he had said this, he cried out in a loud voice, "Lazarus, come out!" The dead man came out, tied hand and foot with burial bands, and his face was wrapped in a cloth. So Jesus said to them, "Untie him and let him go."

Lazarus had been dead four days, and dead men cannot practice their faith; they are capable of naming nothing, and claiming nothing. It was only by the grace of God through our Lord Jesus Christ was Lazarus healed. We are all like Lazarus, dead in sin. Some illnesses are spiritual. They are caused by demonic influences, or by our own spiritual blindness. Jesus told his disciples;" This kind can come out only through prayer and fasting."

In Mark chapter 9, beginning from verse 17 to 29, we read: "Someone from the crowd answered him, "Teacher, I brought you my son; he has a spirit that makes him unable to speak, and whenever it seizes him, it dashes him down; and he foams and grinds his teeth and becomes rigid; and I asked your disciples to cast it out, but they could not do so…Jesus asked the father, "how long has this been happening to him? And he said "From childhood. It has often cast him into fire and into the water, to destroy him; but if you are able to do anything, have pity on us and help us. Jesus said to him, "If you are able! – All things can be done for the one who believes. Immediately, the father of the child cried out, "I believe, help my unbelief!"

When Jesus saw that a crowd came running together, He rebuked the unclean spirit, saying to it,

DRUG FREE HEALING 11 : Medical Science Supporting Scriptures

"You spirit that keeps this body from speaking and hearing, I command you, come out of him, and never enter him again! After crying out and convulsing him terribly, it came out, and the boy was like a corpse, so that most of them said, "He is dead." But Jesus took him by the hand and lifted him up, and he was able to stand. When He had entered the house, His disciples asked him privately:

"Why could we not cast it out? He said to them, "This kind can come out only through prayer and fasting."

God demands our total submission to His absolute will. He demands that we trust implicitly His divine ability to do the impossible in our lives, "Did I not tell you that if you believed, you would see the glory of God?" Just as our Lord told Martha prior to His bringing back to life her brother, Lazarus, the same requirement was evident in the narrative concerning the restoration to life of Jairus' dead 12-year-old daughter.

Mark 5 verses 35 to 42 state: "…While He was still speaking, some people came from the leader's house to say, "Your daughter is dead. Why trouble the teacher any further? But overhearing what they said, Jesus said to the leader of the synagogue "Do not fear only believe. He allowed no one to follow Him except Peter, James and John, the brother of James. When they came to the house of the leader of the synagogue, He saw a commotion, people weeping and wailing loudly. When

He had entered, He said to them, "Why do you make a commotion and weep? The child is not dead but sleeping". And they laughed at Him. Then He put them all outside, and took the child's father and those who were with him, and went in where the child was. He took her by the hand and said to her, "Talitha cum," which means "Little girl, get up!" And immediately the girl got up and begun to walk about.

Trust Jehovah God Completely

When we are seeking healing, we must flush from our system and our minds anything or anyone whose presence will cause us to waver in our faith in the LORD, or impede our relationship with Almighty God Jehovah and His Son our Savior and Lord Jesus Christ. Some of such negative advices forbid any other form of healing except healing by faith. Others discourage the use of conventional medicine, while crediting herbal medicine alone as being the panacea for all ills. Do not do such a thing as follow such fallacies. Avoid such false teachings. Whether we are healed through conventional medical procedures, herbal healing, spiritual healing, they are all God-given. Some may work better than others because Almighty God ordained them that way. Sometimes we may find that a combination of all healing methods: conventional, herbal, dietary, physical exercises, fasting and prayers are the necessary ingredients for restoring our health. Never forget that Almighty God who bore all our diseases, and by whose stripes we are healed, the God who healed the sick by his word and by the power of his touch, the same God "is able to do exceeding abundantly above all that we ask or think, according to the power that works in us. "(Eph 3:20)

It was by His divine choice that our Lord Jesus Christ used a mixture of His saliva and mud as a salve to open the eyes of the blind. John 9:6 tells us this: "He spat on the ground and made mud with the saliva and spread the mud on the man's eyes, saying to him "Go wash in the pool of Siloam…Then he went and washed and came back able to see."

FASTING and PRAYERS

A Seminarian, a farmer, and a cab driver embarked upon fasting to achieve some predetermined personal goals. The Seminarian fasted forty days and forty nights without food and water to pass an impending graduation examination while paying little attention to the scriptural advice, "Study to show yourself approved" (2 Timothy 2:15) The farmer fasted twenty one days during the planting season, and never planted a seed. But the scripture warns, "He who does not work neither shall he eat " (1 Thessalonians 3:10). The cab driver fasted seven days, and went on a long journey with no gas in his car totally in violation of the command, " You must not put the LORD your GOD to the test"(Luke 4:12).

God says, "My people are destroyed for lack of knowledge" (Hosea 4:6). Let us learn not to fast out of presumptuousness.

MARK 9: 23-29

Jesus said unto him, "If thou canst believe, all things are possible to him that believeth. And straightway the father of the child cried out, and said with tears, LORD, I believe, help thou mine unbelief. When Jesus saw that the people came running together, he rebuked the foul spirit, saying unto him "Thou dumb and deaf spirit, I charge thee, come out of him, and enter no more unto him… And the spirit cried and rent him sore, and came out of him, and he was as one dead. But Jesus took him by the hand, and lifted him up; and he arose. And when he was come into the house, his disciples asked him privately,.."Why could not we cast him out?" And he said unto them, "This kind can come forth by nothing, but prayer and fasting."

MATTHEW 6:17-18 KJV

When you fast, anoint your head and wash your face, that you appear not to men to fast, but in secret to your Father. Your Father, Who sees (you) in secret shall reward you openly.

Matthew 17:1-21, Luke 9.28-36 and Mark 9:2-29 told this: Our LORD JESUS while here on earth with HIS disciples took Peter along with the two sons of

Zebedee, James and John atop a high mountain where HE rendezvous with Moses and Elijah. While Jesus was talking, "...a shining cloud came over them, and a voice from the cloud said, "This is my own dear Son, with whom I am pleased – listen to Him!" (Verse 5) When they returned to join the rest of the disciples down the mountain, they were surrounded by a great crowd.

"...A man came to Jesus, knelt before Him, and said, "Sir, have mercy on my son! He is an epileptic and has such terrible attacks that he often falls in the fire or water. I brought him to your disciples, but they could not heal him."

Our LORD called out the demon from the boy, and he was healed at that very moment. His baffled disciples later, asked Jesus how come they were unable to heal him. Jesus told them.

Because of your unbelief: for verily I say unto you, if ye have faith as a grain of mustard seed, you shall say unto this mountain, remove hence, to yonder place; and it shall remove, and nothing shall be impossible unto you. Howbeit, this kind goeth not out, but by prayer and fasting.'"(Matt 17:1-21KJV) Translation. When you trust the power of God to do all things, even if the size of your faith is as the size of a grain of mustard seed, with God all things are possible, and because of that faith, you can even do the impossible as saying to a mountain to move out of here to another place. Even so, however, there are issues such as this type that can be addressed only by prayer and fasting.

WHAT IS FASTING?

What is fasting? Fasting is not self-flagellation by means of voluntary starvation as a tool to force the hand of GOD to do our will, or a means to "attain a higher level of consciousness." Fasting is not involuntary hunger caused by total deprivation and want. Fasting is a determined effort to mortify the flesh in order to heighten spiritual sensitivity. Man, the bible says in Genesis 2:7 was made out of the dust of the earth, and GOD breathed in him the breath of life. And he became a living soul. On salvation he has the indwelling of the Holy Spirit; in his or her regenerated new birth, he becomes Spirit, soul, and body.

Dr Adrian Rogers explains it in a way only he does so cogently. "Have you counted the cost if your soul should be lost? Did you know that when God made you, God breathed into your nostrils what the Bible calls, "the breath of life?" And you became, in the words of the Bible, "a living soul, made in the image of God."

You are not a body; you have a body. The body is the house in which your soul is. The body will one day die. It will be put in the ground and it will decay. But your soul, made in the image of God will last for eternity. When the sun, the moon, the stars have fallen out of orbit, when the sun has become a cinder, when time shall be no more, your soul will be in existence somewhere, either in heaven or hell--timeless, dateless, measureless; your soul, made in the image of God will exist forever and ever and ever and ever. That's why the Lord Jesus Christ asked this question in the word of God. (Mark 8:36) What does a person gain if he wins the whole world and loses his life?

Fasting purposefully means being in prayer along with constant study of the word of GOD. Joshua expresses it succinctly when he echoed GOD'S command to the people of GOD in Joshua 1:8,

"This book of the law shall not depart out of thy mouth; but thou shalt meditate therein day and night, that thou mayest observe to do according to all that is written therein: for then thou shalt make thy way prosperous, and then thou shalt have good success."

FASTING GUIDELINES BY JEHOVAH GOD

GOD has established guidelines for fasting. We complain about our prayers not being answered although we have fasted and prayed without ceasing because we fail to follow those guidelines. This is what GOD said about "True Fasting". Open Isaiah 58: 1-12.

Let us hear the word from GOD.
Isaiah 58 (New International Version)

True Fasting

1 "Shout it aloud, do not hold back.
Raise your voice like a trumpet.
Declare to my people their rebellion
and to the house of Jacob their sins.
2 For day after day they seek me out;
they seem eager to know my ways,
as if they were a nation that does what is right
and has not forsaken the commands of its God.
They ask me for just decisions
and seem eager for God to come near them.
3 'Why have we fasted,' they say,
'and you have not seen it?
Why have we humbled ourselves,
and you have not noticed?'
"Yet on the day of your fasting, you do as you please
and exploit all your workers.
4 Your fasting ends in quarreling and strife,
and in striking each other with wicked fists.
You cannot fast as you do today
and expect your voice to be heard on high.
5 Is this the kind of fast I have chosen,
only a day for a man to humble himself?
Is it only for bowing one's head like a reed
and for lying on sackcloth and ashes?
Is that what you call a fast,
a day acceptable to the LORD ?
6 "Is not this the kind of fasting I have chosen:

to loose the chains of injustice
and untie the cords of the yoke,
to set the oppressed free
and break every yoke?
7 Is it not to share your food with the hungry
and to provide the poor wanderer with shelter—
when you see the naked, to clothe him,
and not to turn away from your own flesh and blood?
8 Then your light will break forth like the dawn,
and your healing will quickly appear;
then your righteousness will go before you,
and the glory of the LORD will be your rear guard.
9 Then you will call, and the LORD will answer;
you will cry for help, and he will say: Here am I.
"If you do away with the yoke of oppression,
with the pointing finger and malicious talk,
10 and if you spend yourselves in behalf of the hungry
and satisfy the needs of the oppressed,
then your light will rise in the darkness,
and your night will become like the noonday.
11 The LORD will guide you always;
he will satisfy your needs in a sun-scorched land
and will strengthen your frame.
You will be like a well-watered garden,
like a spring whose waters never fail.
12 Your people will rebuild the ancient ruins
and will raise up the age-old foundations;
you will be called Repairer of Broken Walls,

Restorer of Streets with Dwellings.
13 "If you keep your feet from breaking the Sabbath
and from doing as you please on my holy day,
if you call the Sabbath a delight
and the LORD's holy day honorable,
and if you honor it by not going your own way
and not doing as you please or speaking idle words,
14 then you will find your joy in the LORD,
and I will cause you to ride on the heights of the land
and to feast on the inheritance of your father Jacob."
The mouth of the LORD has spoken.

    God has a conditional guideline for fasting. He tells us, "If you do this, then you will find your joy...and I will cause you to ride on the heights of the land..."

    Fasting, meditation and prayers accompanied by reading and studying the scriptures increase the sensitivity of the human Spirit to become responsive to the promptings of the Holy Spirit. Let the Spirit direct your lives, and you will not satisfy the desires of the human nature. For what our human nature wants is opposed to what the Spirit wants, and what the Spirit wants is opposed to what our human nature wants. These two are enemies...(Galatians 5:16-19)

"To be controlled by the human nature results in death; to be controlled by the Spirit results in life and peace." (Romans 8:6)

EXEMPLARS OF FASTING

Moses fasted 40 days and 40 nights without eating nor drinking water.(Exodus 34:28)

PURPOSE: To intercede for the nation of Israel for the sin of the people.

"...For I was afraid of the anger and hot displeasure with which the Lord was angry with you, to destroy you. But the Lord listened to me at that time also."

David fasted 7 days. 2nd SAMUEL 12:16-18

PURPOSE: Fasting as an act of contrition and repentance for one's sin. David fasted to plead GOD'S forgiveness of his sins of covetousness and murder, and to intercede for his ailing child born to him by the wife of his general, Uriah whom David cuckolded.

"The LORD caused the child that Uriah's wife had borne to David to become very sick. David prayed to GOD that the child would get well. He refused to eat anything, and every night he went into his room and spent the night lying on the floor... A week later the child died..."

King Jehoshaphat proclaimed a fast.(2 Chronicles 20:3- 4)

PURPOSE: To plead for help in time of trouble, and for guidance.

"...Jehoshaphat was frightened and prayed to the LORD for guidance. Then he gave orders for a fast to be observed throughout the country. From every city of Judah people hurried to Jerusalem to ask the LORD for guidance..."

Ezra called for a national fast Ezra 8:21 KJV

PURPOSE: To come under GOD'S protection from enemies and plead His favor.

"...There by the Ahava Canal I gave orders for us all to fast and humble ourselves before GOD and to ask him to lead us in our journey and to protect us and our children and all our possessions.

Nehemiah fasted. Nehemiah 1: 4 -9

PURPOSE: For success of a mission for GOD'S glory.

"...For several days I mourned and did not eat. I prayed to GOD......Give me success today and make the emperor merciful to me."

(HADASAH) Esther called for 3 days of fasting without food nor water. Esther 4: 15 -16

PURPOSE: For Divine favor.

"...Hold a fast and pray for me. Don't eat or drink anything for three days and nights."

JESUS TO DISCIPLES/MINISTERS

Jesus calls disciples to fast and pray. Matt 6: 21

PURPOSE: For spiritual strength and power to heal.

"However this kind does not go out, except by prayer and FASTING."

OUR LORD JESUS

Jesus fasted 40 days and 40 nights. Luke 4: 1

"Jesus returned from the Jordan full of the Holy Spirit and was led by the Spirit into the desert, where He was tempted by the Devil for 40 days.

PURPOSE: For Spiritual strength to resist temptations by the Devil.

Cornelius prayed and fasted. Acts 10:30 – 31

PURPOSE: As an act of mortifying the body.

"...4 days ago I was fasting until this hour. At the ninth hour I prayed in my house. Behold, a man stood before me in bright clothing, and said, 'Cornelius, your prayer is heard. Your alms are remembered in the sight of God.'"

The church/the faithful/Ministers

The faithful fasted and prayed. Acts 13: 1 -3

PURPOSE: Fasting and prayer as an act of worship and ministry.

"In the church at Antioch there were some prophets and teachers: Barnabas, Simeon (called the Black), Lucius (from Cyrene), Manaen (who had been brought up with Governor Herod), and Saul. While they were serving the LORD and fasting, the Holy Spirit said to them, Set apart for me Barnabas and Saul, to do the work to which I have called them." They fasted and prayed, placed their hands on them, and sent them off."

The Church, Paul and Barnabas fasted and prayed

Paul and Barnabas fasted and prayed before ordaining ministers

PURPOSE: Fasting and prayer for the Holy Spirit to release His anointing on the ministers of God in Christ. For the anointing breaks the yoke.

"...Paul and Barnabas preached the Good News...and won many disciples. They strengthened the believers and encouraged them to remain true to the faith... In each church they ordained elders, and with prayers and fasting they them to the LORD, in whom they put their trust. Acts 14: 21 – 23

Fast with a purpose. Fast that you mean to fast. The Holy Men and women of God in the bible who fasted, there was not a single one of them who did "half fasting." Not one fasted half a day, and not one fasted on banana, nuts or a loaf of bread. You either put your body in subjection to the LORD wholly, or you do not deceive yourself. Eating a heavy meal before sunrise and after sun down is a yearly duty adherents of a certain deity perform. Show devotion to your Jehovah God through his Son Jesus.

HOW LONG SHOULD FASTING LAST?

Let's say, a person, because of deprivation hasn't eaten or taken in any drink for a whole day. Does that mean that person has fasted? Let us be a bit more specific; an earthquake victim in a harrowing life-threatening condition of entombment alive under the rubble of a Cathedral for seven days without food or water; would that person's abstinence from food and drink be considered as fasting? In these two scenarios one person went without food and water for a day, and another seven days. In spite of the length of time each one went without food and water, insofar as matters of the spirit are concerned they were not fasting.

All right. Suppose I decided to deprive myself of food and water for three days to bring down my weight. Would that qualify as fasting? No! None of the scenarios could qualify as fasting, although both the condition and the length of time are common to fasting. Here is why!

Fasting is when we voluntarily deny our bodies the things they desire so that we can purposefully put GOD as center of our focus.

"I beseech you therefore, brethren, by the mercies of GOD, that ye present your bodies a living sacrifice,

DRUG FREE HEALING 11 : Medical Science Supporting Scriptures

holy, acceptable unto GOD, which is your reasonable service. And be not conformed to this world: but be ye transformed by the renewing of your mind, that ye may prove what is that good, and acceptable, and perfect will of GOD.(Romans 12:2) Translation by Today's English Version: "So then, my brothers, because of God's great mercy to us I appeal to you: Offer yourselves as a living sacrifice to God, dedicated to His service and pleasing to Him. This is the true worship that you should offer. Do not conform yourselves to the standards of this world, but let GOD transform you inwardly by a complete change of your mind. Then you will be able to know the will of GOD –what is good and is pleasing to him and is perfect."

During fasting, we are aligning our bodies and souls to the Spirit of God within us to present ourselves as living sacrifices by denying ourselves the pleasures and desires of the body. We must close our minds to what the world says, or does, or hears, or sees. We must keep our minds refreshed by meditating on the WORD of GOD ceaselessly. Fasting and praying are conjoined. We must pray without ceasing as the scripture commands us to do. When we do these things, here is God's promise: Then you will be able to know the will of GOD –what is good and is pleasing to him and is perfect.

To some, fasting one day is all that it takes to put the body under subjection to the Spirit; to another, seven days. To some, twenty-one days, to another 40 days. Cornelius fasted for one day for spiritual renewal and God answered him. Daniel fasted 21 days for spiritual understanding and had a delayed answer. Jesus fasted 40 days and 40 nights to overcome Satan's plots and the Devil fled from Him for a little while. Moses fasted 40 days to intercede for the people of Israel. God heard him. David fasted 7 days to petition God's forgiveness for his sins of adultery, perfidy and murder. God loved him. Our fasting must be purposeful. We must leave how long to fast to the leading of the Holy Spirit. And while we fast and pray, we must pray in the name of our LORD Jesus Christ. He promised:

"Believe me when I say that I am in the Father and the Father is in me. If not, believe because of the things I do. I am telling you the truth: whoever believes in me will do what I do – yes, he will do even greater things, because I am going to the Father. And I will do whatever you ask for in my name, so that the Father's glory will be shown through the Son. If you ask me for anything in my name, I will do it."(John 14:11-14)

We must stand on this promise of the Lord. He will empower us in a way that will baffle us, "Trust in the LORD with all thine heart; and lean not unto thine own understanding. In all thy ways acknowledge him, and he shall direct thy path."(Proverbs 3:5)

We must not ask Almighty God for anything in the name of Jesus and expect an answer when we are habitually committing sin. The key word here is HABITUALLY! Sin is not in the will of God.

When we fast and pray, we must keep our purpose on Jehovah God, and the will of God .James the brother of our LORD wrote this in his letter to "all God's people scattered over the whole world. " But when you pray, you must believe and not doubt at all. Whoever doubts is like a wave in the sea that is driven and blown about by the wind. A person like that, unable to make up his mind and undecided in all he does, must not think that he will receive anything from the LORD. (James 1:6 – 8)

He also wrote this, "You do not have what you want because you do not ask GOD for it. And when you ask, you do not receive it, because your motives are bad; you ask for things to use for your own pleasures. (James 4: 2- 3) Fasting and prayers must therefore be geared toward fulfilling the will of GOD.

In 2 Samuel 12:16 -18, King David prayed to GOD that the child he had through an adulterous relations with Uriah's wife, Bathsheba, would get well. He refused to eat and every night he went into his room and spent the night lying on the floor. His court officials went to him and tried to make him get up, but he refused and would not eat anything with them. A week later, the child died...

Paul, in his 2 letter to Corinthians 12: 7 – 9, wrote that he had a painful physical ailment that acted as "Satan's messenger" to keep him from being puffed up with pride, "Three times I prayed to the LORD about this and asked him to take it away. But His answer was: My grace is all you need, for my power is greatest when you are weak."

Do not become despondent, or dismayed when after all the fasting and prayers you have done, it would seem to you that GOD is not answering your prayers. Sometimes unanswered prayers turn out to be prayers answered. Look around you again and again. When you see that God has worked in a direction opposite to your prayers, you will also ultimately find out that all things have worked out for your good, and for His own glory. That is, fulfilling the will of God.

WHAT IS MEDITATION?

If your answer to this question has to do with the cliche about "emptying one's mind or concentrating on nothing," you have been listening too much to non-biblical philosophies. Turn to Joshua chapter 1 verse 8 KJV, This book of the law shall not depart out of thy mouth; but thou shall meditate therein day and night, that thou mayest observe to do according to all that is written therein; for then thou shalt make thy way prosperous, and then thou shalt have good success".

Study the word. Regurgitate the word. Reflect on the word. Then you will be conversant with God's Fasting Guidelines and His promises. So biblical meditation involves studying and regurgitating God's word, examining and re-examining it with a wholehearted reverential committed mindset to live by it as you breathe in slowly and out the breath of life.

Apostle Paul puts it all together in his letter to the Philippians chapter 4 verses 6-8 in which he states, "Be careful for nothing; but in everything by prayer and supplication with thanksgiving let your requests be made known unto God. And the peace of God which passeth all understanding, shall keep your hearts and minds through Christ Jesus. Now here comes the aspect of meditation. Verse 8:...Whatsoever things are true, whatsoever things are honest, whatsoever things are just, whatsoever things are pure, whatsoever things are lovely, whatsoever things are of good report; if there be any virtue, and if there be any praise, think on these things.

When we put our minds on the awesomeness of God. Continuously thinking about His LOVE and how we too as His children can emulate His LOVE, our minds will have no space to accommodate anger, grudge, malice, jealousy, gossip, foolish talking, jesting, lusting. We ourselves become nothing as our human Spirit reaches to align with the Holy Spirit. When the human Spirit aligns with the Holy Spirit that is, being "in the will of God". Our LORD JESUS made this promise,

"...I am telling you the truth: whoever believes in me will do what I do – yes, he will do even greater things because I am going to the Father...I will do whatever you ask for in my name, so that the Father's glory will be shown through the Son."(John 14:12 – 13).

Medical Science Supports Scriptures On Biblical Meditation

Harvard Medical School Professor emeritus Herbert Benson, M.D, asserts that stress is associated with numerous medical conditions including, "angina pectoris, cardiac arrhythmia, allergic skin reactions, anxiety, bronchial asthma, herpes simplex, cough, constipation, all forms of backaches, headaches, abdominal, pain, joint aches, post-operative pain, and many others." (Benson, 1975, p.32) The author of "The Relaxation Response," documents in this book, more than ten years' pioneering research, and Benson's (1975) conclusions showing how a person can use meditation techniques to "partly relieve or cure most of the common complaints that patients bring to doctors."(Benson, 1975, p.32)

Following a series of studies lasting over ten years, Benson (1975, p.10) and his team of researchers drew an association between the body's nervous system and meditation. Benson (1975, p.10) and his colleagues found that when the human body is under any stressor, the sympathetic nervous system releases a flood of fight-or-flight hormones, made up of "adrenaline and noradrenaline, or epinephrine and adrenaline." (p.9)

These cause increased heartbeat, increased respiratory rate, elevated blood pressure, and increased oxygen consumption. In this way, the body goes under heavy stressors. The researchers concluded that any given number of things could excite the sympathetic nervous system to release the body's adrenaline, and noradrenaline. Such relentless bombardment of the body by adrenaline and noradrenaline hormones was dangerous for the human body. Researchers also found that the opposite reaction occurred when the body was not in the fight-or-flight response. When the sympathetic nervous system was at rest, the parasympathetic nervous system released a flood of hormones including oxytocin that put the body's self-repair mechanism into action.

Benson(1975) and his colleagues believed that just as often as the human body elicited the fight-or-flight responses, so also the parasympathetic system was able release the relaxation response as many times as it is excited enabling the body self-repair as often as possible. Conclusion on the studies led Benson (1975) and his team of researchers to believe that when the sympathetic nervous system to goes, the parasympathetic nervous system puts the body into relaxation. Benson (1975) named the process "the Relaxation Response." (p.8)

The researchers found that the frequent excitation of the "relaxation response" (Benson, 1975) produced the same positive effect on hypertensive patients as patients who took prescription medication. Benson (1975) writes, "The body responds with a dramatic decrease in heart rate, breathing rate, blood pressure and metabolic rate." (p.9) The researchers found that inducing the "relaxation response" by means of meditation had the added benefit of no side effects. On the other hand, high blood pressure medicines prescribed for cardiovascular patients had side effects. Benson (1975) writes, " I noticed a trend among my patients with high blood pressure or hypertension...Once I prescribed medication, I noticed they often complained about fainting...Patients went from feeling fine to being burdened with irritating and disabling side effects, all the result of medicine I had prescribed ."(p.5)

The team of researchers discovered that the hormones that "stress produced – adrenaline and noradrenaline - contributed to...many more medical problems." (p.11) The researchers also found that the "relaxation response" was effective in treating in addition to high blood pressure, " headaches, hypertension, cardiac rhythm irregularities, premenstrual syndrome, anxiety, and mild and moderate depression." (p.11) The author cites "Judaic literature" (p.141) and early Christian sources (p.132 – p.140) to highlight Judeo-Christian roots of Meditation. The researcher makes it clear also, that prayer is an effective acceptable technique for practicing meditation.

In his letter to Timothy 4:8, Apostle Paul counseled, "For physical training is of some value, but godliness has value for all things, holding promise for both the present life and the life to come. " I have added 30 minutes to my daily 60 minutes. In the additional time of 30 minutes, I spend it regurgitating the scriptures while performing breathing exercise.

Long Life and Salvation

In 2013 , Pew Research Center reported by 2050 , Americans would live to 120 years. Researchers further stated that the first babies to live to 150 had already been born. The most pessimistic forecasters, indicated in the New England Journal of Medicine (Olshansky, et al, Mar.17 2005) that by 2060, Americans, and people in the developed world would live to 100 years of age; as though people are not already living to a hundred.

In the middle of those reports, were numerous others emerging from the medical establishment affirming faith in God can prolong life. Those reports included some by researchers at the National Center of Complementary and Integrative Health , announcing after several clinical studies that "church attendance is correlated with increased longevity or better health," according to Harvard Professor, Anne Harrington.

For someone who will be a healthy 120-year old in forty-four years, the news was not a surprise. Methuselah was able to live until he was 969 years. (Genesis 5:5) But his father, Enoch, lived 365 years "walking faithfully with Jehovah; then he was no more because Jehovah God took him. " (Gen.5:24) Both

Enoch and Noah "walked with God," and yet Noah lived 950 years.

Moses whose lamentation over humans' 70 or 80 years' life expectancy is widely cited as though it is an edict from Jehovah Almighty God, died at age 120 years, but David "the man after God's own heart", died at age 70, Hezekiah lived 54 years. He would have died at age 41 had it not been for the grace of Jehovah God that he had a gift of 15 more years. . And yet for another prophet who lived after Moses, David, and Hezekiah, the end of life was as it was with the antediluvian prophet Enoch: "a chariot of fire suddenly appeared, drawn by horses of fire, ...and Elijah was carried by a whirlwind into heaven." (2 Kings 2:11)

Jehovah God is Sovereign. He does what he wants. He is also faithful. He says this: "Those who love me, I will deliver; I will protect those who know my name. When they call to me, I will answer them; I will be with them in trouble, I will rescue them and honor them. With long life I will satisfy them, and show them my salvation." (Psalm 91: 14 -16)

Consult your doctor

Whatever treatment program we choose, we must always make it a point to consult our personal physician. Almighty God also gave doctors the wisdom and the ability to practice their profession. He uses them as instruments for restoring our health. Apostle

Paul who brought a dead boy back to life by the power of the Holy Spirit had a personal physician, Dr. Luke, the author of the gospel by his name, and of the Acts of the Apostles.

I am not qualified to pretend to be like the Apostle, but if getting a personal physician was good enough for him, it should be good for me too. For Paul himself had written in one of his letters to the congregation in Corinth and to us, "Imitate me just as I imitate Christ." (1 Corinthians 11:1)

I sought my doctor's opinion about going herbal, using strictly bible herbs and foods. Dr. Jon Hemstreet was gracious. He said he would see me again in three months to evaluate whether there was any improvement, and advised that I combined my herbal program of treatment with a regimen of balanced diet and daily walking exercises. That was good enough for me. Dr. Hemstreet is a brilliant medico with incredible empathy for his patients.

Competent and methodical, soft-spoken Dr. Jon Hemstreet seems to embody a conviction among some progressive medical professionals that patients are best served when therapy is directed at not only the physiological symptoms but their emotional and spiritual conditions as well. This position is well articulated by another primary care provider, Dr. Christopher Hobbs in his book, "Herbal Remedy For

Dummies." He declares, "As a primary care provider, I see many patients who aren't well-served by today's modern healthcare system – people who are often encouraged to depend on drugs and medical procedure to fix symptoms and conditions without any mention of the personal power they possess to create and maintain health…" The personal power I possess is our Lord Jesus!

Trees for Food and Healing

The same God also healed an individual with speech and hearing impairment by His touch alone as the scripture tells us in Mark 7:31-35 – 31:

"They brought to Him one who was deaf and spoke with difficulty, and they implored Him to lay His hand on him... Jesus took him aside from the crowd, by himself, and put His fingers into his ears, and after spitting, He touched his tongue with the saliva; and looking up to heaven with a deep sigh, He said to him, "Ephphatha!" that is, "Be opened!" And his ears were opened, and the impediment of his tongue was removed, and he began speaking plainly."

Almighty God is gracious. He has made available for our healing when we are ill different varieties of means. He has placed at our disposal plants for food and for healing when we fall sick. This is His word: "There will grow all kinds of trees for food....Their fruit will be for food, and their leaves for healing." (Ezekiel chapter 47 verse 12).

God caused the shadow of the sun to move backward by ten degrees at the request of Hezekiah in order to reassure him that He, Almighty God, would heal Hezekiah of his terminal disease, and told him he would live for fifteen more years. The same God ordered His prophet Isaiah to let Hezekiah apply a lump of figs to his boil and be healed.

We have this account in 2 Kings 20: 1 – 11. It reads, "In those days was Hezekiah sick unto death. And the prophet Isaiah the son of Amoz came to him, and said unto him,' Thus saith the LORD, Set thine house in order; for thou shalt die, and not live. Then he turned his face unto the wall and prayed....And it came to pass, afore Isaiah was gone out into the middle court, that the word of the LORD came to him, saying, "Turn again and tell Hezekiah...Thus saith the LORD, "the GOD of David thy father, I have heard thy prayers...And I will add unto thy days fifteen years...And Isaiah said, Take a lump of figs. And they took a lump of figs and laid it on the boil, and he recovered. And Hezekiah said unto Isaiah, What shall be the sign that the LORD will heal me, and that I shall go up into the house of the LORD the third day? And Isaiah said", This sign shalt thou have of the LORD, that the LORD will do the thing that he has spoken; shall the shadow go forward ten degrees or go back ten degrees?...And Hezekiah answered, It is a light thing for the shadow to go down ten degrees; nay, but let the shadow return backward ten degrees....And Isaiah the prophet cried unto the LORD: and he brought the shadow ten degrees..."

Research

Nutrition researchers found conclusive evidence that eating micro-nutrient diet will prevent, or reverse disease, improve health, and prolong a disease-free life. These scientists believe that eating "micro-nutrient rich" meals can "reduce asthma, ear infections, and allergies, and protect children for the future against diabetes, cardiovascular disease and cancer," (Fuhrman, 2005).

They argue that eating micro-nutrient meals is integral to the protocol for healthy living or longevity. Adhering to micro-nutrient dietary practice will help restore diminished building blocks for improved health and longevity. Dr. Fuhrman (2005), a leading researcher with the National Center for Complementary and Integrative Health (NCCIH), blames the types of foods most people ate in their formative years as "the primary cause of disease and premature death." (Fuhrman, 2005)

The researcher asserts, "We can't smoke with impunity, excessively consume alcohol without paying a price, or eat the typical American diet and not eventually develop atherosclerotic heart disease and cancer." (Fuhrman, 2005)

As the types of foods that people ate in infancy affect their health and growth into adulthood, it will help if mothers feed their babies foods that enhance their children's growth. Feeding children micro-nutrient based foods while bringing them up in the fear and admonition of the Lord will ensure the children's longevity even as their Spiritual salvation is assured. Advocates of micro-nutrient rich dietary practice assert that the biblical injunction in Proverbs 22:6, "train up a child in the way he should go: and when he is old, he will not depart from it," applies as well to the foods parents feed their children. Fuhrman (2005) advises new mothers feed their babies on milk from their own breasts and never on a diet centered on animal's milk. Parents should avoid eating meat, cheese, butter, pasta, and white bread, salt, caffeine, sugar filled snacks and drinks, because those foods are poison; they lay the groundwork for cancer, diabetes, and heart disease. New mothers should not feed their children foods that will inadvertently cause their children to develop later on in life autoimmune illnesses. Parents and their children should keep away from white-colored foods. For better health and longevity, it is good to eat fresh foods, vegetables, beans, raw nuts and seeds, brussels sprouts, broccoli sprouts, kale, berries, grapes, black berries, blue berries, fruits, and turmeric roots. (Fuhrman, 2005)

DRUG FREE HEALING 11 : Medical Science Supporting Scriptures

Scripture instructs that the body is a temple of the Holy Spirit. (1 Corinthians 6:19) It is important that a person does not defile the body with foods that are toxic; it is equally important that a person must not indulge in activities that spiritually corrupt the body.

Restricting one's self to micro-nutrient diet although not a requirement for salvation or spiritual development, it is nonetheless, a discipline that can help a person to structure his or her own spiritual life. The belief that eating micronutrient rich diet helps in restoring diminished building blocks for improved health and longevity, spurred studies at Loma Linda University Medical Center, California (Adventists Health Studies ,n.d).

The studies show that God-believing vegan and vegetarian Seventh Day Adventists, live ten to fifteen years longer than do most Americans. The study considered lifestyles, diet, and belief as significant factors.

Studies, conducted over twelve years of more than 30,000 cohorts, showed that the participants who were over 83 years of age, and who consumed nuts at least five times a week, "had 39% lower risk of death by Coronary Heart Disease. Younger people who ate nuts five times every week, had 48 percent lower risk of death by CHD than those who ate nuts less than once every week" (Higdon & Drake, 2007).

Scientists put together information from five studies, comparing "death rates from common diseases of 76,172 men and women vegetarians, ages 16-89 with non-vegetarians of similar lifestyles and ages. Vegetarians did not eat meat or fish. The death rate from heart attack was lower among the vegetarians than those who were no vegetarians. The death rate by heart attack among regular meat eaters was higher than those who were occasional meat eaters, and lower by 34% among those who ate fish and not meat.

Similar investigations are on-going involving 96.000 Seventh Day Adventists of Canada and America to find out connections, if there are any, between religion, lifestyles, diet and diseases. (Adventists Health Studies, n.d).

Chapter One:
Beginning in the Garden of Eden

In the Garden of Eden, there were three identified by their names. First, there was "The Tree of Life. Next came The Tree of Knowledge of Good and Evil , and the third was The Fig Tree. (Gen 2:9) God did not forbid Adam and Eve from eating of the fruit of the Tree of Life. Indeed, its presence in the Garden of Eden was to underscore God's plan for man; to live forever in paradise. This is not just generic man. I took the name "man" as applying personally and directly to me through the second Adam who is our Lord Jesus Christ. We have this assurance in His revealed word according to John: "To him who conquers I will grant to eat of the tree of life, which is in the paradise of God."(Rev.2:07)

We are told in Genesis 3:7 that after Adam and Eve defied God and ate of the fruit from the Tree of

Knowledge of Good and Evil, "the eyes of them both were opened, and they knew that they were naked; and they sewed fig leaves together, and made themselves aprons."

Fig has been mentioned sixty-four times in the bible. There are good figs, and there are bad figs. Whenever fig is mentioned in the scriptures, it also metaphorically represent the righteous or the unrighteous according to the context in which it appears. (Jer 39:1-18 & Jer. 40:1-6)

In Matthew 21:17-19, figs come off as a picture of productive and unproductive believers. "And leaving them, He (Jesus) went out of the city to Bethany and lodged there. In the morning, as He was returning to the city, He was hungry, and seeing a fig tree by the wayside, He went to it, and found nothing on it but leaves only. And He said to it, "May no fruit ever come from you again." And the fig tree withered at once…"

God is revealing to you and me through His word, and through the message of the fig that while, you or I try to walk a spiritual path, we may find along the way people pretending to be speaking for God. There might even be occasions when we ourselves might become the pretenders. The test for our faithfulness is that our appearances and claims must be seen as matching our deeds, producing fruit acceptable in the sight of God. In other words, what we say or do must be seen by others as a testimony for Christ Jesus. We must walk the walk of the talk we talk. "He who has My commandments and keeps them is the one who loves Me; and he who loves Me will be loved by My Father, and I will love him and will disclose Myself to him." (John 14:21)

Although we may look like fig trees, spiritually speaking, when the LORD of the harvest shall come again, will He find us bearing fruit or will He find nothing on us but leaves? "May no fruit ever come from you again," Jesus told the unproductive fig tree. "And the fig tree withered at once".

If we want to be healed physically, we must first seek from God through Christ Jesus our own spiritual healing, so that we can become like fruit bearing fig trees. "From the fig tree learn its lesson; as soon as its branches become tender and put forth its leaves, you know that the summer is near." As far back as in the Garden of Eden, we had the fig tree to remind us to become fruit bearing fig trees ready for harvesting at the coming of our Lord Jesus Christ. Amen.

The fig, botanically known as Ficus carica L. (family Moraceae), belong to a plant family of more than 1,000 species, widely distributed across the globe, notably including Ficus sycomorus and Ficus religiosa. "There are large figs and small figs, round figs and ovoid figs, spring figs, summer figs, and winter figs, and figs colored black, brown, red, purple, violet, green, yellow-green, yellow and white," states Dianne Onstad, author of the bestselling book Whole Foods Companion. "

Chapter Two: Figs for Food

Some figs are parasites that strangle and kill their hosts; others grow on low trailing shrubs in the desert or on tall trees in tropical forests." Ficus Cariaca universally known as common fig or edible fig can live as long two hundred years. It is often planted along with olive trees, which also are long living plants. It stands 50 ft tall, but more typically to a height of 10 - 30 ft. Fig trees are notorious for being late bloomers, budding new leaves in the dying days of Spring to Summer.

Medicinal Uses:

The latex is applied on warts, skin ulcers and sores. It is taken as a purgative and vermifuge.

The leaf tea is taken as a remedy for diabetes and calcification in the kidneys and liver. Fresh and dried figs for laxative and restorative action. A decoction of the fruits is gargled to relieve sore throat. The fruits poultices are used in treating tumors and other abnormal growths. Figs boiled in milk are used in treating swollen gum. The tiny seeds with their high mucin content help in collecting toxic wastes and mucus in the colon and bringing them out. Studies show that figs help kill pernicious pathogens as they promote the build up of friendly acidophiles bacteria in the bowel, therefore, helping prevent colon cancer. Containing more mineral matter and more alkaline than most fruits, figs are great producers of energy and vitality. Figs help lower cholesterol. Nutritionists highly recommend that figs are regularly added to the daily diet of those allergic to milk because of its highly assimilable calcium content of figs. Figs have delicious sweet taste, being of high sugar content. Ripe figs can be eaten with or without their skin, added to ice cream mixes, stewed, or cooked as puddings, baked in pies, cakes, bread, pastries, or other bakery products. Unripe figs are stewed or used in cakes, jams, or pickles. Dried figs are also used in baked products.

Seed oil: Is edible, but it is also used as a lubricant. Dried seeds contain 30% of fatty acids: oleic, 18.99%; linoleic, 33.72%; palmitic, 5.23%; arachidic, 1.05%. Leaves: Fig leaves are used for fodder, or as a yellow dye. To the perfume industry fig leaves are the source of a substance called "fig-leaf absolute", a dark-green to brownish-green, semi-solid thick liquid which lends the perfume a rugged woody odor.

Latex: The latex contains compounds that are helpful additives used in coagulating milk to make cheese. The latex also contains ficin a protein-digesting enzyme that helps in tenderizing meat. The latex is also used as potters' sealing wax.

Chapter Three : Cypress
Species: Cupressus Sempervirens
Gen 6: 11-21

As one who worked in a library and earned a living by observing people's activities to ensure that nobody violated the library's codes of conduct, I found it amazing how quickly and easily kids of all ages gravitate towards images of animals and plants when they are learning. Go to any library, and you will see the eagerness with which kids move toward books containing images. Even internet-savvy older kids of teenage years are no exception; they are pulled toward images, pictures, and graphics more than anything else. It is not only kids that are enthralled by the power of visual images, however.

DRUG FREE HEALING 11 : Medical Science Supporting Scriptures

In this age of cyber vision, the role of imagery in conveying information that words alone may not adequately express, is as potent as it was in Genesis; the beginning, when GOD used the things he created as earthly metaphors to reveal spiritual things. This form of Divine communication has endured throughout the ages and has been demonstrated in the scriptures page after page, chapter after chapter, and book after book. GOD reveals a glimpse of Himself, and aspects of His incomprehensibility through the things He has created. Thorns and thistles in the scriptures are some of the images symbolizing GOD'S wrath and judgment: "...Because thou hast hearkened unto the voice of thy wife, and has eaten of the tree, of which I commanded thee, saying 'Thou shalt not eat of it; cursed is the ground for thy sake, in sorrow shalt thou eat of it all the days of thy life. Thorns also thistles shalt it bring forth to thee, and thou shalt eat the herb of the field..." (Gen. 3:17-18KJV)

The Gospels are full of instances when Our LORD JESUS CHRIST HIMSELF invoked the imagery of plants to teach spiritual lessons and to underscore Almighty GOD'S love, grace, mercy, goodness, wrath and, or judgment. Here is one example:" Jesus told the parable of the sower who went out to sow seeds. "Some seeds fell on the path, and birds came and ate them. Other seeds fell on rocky ground, where they did not have much of soils and sprang up quickly, since they had no depth of soil. But when the sun rose, they were scorched; and since they had no root, they withered away. Other seeds fell upon thorns, and the thorns grew up and choked them. Other seeds fell on good soil and brought forth grain, some a hundredfold, some sixty, some thirty."

Explaining the meaning of the parable, Jesus said, "When anyone hears the word of the kingdom and does not understand it , the evil one comes and snatches away what is sown in the heart; this is what was sown on the path. As for what was sown on rocky ground, this is he who hears the word and immediately receives it with joy; yet he has no root in himself, but endures for a while, and when tribulation or persecution arises on account of the word, immediately he falls away. As for what was sown among thorns, this is he who hears the word, but the cares of the world and the delight in riches choke the word, and it proves unfruitful. As for what was sown on good soil, this is he who hears the word and understands it; he indeed bears fruit, and yields, in one case a hundredfold, in another sixty, and in another thirty." (Matthew Chapter 13 verses 1-23).

Our first introduction to plants outside the Garden of Eden can be found in Genesis chapter 6 verse 14 when Almighty GOD told Noah: "Make yourself an ark of Cypress tree." Other versions say "Gopher".

Backing up, and reading from verses 11 to 21, the scripture tells us that the earth became "corrupt in

GOD'S sight and was full of violence. GOD saw how corrupt the earth had become, for all the people on earth had corrupted their ways. So GOD said to Noah, "I am going to put an end to all people, for the earth is filled with violence because of them. I am surely going to destroy both them and the earth. So make yourself an ark of cypress wood; make rooms in it and coat it with pitch inside and out...I am going to bring floodwaters on the earth to destroy all life under the heavens, every creature that has breath of life in it. Everything on earth will perish. But I will establish my covenant with you, and you will enter the ark – you and your sons and your wife and your sons' wives with you....You are to take every kind of food that is to be eaten and store it away as food for you and for them."

Cypress as a material for building the ark in keeping with God's instructions to Noah was a symbolic depiction of the Oneness of God the Father Almighty and Christ Jesus, who is the Ark of our salvation.

In John 14: 10 – 11 our Lord Jesus told His disciples; "I am in the Father and the Father is in me. The Father who remains in me does His own work. Believe me when I say that I am in the Father and the Father is in me."

Noah and his family in the ark, was a prediction of our own salvation by at-one-ment through the sacrificial death of Christ Jesus who prayed this in His last prayer while here on earth:

"I have manifested your name to the people whom you gave me out of the world. Yours they were, you gave them to me, and they have kept your word. Now they know that everything that you have given me is from you. For I have given them the words that you gave me, and they have received them and have come to know in truth that I came from you; and they have believed that you sent me. I am praying for them. I am not praying for the world but for those whom you have given me, for they are yours. All mine are yours, and yours are mine, and I am glorified in them. And I am no longer in the world, but they are in the world, and I am coming to you. Holy Father, keep them in your name, which you have given me, that they may be one, even as we are one. While I was with them, I kept them in your name, which you have given me. I have guarded them, and not one of them has been lost except the son of destruction, that the Scripture might be fulfilled. But now I am coming to you, and these things I speak in the world, that they may have my joy fulfilled in themselves. I have given them your word, and the world has hated them because they are not of the world, just as I am not of the world. I do not ask that you take them out of the world, but that you keep them from the evil one. They are not of the world, just as I am not of the world. Sanctify them in the truth; your word is truth.

As you sent me into the world, so I have sent them into the world. And for their sake I consecrate myself that they also may be sanctified in truth. I do not ask for these only, but also for those who will believe in me through their word, that they may all be one, just as you, Father, are in me, and I in you, that they also may be in us, so that the world may believe that you have sent me. The glory that you have given me I have given to them, that they may be one even as we are one, I in them and you in me, that they may become perfectly one, so that the world may know that you sent me and loved them even as you loved me. Father, I desire that they also, whom you have given me, may be with me where I am, to see my glory that you have given me because you loved me before the foundation of the world. O righteous Father, even though the world does not know you, I know you, and these know that you have sent me. I made known to them your name, and I will continue to make it known, that the love with which you have loved me may be in them, and I in them." (John17:6-26)

    In John 14:20 Our Lord Jesus Christ gave this assurance to the disciples, "Because I live, you also will live. On that day you will realize that I am in my Father, you are in me, and I am in you. Whoever has my commands and obeys them, he is the one who loves me. He who loves me will be loved by my Father, and I too will love him and show myself to him."

Our Lord Jesus is like the cypress. For God has said in Hosea 14:8 "...I am like an evergreen cypress, from me comes your fruit." The salvation of Noah and his family from God's judgment by the flood was a picture of believers being buried with Christ to overcome our sinful body. "But if we have died with Christ, we believe that we shall also live with Him. (Rom. 6: 1-8)

The strength, durability, longevity and evergreenness of cypress signify God's omnipotence, omniscience, and timelessness. The upward pointing spires serve as a call to us who believe to look up to God for our strength.

As the Psalmist puts it, "My flesh and my heart may fail, but God is the strength of my life and my portion forever. (Psalm 46:1-3)

The towering height of Cypress, girth and wide spreading buttress roots , and the numerous derived gifts of uses to mankind, are reminders of God's incomprehensibility, providence and grace; " O the depth of the riches and wisdom and knowledge of God! How unsearchable are his judgments and how inscrutable his ways?" (Rom.11:33)

Another scripture gives us this reassurance from Almighty God. He says: "The afflicted and needy are seeking water, but there is none, and their tongue is parched with thirst; I, the LORD, will answer them Myself, as the God of Israel I will not forsake them. I will open rivers on the bare heights and springs in the midst of the valleys; I will make the wilderness a pool of water and the dry land fountains of water.

"I will put the cedar in the wilderness, the acacia and the myrtle, and the olive tree; I will place the juniper in the desert .Together with the box tree and the cypress, that they may see and recognize, and consider and gain insight as well, that the hand of the LORD has done this, and the Holy One of Israel has created it.' (Is.41:17-20)

If your life is fraught with thorns and thistles of sickness, and diseases, of unfulfilled hopes and goals, God has promised that " instead of the thorn bush, the cypress will come up, and instead of the nettle the myrtle will come up, and it will be a memorial to the LORD, for an everlasting sign which will not be cut off." (Is.55:13)

So I for one am determined to trust Him unfalteringly, and depend on Him to keep His promise according to the Prophet Isaiah, "The glory of Lebanon will come to you, the juniper, the box tree and the cypress together, to beautify the place of My sanctuary;

and I shall make the place of My feet glorious . " (Is. 60:13)

Cypress

Altogether, there are about twenty references to Cypress in the bible. The common Cypress is a native of Bible Land. Ethno-botanists say about 3000 genres of plants are found in the Holy Land and its surrounding regions of East Mediterranean and S.W Asia. The common cypress has kinship with such humbler evergreens as firs, pines, cedars, birches and poplars. It is upright, conical in shape, pointing upward. It is strong, long living, enduring several centuries. It grows very large; some species spread to a girth of about 80 feet (24 meters) while raising 150 feet (64 meters) tall. The branches vary in color and shape; some have light-green needle-like leaves and round cones the size of walnuts, and some are candle-shaped evergreens. It is insect, decay and corrosion resistant.

Apart from its wide distribution as a member of the family of conifers in the region, Cypress comes under a variety of names: Bald Cypress, Lawson Cypress, Monterey Cypress, Patagonian Cypress and the like. Many conifers like the Cypress stand upright, rising tall to a height of 130 and are shaped like a cone. Its tiny, evergreen dark green leaves provide a source from which Cypress Oil is distilled. Cypress Oil is also distilled from its branches and the gender specific cones. The male cones are yellowish. Female cones are green when unripe and brown when ripe. The oil has a refreshing camphor-like resinous fragrance. It forms one of the ingredients used in perfumes, after shave lotions and soaps.

Constituents:
Astringent, antispasmodic, anthelmintic, antipyretic, antirheumatic; antiseptic.

Medicinal Uses

The cones and young branches are anthelmintic (anti-parasites), antipyretic (reduces fever), antirheumatic, antiseptic, astringent, balsamic and vasoconstrictive (narrows blood vessels). They are harvested in late winter and early spring, and then dried for later use. Taken internally, cypress is used in the treatment of whooping cough, the spitting up of blood, spasmodic coughs, colds, flu and sore throats. Its astringency and vein constricting properties are potent agents for aroma therapists in the treatment of broken capillaries, and in the reduction of excess fluid such as cellulite and heavy menstruation. Cypress is also used as a tonic to improve circulation, and in the treating hemorrhoids.

External use

Applied externally as a lotion or as a diluted essential oil preferably with almond oil, it astringes varicose veins and hemorrhoids, tightening up the blood vessels. A footbath of the cones is used to cleanse the feet and counter excessive sweating. The extracted essential oil should not be taken internally without professional guidance. A resin is obtained from the tree by making incisions in the trunk. This has a vulnerary action on slow-healing wounds and encourages whitlows to come to a head. An essential oil from the leaves and cones is used in aromatherapy.

Other Uses

An essential oil is distilled from the shoots. It is used in perfumery and soap making. The leaves contain about 2% essential oil whilst the wood contains about 2.5%. An infusion of the wood is used in footbaths to combat perspiration of the feet. Wood - fragrance is hard and durable. It is a popular wood for building, and for cabinet, especially wardrobes, since it retains its fragrance, repels moths and is impervious to woodworm.

Chapter Four : OLIVE

But the dove found no place to set its foot, and it returned to him in the ark... So he put out his hand and took it and brought it into the ark with him.

OLIVE

Genesis chapter 8 verses 6 to 11:

"...At the end of the forty days, Noah opened the windows of the ark that he had made and sent out the raven; and it went to and fro until the waters were dried up from the earth. Then he sent out the dove from him, to see if the waters had subsided from the face of the ground; but the dove found no place to set its foot, and it returned to him in the ark, for the waters were still on the face of the whole earth. So he put out his hand and took it and brought it into the ark with him. He waited another seven days, and again he sent out the dove from the ark; and the dove came back to him in the evening, and there in his beak was a freshly plucked olive leaf; so Noah knew that the waters had subsided."

Two birds were sent out on a mission, one after the other; raven, then dove. The raven did not return to report results of the mission. "It went to and fro until the waters were dried up from the earth". The dove came back: "the dove found no place to set its foot, and it returned to him in the ark, for the waters were still on the face of the whole earth." Both birds were exposed to the same environmental conditions. One was opportunistic in its eating habit; raven. It is an intelligent creature, but greedy. It is omnivorous; it feeds on anything - carrion, insects, food waste, grains, berries, fruits, small animals. By contrast, the dove is an obedient bird, and selective in its eating habits; feeding on seeds, fruits and other plant stuff. It is mournful, meek, peaceable and dependable as a messenger. The species are monogamous. Unlike the raven which trusted in its own wits to survive in the open outside of its master's ark, the dove came back home having found nowhere else to rest its foot. So Noah "put out his hand and took it and brought it into the ark with him." Seven days later, the dove was sent out again. It "came back to him in the evening, and there in his beak was a freshly plucked olive leaf."

    Two birds symbolically stood for us, Christians, who have been saved in the ark of Christ Jesus from the destruction of the flood of God's judgment. The two were sent out. One did not return having been overwhelmed by carrions of false religion, self-righteousness and personal desires. The other returned home with a testimony; carrying in its beak a living evergreen plant-olive- symbol of the Holy Spirit. O Lord, I pray, grant me the grace to follow the example of the dove and not be like the raven. I pray this in the name of my Lord and Savior Jesus Christ. Amen.

Olive

The bible mentions olive trees at least 25 times, and olive oil more than 10 times. The olive tree is one of the most familiar trees in the entire Middle East, and the longest-lived of any fruit tree, surviving a thousand years and more. Olives are large evergreen shrubs with a gnarled trunk, bent and hollow inside, yet the trees continue to produce fruit. They are regarded among the strongest of trees, and often grow wild, but they are also carefully cultivated as orchards, or grafted on rootstock with wild olives, prompting the imagery the Apostle Paul invoked in his letter to Romans 11:16-18: "... And if the roots of a tree are offered to God, the branches are His also. Some of the branches of the cultivated olive tree have been broken off, and a branch of a wild olive tree has been joined to it. You Gentiles are like that wild olive tree, and now you share the strong spiritual life of the Jews..." In this regard, Apostle Paul represented the olive tree as a symbol of the spiritual heritage of the children of Israel. By God's grace, believers now share equal participation in God's promises of eternal life and blessings through faith in Christ Jesus.

In Bible times vast areas of carefully maintained terraces were planted with olives which also thrived on the steep and rocky slopes. (Deuteronomy 32:13)

When trained, olives have knotted trunks with round spreading crowns. Olive trees have unrestrained capacity to endure inclement, rocky and dry environment because of their remarkable root system. Even today the olives are harvested as in Bible times by carefully beating the trees with sticks and then picking up the olives from the ground. A good yield is up to fifteen gallons of raw oil from a single tree. When ripe, the olive is jet black and very attractive.

The Olive Harvest was the last harvest of the year for the children of Israel in Bible times, occurring in October when the people celebrated The Feast of Ingathering. The people depended upon the olive for food and countless other purposes. It was used for religious purposes, and in the lamps in the tabernacle; "Command the people of Israel to bring you pure oil of beaten olives for the lamp, that a light may be kept burning regularly." (Lev.24:2)

It has been used as a facial ointment: "You cause the grass to grow for the cattle, and plants for people to use, to bring forth food from the earth, and wine to gladden the human heart, oil to make the face shine…(Ps 104: 14-15) Olive has been used for healing. "Is any among you afflicted? Let him pray. Is any merry? Let him sing psalms. Is any sick among you? Let him call for the elders of the church; and let them pray over him with oil in the name of the LORD, and the prayer of faith shall save the sick, and the LORD shall raise him up; and if he has committed sins, they shall be forgiven. " (Jam.5:13-15)

The importance of olive in the spiritual and physical lives of the children of Israel is reflected in several bible verses. Disobedience to God would result in a loss of the olive crop (Deuteronomy 28:40). The oil honored both God and men (Judges 9:9) and was a component of the anointing oil of the high priest (Exodus 30:24). A large supply of oil was a sign of prosperity.

The excess oil can be stored for up to six years; such stores were of national concern. For example, in the days of King David, Joash was given the important charge of oil supplies (I Chronicles 27:28).

Constituents:
Gum-resin, benzoic acid, olivile, mannite , oleuropein , palitoleic acid, steric acid, oleic acid, linolenic acid, hydrocarbon, squalen, sterols, carotinoids, tocopherol

Medicinal Parts Used:
Oil of the fruit, leaves, bark

Medicinal Use.

Olives are used as febrifuge, antibacterial, antifungal, antiseptic, antiviral, astringent, tranquilizer, aperients, cholagogue, and as an emollient. They are also used to stabilize blood sugar levels, and in treating viral or parasitic conditions such as giardia, intestinal worms, malaria forming protozoa, microscopic protozoa pinworms, ringworm, roundworm, and tapeworms.

Olive leaves are used as an antiseptic. Olive leaf infusion has been used in treating hypertension, because of its capacity to lower blood pressure, and inhibit oxidation of LDL ("bad") cholesterol.

Olive oil

Olive oil contains monosaturated fats, primarily, oleic acid, squalene, and phenolic compounds that function as antioxidants in the body. Oleuropein, responsible for the bitterness of raw olives, is one of the phenolics. Other simple phenols including tyrosol, lignans and pinoresinol also function as antioxidants. Extra Virgin Oils are higher in these protective compounds than processed oils. Olive oil may act by reducing the LDL ("bad") and raising the HDL ("good") forms of cholesterol in the blood. Olive extracts have been shown to have hypoglycemic activity, and oil reduces gallstone formation by activating the secretion of bile from the pancreas. Olive oil may act as a mild laxative.

The inferior oil is used for soap.
Food

Eating Bible Land Foods so-called "Mediterranean Diet", rich in olive oil, fruits, vegetables, and fish, according to nutritionists, lower the risk of colon, breast, and skin cancer as well as coronary heart disease.

Olives are picked green when they are unripe, or black when ripe. Ripe olives are repeatedly pressed for olive oil. Cold pressed virgin oil is the best quality for culinary consumption. It has high antioxidant content, and it is free from cholesterol. It is valued in salad oils and a good source of edible oil. Olives are used in food preservation.

Olive Tea

To make tea, steep one teaspoon (5 grams) of dried leaves in one cup (250ml) of hot water for 10-15 minutes. Drinking olive leaf tea is beneficial to diabetic patients as it lowers blood sugar level, according to medical experts.

Garlic and Olive Focaccini--Diabetic Version
Ingredient
1 lb. Prepared pizza dough, divided into 4 (4 oz.) balls
2 tablespoon pureed roasted garlic
1 cup olives, halved
1/2 cup shredded asiago cheese
2 teaspoonful chopped rosemary
2 teaspoonful chopped thyme

Black pepper, to taste

Instruction:

Shape each piece of pizza dough into a 5-6 inch disc.
Place in a well-greased baking sheet.
Spread 1/2 tablespoon of garlic puree on each, then dot with 1/4 cup of ripe olives.
Sprinkle with 2 tablespoons of asiago cheese, 1/2 teaspoon of rosemary and thyme.
Then add black pepper to taste.
Allow to rest in a warm place for 30-60 minutes, and then bake in a 400-degree oven for 15-20 minutes until lightly golden.
Serves 4.

Nutritional Fact Per Serving:

Calories 378,
Fat 12g,
Cholesterol 15mg,
Sodium 567mg,
Carbohydrate 53g,
Protein 11g,
Calories from fat 28%,
Sat fat 4g,
Fiber 3g.

Dijon Sautéed Chicken--Diabetic Version

Ingredient

4 (5 oz. each) Boneless, skinless chicken breasts, minced

Kosher salt and coarsely ground black pepper to taste (optional)
1 tablespoonful multigrain wheat flour
2-tablespoonful olive oil
1 (8 oz.) pkg. frozen artichoke hearts
1/2 cup White wine
1/2 cup Low sodium chicken broth
2-tablespoonful Dijon mustard paste
2 tablespoonful chopped tarragon
1 cup spliced ripe olives

Instruction:
Season chicken breasts with salt and pepper to taste, then sprinkle with flour.
Heat 1 tablespoon of oil in a large high-sided sauté pan over medium-high heat.
Place chicken breasts in pan and cook for 3-4 minutes on each side until golden brown and thoroughly done.
Transfer to a clean plate and set aside.
Pour remaining oil into pan and heat.
Carefully, add artichokes and cook over medium heat for 2-3 minutes, stirring occasionally until golden.
Whisk in wine, chicken broth, mustard and tarragon.
Pour in spliced ripe olives and return chicken to pan.
Cook until heated thoroughly. Serves 4.

Nutritional Fact Per Serving:
Calories 318,
Fat 12g,
Cholesterol 85mg,

Sodium 622mg,
Carbohydrate 11g,
Protein 37g,
Calories from fat 35%,
Fiber 3g, Sat fat 2g.

Creamy Dijon Mustard.

Ingredients

4 ounces soft plain tofu
¼ cup Dijon mustard
2 tablespoonful balsamic vinegar
1 tablespoonful capers
1 teaspoonful fresh tarragon or ¼ teaspoonful dried tarragon
2 six-inch scallions, minced
1 tablespoonful chopped flat-leaf parsley
½ cup Homemade Vanilla Glucema Shake
Dash of Tabasco sauce
Freshly ground black pepper, to taste

Instruction

Place tofu food processor and puree.
Add all remaining ingredients and process into a smooth paste.
Store the dressing in an airtight container in the refrigerator until serving time. The dressing can be stored for one day after it has been prepared. Serve with 1 cup of raw, assorted vegetables such as colored peppers, spears of endive, asparagus, fresh grape leaf shoots, celery sticks, fresh fennel.

Nutrition Fact Per Serving

Calories 30	
Calories from Fat 10	
Total Fat 1.5g	2%
Saturated Fat 0g	0%
Cholesterol 0mg	0%
Sodium 190mg	8%
Total Carbohydrate 3g	1%
Sugars 1g	
Protein 2g	
Vitamin A	4%
Iron	4%

Percent Daily Values are based on a 2,000 Calorie Diet

Grapes: Chapter Five
Noah, who was "the first man to plant a vineyard", became drunk on wine, took off his clothes, and lay naked in his tent.

Grape Raisin, Wine, Vine (Vitis vini fera)

Genesis 9:20 Every word of God that is in the bible is important. When that word, a message, or imagery is repeated, it means, it is so important to God, that God wants us to pay a very special attention to it, and meditate on it night and day.

Vineyard and wine were first mentioned in Genesis chapter 9 from verses 20 to 23. The bible made further references to wine about 232 more times, vine and vineyards 198 times, grapes about 30 and vinegar 10 times.

Genesis chapter 9 verses 20 to 23 give an account of how Noah, who was "the first man to plant a vineyard", became drunk on wine, took off his clothes, and lay naked in his tent. "When Ham, the father of Canaan, saw that his father was naked, he went out and told his two brothers. Then Shem and Japheth took a robe and held it behind them on their shoulders. They walked backward into the tent and covered their father, keeping their faces turned away so as not to see him naked. "(TEV).

After his confinement in the ark for one year and ten days while the flood lasted, time eroded Noah's memory of the alienation and rejection he suffered from his compatriots who, time after time had poo-poohed his prophesy about God's coming judgment by flood.

Out of the ark, however, Noah was overcome by loneliness and grief when he found that "all living things upon the earth had perished -- birds, domestic and wild animals and all mankind – everything that breathed and lived upon the land." He must have felt very lonely in spite of being with his family, and all those he took along with him into the ark. In actual fact, Noah was never alone. The bible said, "God walked with him". I believe, however that Noah missed the interaction of humans other than members of his family. Having transferred his focus away from God to his lonely condition, Noah must have felt miserable, very miserable indeed.

When we feel lonely, we begin to hear two voices speak to us. We hear the voice of God, or the voice of the Devil. We can choose to listen to God's voice or the Devil's. To hear God's voice, we must become oblivious to our pressing circumstances and focus on being alone with God. When we seek the voice of God in our moment of strife, His Holy Spirits speaks to us by revelation, inspiration or illumination. We become inspired to redirect our efforts either to ministry or to enterprises that help other people.

Sometimes it is through our loneliness or rather, aloneness that God reveals to us our hidden talents.

The voice of the Devil on the other hand, will try to fill us with unexplained sorrow, and will tell us how worthless we are. Satan then will lure us into all sorts of destructive thoughts and behaviors. To some of us, it is the urge to be suicidal or hurt others. And to some others, it is the seduction of addictions: sexual addiction, pornography, drugs or alcoholism. Proverbs 20:1 states: "Drinking too much makes you loud and foolish. It's stupid to get drunk." Drunkenness is a work of the flesh.

Genesis chapter 9 tells us "God blessed Noah and his sons, and said to them ...Every moving thing that lives shall be food; and as I gave you the green plants, I give you everything." God also said in Ezekiel 47:12, "...There will grow all kinds of trees for food....and their leaves for healing"

Obviously, Noah, who was "the first man to plant a vineyard", did not plant the vineyard for getting drunk nor did he set out overnight to become a drunk. He was well aware of the gift of God to mankind concerning the use of plants. But sin, like grapevines, reproduces by gradual process. Noah gradually slunk into drunkenness, perhaps not by a conscious decision. Satan always devises schemes of deception to turn the people of God away from serving God by counterfeiting what God creates. Noah's drunkenness must have started first by an innocent and casual sip, increasing gradually into a full gulping down. Noah's own son, Ham, seeing his father's nakedness and drunken behavior inside his own tent, went outside to tell it.

This is to show us that those close to us who know our worst secrets may be the very people Satan will use to expose our nakedness although God Himself has already forgiven our sins because of the blood of Jesus His Son. By this narrative, I believe, God is telling me to be careful who gets into the tent of my heart, and who knows intimate details about my life other than God Himself alone. But here is the good news. The action of Shem and Japheth symbolize God's promise that for every agent of destruction that Satan may send our way, God Himself will send two of His own - His Son and the Holy Spirit – to cover our shame. For, God is love, and "love covers a multitude of sins." (1 Peter 4:8)

Shem and Japheth also exemplified obedience to what God commands as filial duty to parents according to Exodus chapter 20 verse 12 and restated in Ephesians chapter 6 verses 1-3; "Children, obey your parents in the LORD for this is right. Honor thy father and mother; which is the first commandment with promise; that it may be well with thee, and thou mayest live long on the earth."

DRUG FREE HEALING 11 : Medical Science Supporting Scriptures

In Ephesians 5:18, (NIV), we are cautioned: "Do not get drunk on wine, which leads to debauchery. Instead, be filled with the Spirit." Webster's American Heritage English dictionary picks up debauchery from the verb, "debauch", meaning, "to corrupt morally, to lead away from excellence in virtue, reduce the value, quality or excellence of, debase. Noah's drunkenness and loose behavior were weaknesses inherent in his Adamic nature like the rest of us, and proof that none of us can be righteous enough before the Holy God. We all are sinners. We are saved only by the grace of God through Christ Jesus. God was the One who imputed righteousness to Noah, and not because Noah was perfect.

God gave us grapes and the products of grapes such as wine for our good. In the parable of "The Good Samaritan," our Lord Jesus Christ himself, more than 2,000 years ago referred to a product of grapes as a healing agent when he stated:"...A man was going down from Jerusalem to Jericho, when he fell into the hands of robbers. They stripped him of his clothes, beat him and went away, leaving him half-dead. A priest happened to be going down the same road, and when he saw the man, he passed by on the other side. So too, a Levite, when he came to the place and saw him, passed by the other side... But a Samaritan, as he traveled, came where the man was; and when he saw him, he took pity on him. He went to him and bandaged his wounds, pouring on oil and wine...." (Further reading, Luke 10:25-37) Apostle Paul advised his protégé Timothy as follows: "Stop drinking only water, and use a little wine because of your stomach and your frequent illnesses." (1 Timothy chapter 5:23).

The wines of ancient time were more like syrups; a few contained a small amount of alcohol. All, as a rule, were taken only when diluted with some water. If undiluted, the percentage of alcohol present was minimal - about 4 or 5 percent.

In "Manners and Customs of Bible Lands', the author, Fred H. Wight told of how the people of Bible Land made a syrup with grape juice by boiling it until "it is as thick as molasses . They call it "dibs" and they are very fond of eating it with bread, or they thin it with water and drink it, "he wrote, adding, "This grape honey was in use in Bible times'.

Our Lord Jesus Christ speaks of Himself as "the true vine, and my Father is the vinedresser. Every branch of mine that bears no fruit, He takes away, and every branch that does bear fruit he prunes that it may bear more fruit...He who abides in me and I in him, He it is that bears much fruit, for apart from me you can do nothing."(John15:1-9)

Grapes contain resveratrol, one of the most potent cancer-fighting compounds ever identified.

Even though the health-giving power of grapes and other bible plants was in evidence since the beginning of time, it was not until very recently, in 1996, that it was proven once again that the Holy Bible has been right all along. Scientists found out that the skin of purple grapes contain a powerful chemical known as resveratrol, which is one of the most potent cancer-fighting compounds ever identified.

Originally isolated in a tropical legume, this compound was found later in grapes (particularly red). It can inhibit tumor formation in three ways - stopping DNA damage, slowing/halting cell transformation from normal to cancerous, and slowing tumor growth. Resveratrol has anti-inflammatory properties and may be very useful for colon cancer prevention, and a wide variety of other tumors.

Resveratrol may be important in reducing heart disease. Red wine consumption has been associated with lower LDL ("bad") and higher HDL ("good") forms of cholesterol and resveratrol may be the active principal involved. In her book, **Nutrition For Dummies**, Carol Ann Rinzler reports; " A study by 1700 heart patients at the Institute of Preventive Medicine, Kommunehospitalet in Copenhagen, Denmark, showed that people who drank a moderate amount of wine were less likely to develop Alzheimer's disease. By contrast, however, high drinkers of hard liquor had a higher risk of dementia. Another author Dr Judith Sumner, wrote this in her book **The Natural History of Medical Plants,** "laboratory studies show that resveratrol can stop the growth of human leukemia cells that are grown in cultures. "

Resveratrol may also be useful in controlling high levels of cholesterol, and in preventing the formation of blood clot. Grapes also help in fighting chronic inflammatory conditions such as arthritis and irritable bowels. According to Dr. Christopher Hobbs author of **Herbal Remedies For Dummies**, "The seed extracts contain potent antioxidants compounds called oligomeric proanthocyanidins (CPCs) which some researchers claim may slow down the aging process. "

Grapes come in many colors and sizes. The species has many varieties that are eaten as fruit, pressed for juice, dried as raisins or fermented into wine for drinking, flavoring food , for medicinal and religious use. The most popular varieties are the seedless. Grape juice is evaporated into grape honey. Pressed grape residue is used to make cream of tartar. Grape leaves used as food wrap.

Pressed grape seeds yield light vitamin-rich fine culinary oil. It is ideal for aromatherapy massage. Grapes are useful help in restoring energy to the convalescent. They are the basis of some blood-cleansing diets. Chewing the seeds may stimulate anticarcinogenic activity. The seeds of purple grapes contain powerful antioxidant compounds known as oligomeric proanthocyanidins (OPC) which are claimed to slow down the aging process.

Grapes also help in fighting chronic inflammatory conditions such as arthritis and irritable bowels. The branch sap provides eyewash. Wine in moderation is regarded as a tonic, and readily absorbs properties of steeped herbs.

Medicinal Uses

Grapes are useful help in restoring energy in convalescents. In some quarters, medical experts have claimed that imbibing a moderate amount of wine relaxes muscles and mood, expands blood vessels to lower blood pressure, and temporarily lower risk of heart diseases either by reducing stickiness of blood platelets, or by relaxing blood vessels, making them temporarily larger, or by increasing amount of HDLs." Wine is an antiseptic, sedative, analgesic – all three reasons for its use by the Good Samaritan. Ellagic acid occurs in grapes, and may have a number of human health effects. It has anti-cancer properties, and may act as a free radical scavenger.

The branch sap : Provides eyewash.

Leaf: Is used as tea to treat diarrhea, hepatitis, thrush and stomachache.

Leaf poultice: Applied externally for sore chest, headache, rheumatism, and fevers.

Grapeseed: Varieties containing seeds when chewed and swallowed with the sweet pulp are believed to help in protecting one's internal organs against stress and environmental toxins. Chewing the seeds may stimulate anticarcinogenic activity. The seeds of purple grapes contain powerful antioxidant compounds known as oligomeric proanthocyanidins (OPC) which are claimed to slow down the aging process.

Juice: Purple grape juice contains the same powerful disease-fighting antioxidants called flavonoids that are believed to give wine many of the heart-friendly benefits.

Wine: It contains antiseptic, sedative and analgesic properties.

Vinegar taken one teaspoonful three times daily and applied to the groin area and other affected parts of the body will stop itches, skin lesions and measles.

Food

Grapes are used to produce raisins for condiments, sweeteners in bread, cakes and pastries, juices, wines and vinegars for culinary preparations. Young leaves infusions are used as beverages and food additives.

Chicken and Grape Leaves in Phyllo Recipe
Ingredients
¾ lbs sliced mushrooms
2 cloves garlic, minced
3 cloves of raw garlic paste
2 tsp olive oil
4 large pickled grape leaves
¼ tsp crushed dried mint
¼ tsp crushed dried thyme

¼ tsp crushed dried sage
8 sheet frozen phyllo dough
2 tsp dark uncooked honey
2 medium size whole chicken breast, cleaned, skinned, deboned and halved lengthwise.

Instruction

Cook mushrooms and garlic in oil 4 to 5 minutes or until tender, then set aside.

Remove and discard stems from grape leaves, and rinse thoroughly.

Stack and roll up leaves as for jelly roll.

Cut into 1/8" slices, then crosswise into pieces.

Mix in bowl mushroom, garlic mixed with grape leaves, mint, thyme and sage.

Take 4 phyllo sheets.

Mix honey, and vinegar with garlic paste into a fine dressing consistency.

Brush sheets of phyllo with a liberal amount of garlic-honey dressing, then stack up sheets.

DRUG FREE HEALING 11 : Medical Science Supporting Scriptures

DRUG FREE HEALING 11 : Medical Science Supporting Scriptures

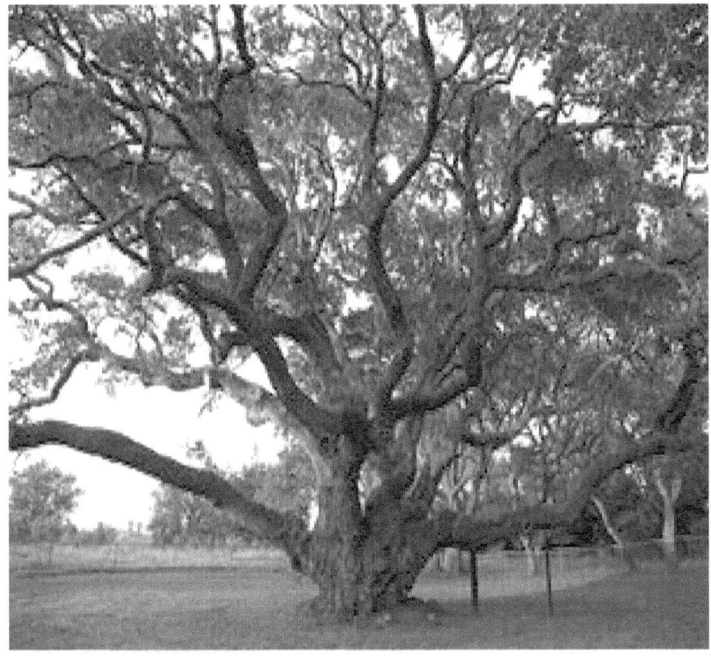

Oak : Chapter Six
"The Lord had said to Abram, "Leave your country, your people and your father's household and go to the land I will show you. "I will make you

into a great nation and I will bless you; I will make your name great, and you will be a blessing.
Genesis 11
The Earth's Habitation After The Flood

Abraham, the patriarch of Semitic people, and of believers by adoption through faith in Christ Jesus, was the eleventh generation of offspring counting down from Noah, and twentieth counting down from Adam.

The ancient city of Ur was Abram's hometown. The city was located in southern Mesopotamia, near the Euphrates River, about 150 miles southeast of Babylon. Today, Ur finds itself in southern Iraq, about 100 miles northwest of the Kuwait border. Here is the bible's account about this man, and of his calling by God: "... Terah became the father of Abram, Nahor and Haran. And Haran became the father of Lot. While his father Terah was still alive, Haran died in Ur of the Chaldeans, in the land of his birth. Abram and Nahor both married. The name of Abram's wife was Sarai , and the name of Nahor's wife was Milcah; she was the daughter of Haran, the father of both Milcah and Iscah. Now Sarai was barren; she had no children. Terah took his son Abram, his grandson Lot son of Haran, and his daughter-in-law Sarai, the wife of his son Abram, and together they set out from Ur of the Chaldeans to go to Canaan. But when they came to Haran, they settled there. "Terah lived 205 years, and he died in Haran." (Genesis 11:27-32) The account continues, "The Lord had said to Abram, "Leave your country, your people and your father's household and go to the land I will show you. "I will make you into a great nation and I will bless you; I will make your name great, and you will be a blessing. I will bless those who bless you, and whoever curses you I will curse; and all peoples on earth will be blessed through you. So Abram left, as The Lord had told him; and Lot went with him. Abram was seventy-five years old when he set out from Haran. He took his wife Sarai, his nephew Lot, all the possessions they had accumulated and the people they had acquired in Haran, and they set out for the land of Canaan, and they arrived there…Abram passed through the land to the place at Shechem to the oak (Terebinth) of Moreh. At that time, the Canaanites were in the land. The Lord appeared to Abram and said, "To your offspring I will give this land. So he built an altar there to The Lord, Who had appeared to him." (Genesis 12:1-7)

"…So Abram moved his tent, and came and settled by the oaks of Mamre which are at Hebron, and there he built an alter. " (Genesis 12:18)

While Abraham was sitting at the entrance to his tent in the heat of the day near the great trees of Mamre, three men appeared to him, bringing him confirmation of God's promise that Sarah would indeed bear him a son (Genesis 18:1-15). The three men, who Abraham recognized as a manifestation of God's presence, brought a message foretelling of the coming destruction of Sodom and Gomorrah, where Abraham's nephew Lot was living.

The Oak of Mamre, also known as Abram's Oak, is a prickly evergreen or Kermes Oak, a native of Bible Land. It belongs to the genus Quercus comprising numerous species, which include Quercus ilex also known as the Common Oak and Quercus robur. They are hard woods with remarkable medicinal properties. Oaks generally, whether they are Common Oaks, Italian Oaks, English Oak, American Oak or African Oak are known to be possess identical medicinal properties, and have been used for treating a variety of health conditions.

Chemical constituents:
Tannins, sodium sulphur, calcium, abundant traces of minerals, also Vitamin B-12, gallic acid, ellagitannin.

Medicinal Uses:
Parts used: Bark and Root

A decoction of the bark is an excellent astringent. It also is good in purging intestinal parasites. The tannins anesthetize them and they are passed out. It is useful in treating hemorrhages, and used as a good substitute for quinine to treat intermittent fever. It is used also to treat chronic diarrhea and dysentery. It is a healing agent as a compress or wash for wounds. Oak decoction used as a compress will lessen the pain from most open wounds. It helps to cleanse the puss out of wounds and prevents infection.

For chronic constipation sufferers, a large glass of warm oak bark decoction taken orally, followed by an administration of high enema is the remedy. Oak decoction taken orally helps cleanse the mucous out of the colon, stops internal bleeding, and heals bleeding ulcers. It works well as a compress for varicose veins. It is also an excellent liver flush, helping in expelling gallstones. Taking a decoction of oak bark or will help fight infections, increase, circulation.. Its main use is for varicose veins, hemorrhoids, pinworms, strep throat, and bleedings.

Dosage

Decoction of up to 8 ounces at one time can be taken when needed to treat an extreme case of constipation. 1-2 ounces at a time may be used for bleeding ulcers.

To make an effective decoction, boil one ounce of bark in a quart of water until it is down to a pint. The decoction is also used as gargle in cases of chronic sore throat, and for bleeding gums and piles.

Acorn : A decoction of acorns and bark in milk is used as an antidote to poisonous herbs and medicines.

Wheat: Chapter Seven

"Having taken the bread, Jesus gave thanks and broke it, giving it to them and saying, "This is My Body, which is given for you; do this in remembrance of Me. " (Matt. 26:26) Jesus also said, "I AM the Bread of Life; he who come to Me will not hunger in any way." (John 6:35)

Bread, Flour, Products of Wheat
Genesis 18: 1-6

"..The LORD appeared to Abraham by the Oaks of Mamreh, as he sat at the entrance of the tent in the heat of the day. He looked up and saw three men standing near him. When he saw them, he ran from the tent entrance to meet them and bowed down to the ground. He said: "My lord, if I find favor with you, do not pass by your servant. Let a little water be brought, wash your feet, and rest yourselves under the tree. Let me bring a little bread that you may refresh yourselves, and after that you may pass on since you have come to your servant. So they said, "Do as you have said." And Abraham hastened into the tent to Sarah, and said, "Make ready quickly three measures of choice flour, knead it, and make cakes…"

DRUG FREE HEALING 11 : Medical Science Supporting Scriptures

References to bread and flour – products from wheat – have occurred more than three hundred times in the scriptures. Webster's 11 New College Dictionary defines bread as "leavened staple food made from flour or a mixture that is shaped into loaves and baked." The dictionary also states, "Food in general, livelihood, something that nourishes."

There is the "refined, enriched" white bread, and there is whole wheat bread. So-called "enriched white bread which has had all of its original vitamins and minerals removed, has nothing left but raw starch of such little nutritive value that even most bacteria will not voluntarily eat it, " comments the noted nutritionist and author, Dr. Dianne Onstad, in her bestselling book, "Whole Foods Companion".

To God's people, bread is not just a meal; it has spiritual and historical significance. They eat bread; unleavened, as a part of a festival meal because Almighty God decreed it for them to memorialize their deliverance from Egypt, and as a prefigure of our redemption from sin and deliverance from the bondage of Satan through our Lord Jesus Christ.

Exodus chapter 12:12-20, read: "This day shall be a day of remembrance for you. You shall celebrate it as a festival to the LORD; throughout your generation, you shall observe it as a perpetual ordinance. Seven days you shall eat unleavened bread; on the first day you shall remove leaven from your houses, for whoever eats leavened bread from the first day until the seventh day shall be cut off from Israel. You shall observe the festival of unleavened bread. For on this day I brought your companies out of the land of Egypt; you shall observe this day throughout your generation as a perpetual ordinance. In the first month, from the evening of the fourteenth day until the evening of the twenty-first day, you shall eat unleavened bread. For seven days no leaven shall be found in your houses; for whoever eats what is leavened shall be cut off from the congregation of Israel, whether an alien or native of the land. You shall eat nothing leavened; in all your settlements you shall eat unleavened bread..."

Almighty God's command to his people to do away with leaven "from the first day until the seventh" is a physical reminder to all of us to become spiritually unleavened at all times by removing the leaven of sin from our lives. For unleavened bread is symbolic of sincerity and truth. It memorializes the resurrected body of Christ Jesus living in us who believe in Him. Leaven is a symbol of corruption, hypocrisy – sin. In 1 Cor. 5:8, believers have been urged to "keep the feast, not with old leaven, neither with the leaven of malice and wickedness; but with the unleavened bread of sincerity and truth."

The leaven of malice is a dangerous deadly disease of the spirit that destroys our body's ability to heal. When we hold on to old grudges, wrongs and refuse to forgive others who wrong us, we block the channel of healing that Almighty God has in place for us. "If you forgive others the wrongs they have done to you, your Father in heaven will also forgive you. But if you do not forgive others, then, your Father will not forgive you the wrongs you have done." These are the words of the Creator of the Universe Himself, our Lord Jesus Christ as was reported by one of His disciples in a book bearing the disciple's name –Matthew-- chapter 6 verses14 and 15.

Nurturing malice and the lingering sinful attitudes rooted in the desire for money, sex or power, are like festering spores beneath our skin. In time, we will be dead by their poison. Outwardly, we may appear as recovering from our sicknesses because of the medications we may be taking, or because we exercise regularly. We may credit the efficacy of bible herbs and foods for our healing. But let us not be surprised if we find our recovery to be short-lived when we remain without the spiritual nourishment of unleavened bread. We can look forward to being redeemed from Satan's bondage of sickness and death when we make every effort to put out from our lives the leaven of sin by conducting "ourselves properly, as people who live in the light of day – no orgies or drunkenness, no immorality or indecency, no fighting or jealousy." (Rom. 13:13)

"If thou wilt diligently hearken to the voice of the LORD thy God, and wilt do that which is right in His sight, and wilt give ear to His commandments, and keep all His statutes, I will put none of these diseases upon thee, which I have brought upon the Egyptians; for I am the LORD that healeth thee" (Ex. 15:26 KJV)

Desiring to be healed of my physical and emotional disabilities, I recognized that I needed to be first healed of my spiritual infirmities, knowing that we are all spiritually infirmed. "All of us have sinned and have come short of the glory of God."(Rom. 3:23)

Without the unleavened bread of Jesus Christ being the hallmark of my life, I am nothing but a living dead. Life is short. Sin cuts it shorter. I believe we are healed when we take God at His word. We take God at His word when we trust Him totally and surrender all of ourselves to Him totally. We surrender all to Jesus when we let Him into our heart. When Christ is in our hearts, like Paul, we can affirm that we "can do all things through Christ who strengthens" us. (Phil 4:13).

Doing all things includes believing without a doubt that "by His stripes we are healed. We are healed because Jesus is the bread of life; in Him, we have our being.

Bread symbolizes the body of Jesus Christ; "The evening before Jesus was crucified, He took bread and the cup, saying, "This is my body, which is for you...This cup is the new covenant in my blood."

DRUG FREE HEALING 11 : Medical Science Supporting Scriptures

Whenever we celebrate the Lord's Supper, we partake of bread and the cup in remembrance of our Savior, proclaiming His death until He comes. The LORD'S Supper is a participation in the death and resurrection of our LORD, who gave His body and shed His blood so that we might be forgiven our sins. (1Cor.11:23-26) We also read: "Having taken the bread, Jesus gave thanks and broke it, giving it to them and saying, "This is My Body, which is given for you; do this in remembrance of Me. In the same way also, the cup, after having eaten, Jesus said, "This cup is the New Covenant in My Blood, which is poured out for you." (Matt 26:26-28) Jesus also said, "I AM the Bread of Life; he who come to Me will not hunger in any way." (John 6:35)

Uses

The world consumes bread more than any other products of grain. Many types of breads are baked and eaten all over the world as staples: wheat bread, whole wheat bread, wheat bran bread, white bread, bread for hot dogs, hamburger buns, cakes, cereals, or pastas. Health conscious consumers prefer wheat bread because wheat has the reputation of stimulating the liver, thus, enabling the liver to cleanse itself of toxins. Refined white wheat bread can cause some people an allergic reaction. If you have a feeling that your body's metabolism is warring against you when you consume bread or foods of which refined wheat flour is the principal ingredient, you are getting a message from your body that your liver has collected too much toxins.

Refined wheat has very little to offer nutritionally. It losses a significant amount of bran and germ during processing. It also losses 80 percent of its vitamin content, and 93 percent of fiber. Although in a popularity contest, refined white bread wins hands down, the healthiest of breads are wheat germ, wheat bran and whole wheat.

So-called "enriched white bread which has had all of its original vitamins and minerals removed, has nothing left but raw starch of such little nutritive value that even most bacteria will not voluntarily eat it, " comments the noted nutritionist and author, Dr. Dianne Onstad, in her bestselling book, "Whole Foods Companion". White bread contains only 0.5 grams of fiber per slice, compared to that of 2 grams of fiber per slice of whole wheat bread. So if white bread gives you an allergy, try eating whole wheat bread, wheat germ or wheat bran. Whole wheat contains bran and germ with traces of barium and vanadium both of which are essential to the health of the heart. The fiber in the wheat helps in lowering cholesterol, and, in getting clogged up bowel running again; in this way, reducing the risk of rectal and colon cancer. Eating wheat sprout and drinking wheat grass tea are excellent liver sweep.

When you go out to buy your loaf of whole wheat bread, look for the one that is labeled "100%

whole wheat flour". Do not settle for just "wheat flour", a nutritionist advised. Look up the ingredients and remember that the first item on the list is always the dominant ingredient. Don't think that just because the bread looks brown, it is whole wheat.

Some so-called wheat bread contain brown caramel coloring. Wheat germ, that is, the heart of wheat, and wheat bran, help in fighting off some cancers and heart attacks. One cup serving constitutes more than one hundred percent of the Recommended Daily Allowance (RDA) for its vitamin E.

Researchers in St. Luke's Medical Center in Chicago concluded that people with high cholesterol level who eat about six to eight tablespoons daily of raw wheat germ will experience the lowering of harmful cholesterol LDL by 15.5% and 11.3% of triglycerides.

Wheat Sprouts Bread
Preparation of this recipe is time consuming: it takes days. Sprouts have to be grown. The main ingredients are wheat berries. They can be obtained from your local health foods store. Baking at high oven temperatures may destroy the sprout enzymes. Bake in a very low temperature for about a duration of four hours.
Original recipe yield: 2 small loaves.
Ingredients
6 cups wheat berries
6 cups water to cover

2 tablespoons cornmeal
½ cup dark (uncooked) honey

Instruction

Rinse the wheat berries in cool water.

Soak in cold water in a large bowl and cover the bowl.

Allow to soak for about 12 hours. The berries will soak up a considerable amount of water. Strain the berries and cover the berries to prevent from drying up.

Place in a dark location away from light.

Rinse the berries 3 times a day until sprouts begin to show.

Growth will continue until reaching about ¼-inch height.

Put in food processor.

Add cornmeal.

Mix with honey.

Blend for 10 minutes until well kneaded.

Remove and roll into desired loaf shapes.

Sprinkle an insulated cookie sheet with a little bran or cornmeal, and put the loaves on it.

It is not necessary to pre-heat the oven.

Bake at 350 degrees F (175 degrees C) for 30 minutes.

Then turn the oven down to 325 degrees F (165 degrees C), and bake for additional 2 hours and 15 minutes.

Remove bread from oven. Allow to cool down. Because of the high moisture content, refrigerate for consumption.

Lentils: Chapter Eight

Esau came back home from one of his characteristic open country jaunts very hungry, and it was just at the time Jacob had finished preparing for himself a sumptuous dinner of red lentil stew with bread.

Lentils . Lens esculentas : Gen 25 through Genesis 27

Esau and Jacob, the bible's best-known fraternal twins, famous for giving lentil stew its acclaimed reputation qualify to be dubbed the ideal poster boys for the children of dysfunctional homes, parental favoritism and victims of sibling rivalry anonymous.

Born of Isaac and Rebekah, and grandsons of Abraham and Sarah, the twins, twenty-second down the generational ladder from Adam and Eve, were everything else but identical in disposition. Their personalities and temperaments were as dissimilar as daylight is from darkness. One son was hairy, preferring the benefits of immediacy to unforeseeable gains in an indeterminate future. That one also loved the freedom of the rugged outdoors coupled with the manly game of hunting as much as he disdained the sedentary and culturally effeminate domestic life that thrilled his younger brother. Their father, Isaac who had a taste for wild game, loved Esau, the elder of the two. The other son, Jacob, was their mama's favored baby. He was smooth and quiet, and loved to play house "staying among the tents". Their mother, Rebekah, loved him, and even condoned the child's propensity for scheming and manipulating others.

Open Genesis chapter 25. Read verses 27 to 34, and skip to chapter 26 verse 34, read through chapter 27. The lesson of Genesis chapter 25 verses 27 to 34 through chapter 27 is not merely an account of Esau selling his birthright for a loaf of bread and lentil stew. God is showing us by the example of the life of Isaac and his household how not to treat our spouses, our children and members of our families. By exposing the weak links in the house of Isaac and Rebekah, God's word is putting us on our guard against factors that cause a breakdown of the family. My bible warns fathers and mothers, "do not exasperate your children; instead, bring them up in the training and instruction of the LORD." (Eph.6:4)

Do you play a favorite baby card with your children, calling one, a "mama's own baby", and another "a daddy's child"? You are setting your family up on a course of catastrophic end.

Turn again to Genesis chapter 25. Let's begin reading from verse 24 to 34. Verses 24 to 28 read: "When the time came for her to give birth, there were twin boys in her womb. The first to come out was red, and his whole body was like a hairy garment; so they named him Esau. After this, his brother came out, with his hand grasping Esau's heel; so he was named Jacob. Isaac was sixty years old when Rebekah gave birth to them. The boys grew up, and Esau became a skillful hunter, a man of the open country, while Jacob was a quiet man, staying among the tents. Isaac who had a taste for wild game, loved Esau, but Rebekah loved Jacob."

So what happened to loving your children equally and unconditionally? What happened to God's injunction? "Do not exasperate your children?" We must not look far afield for semblances of Jacob and Rebekah. In some of us can be seen the character of Jacob or Rebekah. Some of us exhibit biased judgments and preferences in our daily deliberations; the same bias shows up in our general relationships. Sometimes, the manifestation of these biases is subtle; sometimes, it is institutionalized. It shows up in our homes ; we find siblings turning against each other; wives and husbands turn themselves into total strangers, and if they both get into the same bed at all, the couple are separated by a thick invisible cold wall. In churches, we group ourselves into cliques, special affiliations, and fall on our faces favoring one preacher against another.

Our local and national governments demonstrate similar evidence of favoritism. It is even expressed through our national psyche; through the different standards by which we treat boys and girls, men and women. We glorify women and demonize men. It is now a trend in show business to depict men as morons on sitcoms. We set aside a special day in the year that we are all expected to "Take Our Daughters To Work", ignoring the needs of our sons for attention as well. Any wonder that some among the young male population are suffering a chronic case of identity crisis? We "sow the wind and reap the whirlwind". (Hosea 8:7)

Favoritism breeds resentment, connivance and manipulation, hostility and rebellion. This is called Yitzak-rebekasis. Never mind. Don't look it up in the dictionary. You will not find it there. I will tell you what Yitzak-rebekasis means. If you are in a relationship that is held up in public as a model but behind closed doors, you are short-circuited on communication with your mate, you are suffering Yitzak-rebekasis. If the bed you both share has between you an invisible cold dividing island, you have Yitzak-rebekasis. If you use children as pawns for an advantage over your spouse, you have Yitzak-rebekasis. If as a leader, you play one group of people against another, blacks against whites, citizens against immigrants, you have Yitzak-rebekasis. If you are a preacher, a religious broadcaster and you like to play one political party against the other, conservatives against liberals, and democrats against republicans, you have Yitzak-rebekasis.

You may then ask that if Isaac and Rebekah's lives were so flawed, how was it that they became the ancestors of God's covenant people? You and I are no different than they were. God chose them in spite of their flaws so that they could become a picture of God's salvation plan for humankind; that salvation is by grace through faith in Christ, <u>and</u> not of ourselves, "it is the gift of God, not of works lest any one should boast". (Eph 2:8-10)

Bread and lentil stew may provide a temporary respite for our hunger, but faith in Jesus Christ will give our souls everlasting nourishment. In the Jacob and Esau saga, the bible relates in verses 29 to 34 of Genesis chapter 25 that Esau came back home from one of his characteristic open country jaunts very hungry, and it was just at the time Jacob had finished preparing for himself a sumptuous dinner of red lentil stew with bread. "Quick, let me have some of the red stew. I'm famished." Esau told Jacob.

"First sell me your birthright." Jacob replied. "Look, I'm about to die" Esau pleaded, adding, "What good is the birthright to me?" But Jacob insisted, "Swear to me first."

So Esau swore an oath to Jacob, selling his birthright to his younger twin brother. Jacob as a result, gave Esau some bread and lentil stew. Esau ate and drank, and then got up and left." The bible tells us, "Esau despised his birthright."'

Where were the parents when their sons were haggling with each other over food? What happened to a father's responsibility to provide food, and a mother's obligation to prepare the food for the family? "Can a woman's tender care cease toward the child she bears...?" These are lines from an old hymn.

How about Isaac? It would seem Isaac had become detached from his responsibilities as head of the family. If he was the head of anything at all, it was of a dysfunctional family. In spite of the evidences of Almighty God's grace upon his life, Isaac, unlike his father Abraham, was at best, flaky in his faith. Rebekah turned out to be no Sarah who obeyed Abraham and "called him master" according to 1 Peter 3:6.

Rebekah had become derelict in her responsibility as a wife and mother, not caring to "knead and bake some bread" as Sarah, her mother-in-law did. She chose to wear the pants; to be the "head of the household." Her can-do-for-myself attitude destroyed the love and cohesiveness that glued her marriage with Isaac when they first met.

Before her pregnancy, for twenty years, Isaac her husband, interceded by prayers for her that she might be blessed with a child. But once the prayers were answered, making her the mother of Esau and Jacob, Rebekah became a changed woman. She favored Jacob over Esau, and taught Jacob creative brinkmanship; cheating and stealing through cunning manipulation and scheming. Genesis 27, verses 1 to 27 are instructive. But what was the birthright that Esau sold to Jacob for lentil stew and bread?

American Heritage Dictionary defines birthright as "a privilege that is one's due by birth...a special privilege accorded a firstborn." The firstborn enjoyed a special position of authority in the family. The firstborn ranked next as the father's delegated authority, and took a special place over the younger siblings. The firstborn was "lord" over his younger brothers. (Gen 27:37) The firstborn received from the father's legacies "a double portion of all that he hath; for he was the beginning of his strength; the right of the firstborn is his." (Deut.21:15-17). That is to say, if a father had four children, the possession would be divided into five parts with the firstborn taking two parts while the others take one part.

Spiritually speaking, the firstborn was sanctified for the service of God and for headship, symbolically representing the priesthood and kinship of our LORD Jesus Christ. "For those whom he foreknew he also predestined to be conformed to the image of His Son, in order that He might be the firstborn among many brethren..." (Rom 8:29)

Spurning his birthright, Esau rejected service to God. Unlike his father Isaac or his grandfather Abraham, Esau showed that he did not trust God for provision of his needs. He trusted in his own strength and skills for his own supplies. He trusted man to satisfy the needs of his flesh. His comment, "I am about to die, of what use is a birthright to me?" exposed his spiritual myopia. Esau did not have any faith that God had power to sustain him. Instead, he desired a fast-food type of a quick temporary solution to his problems; the satiation of his hunger by bread and lentil stew.

There is a bit of Abraham and Sarah, Isaac and Rebekah, Jacob and Esau in each one of us. We all have in us, elements of deceit and graft, greed and conceit. None of us is perfect. Despite our human failings, God has made provision for our salvation through His firstborn, our LORD Jesus Christ.

Salvation, translated from Hebrew and Greek, according to the New Scofield Study Bible, "implies the ideas of deliverance, safety, preservation, healing and soundness. Salvation is the great inclusive word of the Gospel, gathering into itself all the redemptive acts and process; and justification, redemption, grace, propitiation, imputation, forgiveness, sanctification and glorification." Jesus is the bread of life, the best lentils that will not only fill us up, but also restore our bodies to life everlasting. What the scriptures are telling us is that we must not be like Esau, content with healing the body alone. We must also seek the healing of our spirit. Lentils have the properties that provide nutrients to our bodies. Jesus Christ is the lentils for our souls.

Lentils

A long time ago in bible land in Egypt, people served lentils liberally because they believed that eating lentils enlightened the mind , opened hearts and made people cheerful. Lentils are small disk-shaped beans of legumes family contained two in a pod. Lentils have many colors. There are black lentils, white lentils, yellow lentils, and green lentils. There are more than 50 varieties.

 Lentils Sprouts

Constituents:

The nutritional constituents of lentils include protein, starch, fiber, folate and iron. When you consume half a cup of lentils, you have just given 5 grams of fiber, 89% of RDA for folate and 33% RDA for iron. Vitamins A, B1, B2, B3, B5, B6, B12, B15, B17, C, and K Minerals: boron, calcium,chlorine, copper, iron, magnesium, molybdenum, phosphorus, potassium, selenium, sodium, sulphur, and zinc.

Lentils are antioxidant, cardio-tonic, depurative, hypoglycemic, nutritive, tonic. Lentils have all 8 essential amino acids. The fiber component helps in lowering cholesterol level by stabilizing blood sugar. Women who eat beans and lentils frequently have a significantly lower risk of developing breast cancer than women who seldom eat them, according to a study reported in the International Journal of Cancer (2005; 114: 628-33)

Medicinal Use

Lentils have been used to cleanse and stimulate the kidneys and the adrenal system. Eating lentils is believed to strengthen the heart and circulation, boost energy and increase vitality. Eating lentils regularly helps lower LDL cholesterol, blood pressure, blood sugar and regulates insulin levels.

Food

Lentils are easily digested. They neutralize muscle acids, help build glands and blood tissue in the body. They are good for the heart. Lentils sooth stomach ulcers.

Are you trying to lose weight? Add lentils to your daily diet. Lentils can reduce your appetite. Lentils are used in soups, casseroles, curries, purees, spreads, stuffing and other dishes, to provide bulk and nutrition.

To cook lentils to be soft will take about 30 minutes. If the dried seeds are pre-soaked in water, they will cook even quicker.

Season lentils with garlic, onions, chives, coriander, cumin, curry or curry tree leaves, chillies, capsicum, yogurt.

Cooked lentils, pureed with herbs or spices, make delicious dips to serve with crackers, biscuits or carrot and celery sticks. Young, green, fresh lentil pods are eaten raw or steamed like green beans, while lentil sprouts are added to salads, soups, breads and savory dishes. Sprouts are sweet in flavor, similar to fresh, green beans. If the sprouts are eaten in large quantities at a time, you may have excessive gas. Lightly steam to neutralize the wind-causing substance.

Recipe
Lentil sprout spread.
Sprout 1/2 cup lentils for 2 days
1/2 cup sesame seeds 1-2 days.
Put in a food processor,
Add a ripe avocado
Add a clove of garlic
Add herb salt or fresh herbs to season,
Blend until smooth.
Use the spread on bread or savory biscuits.

Lentil fritters
Combine 1 cup sprouts, chopped or blended finely in a food processor,

1 cup grated, tasty cheese,
2 tablespoon olive oil,
A pinch of pepper,
Add a small bulb of onion, chopped
Add ½ cup beef stock
Add 1 cup fresh, whole meal breadcrumbs.
Blend
Pour two tablespoonful olive oil in frying pan and put on stove over low heat
Drop tablespoonful of mixture into an oiled frying pan, and brown on both sides. Ready to serve

Lentil stew
(Serves 4)
Ingredients:
250 grams lentils
1 green pepper
1 onion cut in half
1 carrot, peeled and cut into slices
1 small potato, peeled and cut into pieces
4 tablespoonful tomato sauce
2 cloves garlic
100 grams chorizo sausage, cut into pieces
100 grams streaky bacon cut into pieces
1 bay leaf
1 teaspoon paprika

Instruction
Soak the lentils in cold water for six hours and rinse.

Put in a saucepan.
Add the onion, carrot, chopped pepper, garlic, chorizo sausage, bacon, bay leaf, paprika and salt.
Mix.
Add enough water to cover.
Put on the stove and cook very slowly, lid on for around 25 minutes.
Check regularly to ensure the stew is not drying up Add more water if necessary.
Add the potato and the tomato sauce.
Continue to cook until everything is ready.
Remove the bay leaf. Serve.
If the stew is too runny, mash a couple of pieces of potato and add to the lentils to thicken.
This dish is perfect for the pressure cooker, but be careful to put in enough water so it does not dry up.
Nutrition fact
Calories: 350
Total Fat: 11.2g
Cholesterol: 26mg
Sodium: 477mg
Total Carbs: 45.3g
Dietary Fiber: 11.1g
Protein: 17g
Lentil Stew: This is an easy dish to serve your vegetarian family members and guests as a main dish or as a side dish with fish or pasta. It works nearly as well with split-peas.

Ingredients

3 tablespoonful olive oil
1 tablespoonful. chopped garlic
1.5 quarts pareve broth (chicken or vegetable flavor)
2 cups dry lentils
1/2 cup chopped tomatoes
1 pound red potatoes, peeled and cut into 1/2 inch pieces
1/4 cup lemon juice
12 ounces fresh spinach leaves, cleaned and roughly broken up
Add pepper to taste
1/2 cup chopped fresh mint
1/4 to 1/2 cups crumbled feta cheese
1/2 cup chopped fresh parsley

Instruction

Sauté garlic in 3 tablespoonful. oil, just for 30 seconds.
Add stock, lentils, tomatoes, and bring to a boil.
Reduce heat, cover, and simmer 10 minutes.
Add potatoes, cook 15 minutes.
Add lemon juice, spinach et al.
Simmer 2 minutes.
Fold in mint and parsley.
Ready to serve.

Lentil soup with leeks and honey (really delicious)

500gr lentils
2-3 leek stalks
2-3 bay leaves

5 tablespoonful olive oil
vinegar
2-3 soup spoonful of honey

Instruction

Cut the white part of the leeks into fine slices and wash them very thoroughly.
Cover the bottom of a big pot with olive oil.
Heat it up and put the leeks in.
Stir fry until golden, then add the lentils.
Turn them a couple of times and add enough water to cover the lentils .
Add bay leaves.
Let the lentils boil until they all settle to the bottom of the pot. Add 5-tablespoonful olive oil, some vinegar, some honey and pepper to taste.

DRUG FREE HEALING 11 : Medical Science Supporting Scriptures

Mandrakes: Chapter Nine
Reuben brought the mandrakes home to his mother because he knew she wanted to get pregnant again 'after she ceased bearing" following the birth of Judah.

Mandrake – Mandrago officinarum
Gen chapters 25 through chapter 33

Was there ever a point in your life when you felt so sick, rejected by those you called your friends, and were all alone; when nothing worked right, and you felt so stifled you wanted to die, a time when you questioned your own faith in God, and the reason for your being? Then you called on God, promising to serve him in every possible way, but after your prayers were answered, did you go right back doing those lousy things you used to do which you ought not to have done, and left undone those things that you ought to have done?

I don't know about you, but in my life, there were many of those occasions. I have had many moments when I felt very much like that, or worse than the feeling Apostle Paul expressed in Rom 7:15-25; " I do not understand my own actions…I do not do what I want to do, but I do the very things I hate… For I know that nothing good dwell within me, that is, in my flesh. I can will what is right, but I cannot do it. For I do not do the good I want, but the evil I do not want is what I do." But that might very well be the confession of the patriarch Jacob also.

Reading from Genesis chapter 25 to chapter 33, we find that Rebekah was doing a good job in teaching her son, Jacob, how to live by deceit and trickery. This conversation with Jacob illustrates her interpretation of "bringing up a child in the discipline and instruction of the LORD" (Eph.6:4).

She told Jacob; " I heard your father say to your brother Esau, 'bring me game, and prepare for me savory food to eat, that I may bless you before the LORD before I die. Now, therefore, my son, obey my word as I command you.' Go to the flock and get my two kids, so that I may prepare from them savory food for your father such as he likes; and you shall take
it to your father to eat, so that he may bless you before he dies."

Her son appeared to demonstrate a streak of level headedness and caution which he probably inherited from his grandfather Abraham when he told his mother this: "...My brother Esau is a hairy man, and I am a man of a smooth skin. Perhaps , my father will feel me, I shall seem to be mocking him, and bring a curse on myself and not a blessing." But Rebekah swiftly suppressed her son's objection saying "Let your curse be on me, my son. Only obey my word, and go, get them for me." (Gen. 27:5-13)

With his mother's connivance, Jacob tricked his father and stole his brother's birthright. Teaching her son further acts of deception and trickery, Rebekah told Jacob; "Your brother Esau is consoling himself by planning to kill you. Now therefore, my son, obey my voice; flee at once to my brother Leban in Haran, and stay with him awhile, until your brother's anger against you turns away, and he forgets what you have done to him; then I will send, and bring you back from there."

Although the motive for Jacob's flight to Haran , to his uncle Leban, was to escape Esau's vengeance against his brother, Rebekah told her husband a different story; "Then Rebekah said to Isaac, "I am weary of my life because of the Hittite women. (Esau had two Hittite wives). If Jacob marries one of the Hittite women such as these one of the women of the land, what good will my life be to me?"

When Jacob went away from the protection of his scheming mother, he found that his life came to a dead end.

Like Jacob, there come a time in our lives when we too, do find ourselves to be at a dead end ; a dead end to issues of our health, a dead end in our relationships, a dead end of our financial standing, a dead end in our worshipping of, and dependence on the LORD. For, no matter who is sheltering us from our misdeeds, missteps and miscalculations, from our bad choices, decisions and judgments, there will come a time when each one of us will be held accountable for every misguided word, thought or deed. As the scripture says; "But I tell you that men will have to give account on the Day of Judgment for every careless word they have spoken. "(Matt.12:36)

There is good news, however. In our moments of desolation and strife, God is faithful. He is gracious and merciful, when we call unto him, he has promised, "I will answer you, and will tell you great and hidden things that you have not known." (Jer.33:3)

The problem with us is that we are just as likely to forget our promises to God during out times of trouble, and return to our sinful ways as easily when our prayers are answered, as we might have been if our hopes were dashed. Jacob too was an imperfect man like the rest of us. He came to that moment of desperation as he fled, dreading his brother's revenge. He made a vow to God., saying; "If God will be with me, and will keep me in this way that I go, and will give me bread to eat and clothing to wear, so that I come again to my father's house in peace, then the LORD shall be my God, and this stone, which I have set up for a pillar, shall be God's house; and of all that you give me I will surely give one tenth to you." (Gen. 28:20-27)

No sooner were his prayers granted than Jacob forgot his vows to the LORD, and returned to the dubious and cantankerous behaviors he learnt from his mother.

We have been forewarned by God's word: "When you vow a vow to the LORD, do not delay in paying it; for he has no pleasure in fools. Pay what you vow. It is better that you should not vow than that you should vow and not fulfill it. Let not your mouth lead you into sin, and do not say before the messenger that it was a mistake, why should God be angry at your voice, and destroy the work of your hand?"(Eccl. 5:4-6)

God expects our faithfulness to him is demonstrated without making unwarranted promises as Jacob did.

Some of us have made vows to God because we are physically sick, some of us made such vows while we are emotionally sick, some financially sick, and some of us because we are spiritually sick. Whatever is the symptom of our sickness and the reason for such vows, God expects us to keep our vows. When we come out as new believers and give ourselves to Christ, God expects us to turn away from our old ways of sin; to lie no more, to cheat no more, to commit adultery no more and no more to indulge in fornication, murder, robbery and worship false gods no more.

Some preachers maintain that once we accept Jesus Christ as our Savior , not only has God forgiven our past sins, but also our sins of the present and the sins we will commit in the future because all our sins are already paid for by the blood for Jesus Christ. By this assertion, there is the implication that the vows we have made coming to Jesus can be violated; that we are at liberty to sin many times, and the LORD will forgive us. Poppycock!

"What shall we say then? Are we to continue to sin that grace may abound? By no means! How can we who died to sin still live in it?" (Rom. 6:1-2)

Being a Christian is a commitment to follow Jesus. Our Lord Jesus Christ tells us therefore, "You have heard that it was said to our people long ago, "When you make a vow, don't break that vow. Keep the vows that you make to the LORD." But I tell you, never make a vow. Don't make a vow using the name of heaven, because heaven is God's throne. Don't make a vow using the name of Jerusalem, because that is the city of the great King "God). And don't even say that your own head is proof that you will keep your vow…Let your word be "Yes, Yes," or "No, No", anything more than this comes from the evil one. (Matt 5:33-35 and 37). Our Lord Jesus commanded us to live in a way that it will not be necessary for us to make vows to show our sincerity.

Jacob had the break of his life for which he had prayed. By the mercy and grace of God, he arrived safely at the home of his uncle, Leban. God blessed him, and he had more than food, clothing and shelter. He had fled Beersheba alone. Now, having arrived in

Haran, he had become a family man. But he forgot his vows to God. He looked the other way as his family and his wives' relatives steeped themselves in the idolatry and superstitions of the people of Haran.

Within a month after he arrived in his uncle's home, according to Genesis chapter 29:14-26, his uncle offered to hire him, an offer Jacob accepted on condition that after seven years of service, Laban would grant him a pension by permitting him to become the husband of Leban's younger daughter, the beautiful Rachel.

At the end of his term of service to his uncle , instead of giving thanks to God for sustaining him, and trusting God with the desires of his heart, Jacob complained bitterly that his uncle tricked him, "What is this you have done to me?" Did I not serve with you for Rachel? Why then have you deceived me? But Laban responded that it was against the custom of his country that the younger child married before the firstborn did. (Gen.28:25-26) Jacob had to agree to marry Leban's older daughter, Lea and work for his uncle for an additional seven years to qualify to become Rachel's husband as well.

Sometimes, when answers to our prayers for healing are not exactly what we expected, we become disillusioned and fail to praise God. We must still give thanks to God for what we have. We must give thanks for what we do not have, but expect to have. We must thank God for the good times, and thank God for the bad times. For, in God's economy, our ways are not his ways of doing things. If we persevere, and stand firm in our faith, taking God at His word, we shall surely see the salvation of the LORD. For, ultimately, Laban gave away his younger daughter Rachel in marriage to Jacob it was after an additional seven years of Jacob's service to him.

As we seek healing, we must be aware that we will also have to undergo many tests in life. There will be medical tests, spiritual tests, physical tests, emotional tests, ethical tests or psychological tests. In all things we must be determined to stand up to the test and like the Apostle Paul, stand out to proclaim " In all things we are more than conquerors through him who loved us...Neither death, nor life, nor angels, nor rulers, nor things present, nor things to come, nor powers, nor height, nor depth, nor anything else in all creation, will be able to separate us from the love God in Christ Jesus our Lord."(Rom. 8:37-39)

Under all circumstances, we must let Christ be reflected through us by our deeds even more so than by our words. Jacob made a vow before God to serve Him if He blessed his journey with "bread to eat and clothes to wear." He knew his father-in-law Laban was an idolater. He knew that his wives were brought up in an environment of idol worshipers. But he, Jacob, the prophet of God, and the child of the covenant through whom God's promise of salvation would be fulfilled, did nothing about witnessing for the LORD. He compromised.

It is not enough to do no sinful action. It is not enough to claim to live by the word. It is equally sinful to do nothing about wrongful deeds by others when it is in our power to stop or correct it. Doing nothing is compromising.

Jacob had three sons by his first wife, Leah, but Rachel, the younger sister of Leah had no child. "When Rachel saw that she bore Jacob no children, she envied her sister; and she said to Jacob, "Give me children, or I shall die" to which Jacob would snap out, "Am I in the place of God, who has withheld from you the fruit of the womb?"

As a son of Rachel's aunt Rebekah, who herself had had an issue with infertility, but was later blessed to become a mother of twins following twenty years of intercessory prayers by her husband Isaac, Jacob's father, Jacob was obligated to encourage his wife in the LORD. It was his responsibility to console his wife by the precedent God Himself had set in the story of the birth of his own father Isaac by Rachel's aunt Sarah in her old age. Rather, Jacob directed his efforts to helping God be God in fulfilling His covenant to bless him. Jacob devised schemes to outwit his devious uncle and father-in-law, Laban. In the process, his own family had become mired in the idolatry and superstition of the people of Padanaram.

Genesis 30:14-16: "In the days of wheat harvest, Reuben went and found mandrakes in the field, and brought them to his mother, Leah. Then Rachel said to Leah, "Please give me some of your son's mandrakes." But she said to her, "Is it small matter that you have taken away my husband? Would you take away my son's mandrakes also? Rachel said, "Then he may lie with you tonight for your son's mandrakes. When Jacob came back from the field in the evening, Leah went out to meet him, and said, "You must come in to me, for I have hired you with my son's mandrakes."

Reuben who had had no spiritual direction from his father was distracted by the presence of mandrakes in the wheat fields. Mandrakes had no business being in the wheat fields. But when you compromise with the enemy, you create a fertile ground for the enemy to grow. The enemy had a plan and Reuben succumbed because everybody was doing it.

Have you been tempted to do something that is wrong by Christian standards, but you went along with the rest and did it anyway because everybody else was doing it?

Mandrakes had a reputation in idolatrous Haran for possessing magical powers for procreation. It was also regarded as an aphrodisiac, in spite of its deadly toxicity. Reuben brought the mandrakes home to his mother because he knew she wanted to get pregnant again 'after she ceased bearing" following the birth of Judah. He brought the mandrakes to his mother because everybody who was anybody who had a child credited mandrakes for the conception.

Mandrake is the common name for members of the plant genus Mandragora belonging to the nightshades family (Solanaceae). The structure of the plants from the leaves down to the roots resembles male and female human figures.

Mandrakes were used by pagan communities in magical spells and witchcraft. They were frequently made into amulets believed to bring good fortune, and to cure sterility.

Mandrakes fostered the superstition that if a person uprooted the plants by the hand, that person would die. The roots were tied by rope to the bodies of dogs that would pull up the roots from the soil. Preposterous claims were attributed to the plant that it would shriek in pain when being pulled from the ground, and that those that heard its cries instantaneously became mad, deaf or dead. Use of roots and leaves may cause hallucination and insanity.

Uses:

Mandrake roots were used as a sedative. They were among the oldest narcotics. It has a long history as an anesthetic.

Sheaves of Grain: Chapter Ten
Judgment time is equated with the process of threshing wheat.

Sheaves (of Wheat)
Triticum aestivum
Gen.31 to chapter 44

"Once Joseph had a dream, and when he told it to his brothers, they hated him even more. He said to them, 'Listen to this dream that I dreamed. There we were binding sheaves in the field. Suddenly my sheaf rose and stood upright; then your sheaves gathered around it, and bowed down to it.'" (Gen 37:5-7) " ...I fell asleep a second time and I saw in my dream seven ears of grain full and good, growing on one stalk..."(Gen.41:22) "Let them gather all the food of these good years that are coming, and lay up grains under the authority of Pharaoh for food in the cities, and let them keep it." (Gen 41:35) And in verses 47-49, we are told: "During the seven plenteous years the earth produced abundantly. He gathered up all the food of the seven years when there was plenty in the land of Egypt, and stored up food in the cities; he stored up in every city the food from around it. So Joseph stored up grain in such abundance – like the sand of the sea - that he stopped measuring it; it was beyond measure."

Grains grow on stalks. In the dream of Joseph, the bible did not tell us what types of grains were on the stalks of the sheaves. But somewhere seven chapters back, from Genesis chapter 37, it is written: "In the days of wheat harvest Reuben went…in the field." Further up in chapter 41 verses 22, 35 and 49, "grain" has been mentioned several times. In fact, at one point, the bible reports that Joseph stored up "grain" in such abundance – like the sand of the sea- that he stopped measuring it; it was beyond measure." It was impossible to escape sheaves where grain was in abundance. It is reasonable to surmise that the sheaves in Joseph's dream were of grains of varied descriptions. "Father of many nations", recalls God's covenant with their great-grand father. Sheaves of wheat, sheaves of corn, of barley, spelt, oats, rue or rye, and , perhaps, even sheaves of weeds – tares in the mix.

      Wherever there was food in abundance for God's people, there mysteriously emerged also tares and weeds, poisonous weeds. For untrained eyes, the sheaves would all appear to be like grass. It would be tough on the person without experience in farming to identify one crop from the other. Identifying wheat from the tares would be impossible because they all look alike. However, that would be a very small matter to an experienced farmer. God was laying out a picture of the future about Christ's mission during His second coming. Judgment time is coming when Jesus Christ will separate the sheep from the goats, the wheat from the tares; that is, true Christians from false Christians, true Church of Christ from false Church of Christ. Judgment time is equated with the process of threshing wheat.

To correctly identify the wheat and the tares by the marketplace, the grain has to be separated from the stalk on which it grows, and from the chaff that covers it. This would call for the sheaves to be subjected to the process of threshing.

According to the New American Heritage Dictionary, threshing means "to beat the stems and husks of grain or cereal plant with machine or flail to separate the grains or seed from the straw." It is a rigorous examination. A time will come when we will all face God's rigorous examination. "Are you ready when the LORD shall come?"

If you were to die today, do you know which side of eternity you would go? When Joseph told his brothers of his dream predicting God's ultimate judgment upon them using Joseph himself as God's instrument of justice, his brothers' bruised egos were so damaged that they were blinded by rage, that they failed to see God's big picture of salvation for the world. However, 13 years later, the sons of Israel saw the judgment of God upon them. We read this from Genesis chapter 44: " Judah said: "What can we say to my lord? What can we speak? How can we clear ourselves? God has found out the guilt of your servant; here we are then my lord's slaves, both we and also the one in whose possession the cup has been found."

Just as Joseph symbolized Christ before whom the children of Israel were brought to judgment, so it is also that the time will come when all of us will "appear before the judgment seat of Christ, so that each may receive recompense for what has been done in the body whether good or evil."   (2 Cor. 5:10)

Some sheaves are nothing, but weeds fit for the fire. Sheaves reveal their special crops; the grains for sustenance. Some grains are of wheat, some grains are of barley, oats, or spelt, millet, or rice. Each one of us is to fulfill the rolls God ordained for us. Each one is to bring what sustains the spirit to mankind; to lead somebody to Jesus Christ just as grains provide nutrients for the human body.

"There was famine in every country, but throughout the land of Egypt, there was bread. When all the land of Egypt was famished, the people cried to Pharaoh for bread. Pharaoh said to all the Egyptians, "Go to Joseph; what he says to you do"

In the marriage in Cana (John 2:1-11) Jesus also was invited to the marriage, with his disciples. When the wine failed, the mother of Jesus said to him, "They have no wine." And Jesus said to her, "O woman, what have you to do with me? My hour has not yet come." His mother said to the servants, "Do whatever he tells you."

Joseph was archetype of Jesus Christ. Out of the house of Israel came one called to save the world from famine, to open the storehouse for the distribution of grain to all.

There is famine all over the world today. We all have work to do in providing all the world spiritual nutrients. Amidst the rise of religious extremism, war and terrorism, God has called us to be His sheaves of grain. It is not enough to call ourselves Christians just because we attend Catholic masses, Pentecostal revivals, Presbyterian worship, Baptist meetings, Evangelical crusades or Methodist services. God wants us to be sheaves of grain in Christ. God wants us to be soul winners for his kingdom, and not bench-warmers in church. As Christians, we place far too much value upon our religious denominations rather than on the author and finisher of our faith, Jesus Christ our Lord who has called us. We have been called to be whole grain Christians. We must become sheaves of wheat in the LORD, or sheaves of barley, sheaves of oats, millet or rye according to our special spiritual gifting.

Constituents

Wheat grass contains minerals like calcium, iron, magnesium, phosphorus, potassium, sodium, sulfur, cobalt and zinc. Chlorophyll, one of the main constituents of wheat grass is very beneficial for the body. It is also a rich source of vitamin A, B and C. Between 65 and 90 percent of the calories in grains come from complex carbohydrates constituting two-thirds of everyone's daily caloric consumption. Grains are rich in both soluble fiber which lowers blood-cholesterol levels, and insoluble which helps to prevent constipation and protects against some forms of cancer.

People living in areas where unrefined whole grains make up a significant part of the diet are known to have a lower incidence of intestinal and bowel problems, such as colon cancer, diverticulosis, and hemorrhoids.

Grains contain significant amounts of B vitamins, riboflavin, thiamin, and niacin, vitamin E, iron, zinc, calcium, selenium, and magnesium. Health experts advise everyone – men and women, young and old – to eat more "whole grains" and to cut back on "refined grains". Whole grains include wheat, corn, rice, oats, barley, quinoa, sorghum, spelt, rye – and even popcorn!

In their natural state growing in the fields, whole grains are the entire seed of a plant. This seed which industry calls a "kernel" consists of three key parts; the bran, the germ, and the endosperm. The bran is the multi-layered outer skin of the kernel, and is tough enough to protect the other two parts of the kernel from assaults by sunlight, pests, water, and disease. It contains important antioxidants, B vitamins and fiber. The germ is the embryo, which, if fertilized by pollen, will sprout into a new plant. It contains many

B vitamins, some protein, minerals, and healthy fats. The endosperm is the germ's food supply, which provides essential energy to the young plant so it can send roots down for water and nutrients, and send sprouts up for sunlight's photosynthesizing power. The endosperm is by far the largest portion of the kernel. It contains starchy carbohydrates, proteins and small amounts of vitamins and minerals. Whole grains contain all three parts of kernel. Refining normally removes the bran and the germ, leaving only the endosperm. Without the bran and germ, about 25% of a grain's protein is lost, along with at least seventeen key nutrients.

Processors add back some vitamins and minerals to enrich refined grains, so refined products still contribute valuable nutrients. But whole grains are healthier, providing more protein, more fiber and many important vitamins and minerals.

Wheat and wheat products are major parts of the diet for over a third of the world's people. Wheat is present in one form or another at almost every meal all over the world. The products come in the form of breads, cookies, cakes, crackers, macaroni, spaghetti, and other kinds of pasta. There are many varieties of wheat, at least thirty, of which there are three ; durum wheat, club wheat and bread wheat cultivated in the Spring or Winter, thus the names, Spring Wheat and Winter Wheat.

Medicinal Benefits

The wheat, as produced by nature, contains several medicinal virtues. Every part of the whole wheat grain supplies elements needed by the human body. Starch and gluten in wheat provide heat and energy. The inner bran coats provide phosphates and other mineral salts. The outer bran, the much-needed roughage - the indigestible portion that helps easy movement of bowels - the germ, vitamins B and E. Protein of wheat helps build and repair muscular tissue. The wheat germ, which is removed in the process of refining, is also rich in essential vitamin E, the lack of which can lead to heart disease.

The loss of vitamins and minerals in the refined wheat flour has led to widespread prevalence of constipation and other digestive disturbances and nutritional disorders. The whole wheat, which includes bran and wheat germ, therefore, provides protection against diseases such as constipation, ischemic, heart disease, disease of the colon called diverticulum, appendicitis, obesity and diabetes.

Dr. Ann Wigmore, founder director of the Hippocrates Health Institute, Boston, U.S.A. and a leading proponent of the 'wheat grass therapy' has been quoted as saying," guided by spiritual mentality and nourished only by live uncooked food, the body will run indefinitely, unhampered by sickness".

Wheat bran which is lost during milling has more nutritional value than the finished product of refined white flour. The chlorophyll present in wheat grass serves as a body cleanser to rebuild and neutralize toxins. Wheat grass juice furnishes the body with vital nourishment, providing extra energy to the body. This juice contains nearly 70 per cent of chlorophyll. It is also a rich source of vitamin A, B and C. It also contains minerals like calcium, iron, magnesium, phosphorus, potassium, sodium, sulfur, cobalt and zinc. Chlorophyll, one of the main constituents of wheat grass is very beneficial for the body. Chlorophyll, due to its high vitamins and mineral contents, purifies blood.

Constipation

The bran of wheat, which is generally discarded in milling of the flour, is more wholesome and nourishing than the flour itself. It is an excellent laxative. The laxative effects of bran are much superior to those of fruits or green vegetables as cellulose of the latter is more easily broken down by bacteria while passing through the intestine. The bran is highly beneficial in the prevention and treatment of constipation due to its concentration of cellulose which forms a bulk-mass in the intestines and helps easy evacuation due to increased peristalsis. The chlorophyll content present in wheat grass enhances heart and lung functions. Capillary activity also increases while toxemia or blood poisoning is reduced. Due to increased iron content in the blood and hemoglobin, lungs function better, oxygenation improves and the effect of carbon-dioxide is minimized. It is for this reason that wheat grass juice is prescribed for circulatory disorders.

Tooth Disorders

Wheat is valuable in the prevention and cure of pyorrhea. Wheat grass juice acts as an excellent mouth wash for sore throat, prevents pyorrhea, tooth decay and relieves toothache.

Skin Diseases

Chlorophyll that wheat contains, arrests growth and development of harmful bacteria. When poultice of wheat grass is applied externally to diseased skin or ulcerated wounds it is proven to retard bacterial activity. Wheat flour can also be applied as a dusting powder over burns, scalds, itching body parts and burring eruptions. Whole-wheat flour, mixed with vinegar, boiled and applied outwardly removes freckles. Poultice of wheat grass juice can be applied on the infected area, as it is an able sterilizer.

Digestive System Disorders

Wheat grass juice used as an enema helps detoxify the walls of the colon. The general procedure is to give an enema with lukewarm or neem water. After waiting for 20 minutes, 90 to 120 ml. of wheat grass juice enema is given. This should be retained for

15 minutes. This enema is very helpful in disorders of the colon, mucous and ulcerative colitis, chronic constipation and bleeding piles.

Ingesting

Chewing wheat grass is the easiest method of ingesting wheat grass juice. As an alternative to chewing, wheat grass should be finely ground in a blender with some water added to it to enable the extraction of the wheat grass juice. This juice should be taken within 10 to 15 minutes after extraction. Wheat grass juice should be mixed thoroughly with saliva before being swallowed slowly. This juice should be drunk an hour before a meal and two to three hours after the meal. Wheat grass is grown by soaking a good variety of wheat for eight to 10 hours.

Wheatgrass Juice
Recipe

Grow wheatgrass by soaking wheat in water for eight to 10 hours.

Drain water.

Allow 15 hours for grain to sprout.

Spread sprouts in trays –any earthenware pot or wooden trays – over compost manure.

Cover sprouts with dark material, or tray.

Keep away from sunlight.

Sprinkle sprouts with water twice a day for seven to ten days until sprouts grow about seven inches tall.

Cut wheat grass.

Put in juicer or blender.
Add water as desired.
Add dark honey to taste.
Take a glassful three times a day two hours before meals. Chew wheat grass thoroughly before swallowing.

Honey: Chapter Eleven

"Pleasant words are as honeycomb, sweet to the soul, and health to the bones." (Prov. 16:24 KJV)
Honey
Genesis chapter 43 verses 1- 4 and verses 11 – 14:

"Now the famine was severe in the land. And when they had eaten up the grain that they had brought from Egypt, their father said to them, "Go again, buy us a little more food." But Judah said to him, "The man solemnly warned us, saying." You shall not see my face unless your brother is with you… Then their father Israel said to them, "If it must be so, then do this: take some of the choice fruits of the land in your bags, and carry them down as a present to the man – a little balm and a little honey, gum, resin, pistachio nuts, and almonds. Take double the money with you…may God Almighty grant you mercy before the man…"

Here's an account from King James Version; "And the famine was sore in the land. And it came to pass, when they had eaten up the corn which they had brought out of Egypt, their father said unto to them, Go again, buy us a little food. And Judah spoke unto him, saying, "The man did solemnly protest unto us, saying, "Ye shall not see my face, except your brother be with you"...And their father Israel said unto them, "If it must be so now, do this; take of the best fruits in the land in your vessels, and carry down the man a present, a little balm, and a little honey, spices and myrrh, nuts and almonds: and take double money in your hand; and the money that was brought again in the mouth of your sacks, carry it again in your hand; peradventure it was an oversight; Take also your brother, and arise, go again unto the man; And God Almighty give you mercy before the man, that he may send away your other brother, and Benjamin. If I be bereaved of my children, I am bereaved."

We are seeing a broken man, Israel, transformed from being a taker and a cheat to a giver, having been subdued by a severe famine, and events of his reclining years that he could not manipulate. We are seeing the conversion of Jacob to a father who loved all of his children and not the uncaring, irresponsible, deadbeat father, and head of a dysfunctional family that he once was. Israel was no longer the spiritually detached head of a household. He was no more the rash, irascible, and undemonstrative husband who was unresponsive to the emotional needs of his wives causing one of the wives - Bilhah – to have sexual intercourse with Jacob's own son, Reuben. Jacob had become Israel. He was a man being transformed by Almighty God.

While on his way from Haran back to Canaan, Jacob had an encounter with Almighty God who gave him a new name, Israel and a transformation began to take place in his life. When Almighty God comes your way, you will never be the same again. Jacob became a new creation in the Lord.

"If any man be in Christ, he has become a new creation. The old is passed away. All things have become new." (Corinthians 5:17)

Israel had become a man bowed to the will of God. Despite the severe famine, and his miseries, Israel had determined to turn his back on his own past life of duplicity and selfishness to become a giver instead of the taker that he was. He was resolved to give not just what was demanded of him, but double. He would give only "the best fruits in the land." He gave "the choice fruit". He told his sons carry along with them as present to the man, he did not know was his own son, Joseph "a little balm, and a little honey, spices and myrrh, nuts and almonds: and double money".

That scenario would be reenacted a thousand years later by wise men from the east visiting the infant Jesus Christ in Bethlehem. Matthew 2:11; "And when they were come into the house, they saw the young child with Mary his mother, and fell down, and worshipped him: and when they had opened their treasures, they presented unto him gifts; gold, frankincense, and myrrh."

The lesson we are learning from the life of Jacob is that nobody is too far gone in sin that the Lord cannot use him or her to be His witness. But each of us must demonstrate the willingness to be used by God regardless of our sinful past.

Believe that God can accomplish the very best in the worst of people or situations. Put your hope in Him. Talk about the good things that He can do. Pleasant words are hopeful words, and they are like "a honeycomb, sweet to the soul and healing to the bones." (Prov 16:24)

Let us pray! Almighty God Jehovah, Creator of the universe, I pray in the name of our Lord and Savior Jesus Christ that you grant me the grace to apply to my life the lesson from the life story of Jacob; to always remember your covenant through Jesus Christ your beloved Son that you are able to use the worst of me to accomplish my best in the worst of situations in order to fulfill your plan and purpose.

Grant me the favor, O God, therefore, never to look back at my past, and never to give in to the evil tricks of the Enemy to be reminded of my worthlessness, and of my past duplicitous, neglectful, judgmental, insensitive and irresponsible life, but to be yielded to your will, knowing that all things work together for the good of those who love the LORD. Help me, Almighty God to be transformed by the renewing of my mind to the new creation that you made me through Christ Jesus, so that like Israel, I too, will cease to be a taker, but, instead, become a giver. Fill me with the spirit of giving; to be a giver in my good times, and give also, even if my life is besieged by severe famine. Help me to give still, though the grains of my resources might be depleted, or I am oppressed by demands beyond my ability. Help me to give, not just what is expected from me, but more than double the demand. Help me to be able to give the choice fruits of my heart and of my life, to give to your church for the work of your kingdom here on earth, give to my fellow man in need, to be a little balm of encouragement for the one in the throes of despair, and a little honey of love to the one alone and unloved.

Grant me the grace O God to be a gum, providing glue to fractured relationships, becoming a spiritual preservative of myrrh, and a resin of frankincense to edify by prayers someone in need of spiritual uplifting, pistachios of nourishment, and almonds to energize those debilitated.

When the going is tough, grant me the mercy and grace, Almighty God, to have the faith to lean on you at all times, and to be encouraged in knowing that with you, all things are possible. For it is you alone who are able to do exceeding abundantly above all that I can ask or think, according to your power that works in me. Help me also to live the words of the songwriter of the hymn my mother taught me to sing when I was but four years old;

> "I'm walking arm in arm with Jesus,
> I trust in him to lead the way,
> I know that if I only cling to Him,
> He'll never let me go astray.
> For I am walking, with Jesus
> Walking all alone,
> All along the way.
> For I am walking with Jesus,
> Walking with Jesus all alone!

I pray, O God, for courage to face the challenges that may come my way while trying to bring honey to somebody's life; grant me the courage to accept the sacrifices that may be demanded of me. To you be the glory and honor and praises forever and ever through Jesus Christ I pray. Amen!

Honey from Apis Mellifica (Honey bee)

There are more than 20,000 species of bees, but only 5 kinds produce honey. To make one pound of honey, 160,000 honeybees would make as many as two million trips to flowers so that they could collect four pounds of nectar to produce honey one fourth the quantity of nectar collected. One honeybee would take an entire lifetime to produce a teaspoon of honey.

Constituents

Honey is the only food that will not spoil. It may crystallize in cold weather or over a time, but will melt under heat. It is a source of rapid energy. It contains live enzymes vital for the proper functioning of our body systems. Its other constituents include glucose, fructose, proteins, antimicrobials, hormones, organic acids, and carbohydrates. Honey is composed of a complex mixture of vitamins, namely; vitamin B6, vitamin B-12, vitamin C, vitamin A, vitamin D, vitamin E, and vitamin K as well as thiamin, riboflavin, niacin, foliate, and pantothenic acid. Honey is rich in minerals such as calcium, copper, iron, magnesium, manganese, phosphorous, potassium, sodium, and zinc. Honey as a simple sugar, breaks down easily requiring the body less work in converting the sugar to energy, unlike refined white sugar that has been proven to be carcinogenic, inhibits calcium absorption in the intestines, and weakens the strength and ability of the vitamins and minerals that honey has put in the body.

Medicinal Uses

Honey is antibiotic, antiviral, anti-inflammatory, anti-anemic, tonic, laxative, anti-allergenic, expectorant, and anti-carcinogenic. It is an overall tonic to all systems in the body, and is of special use in the intestinal and skeletal systems. Because of its anti-microbial properties, honey is effective in healing wounds. It has proved useful in burns and sunburn. The glucose in honey speeds up the body's absorption abilities of calcium, zinc, and magnesium, thus, providing a quick energy boost. Honey mixed with vinegar can soothe arthritic joints. Honey has been used throughout the ages to heal wounds. When honey mixes with the fluids from the body in the wound, it actually causes those cells to release hydrogen peroxide to cleanse the wound and promote healing. Honey has also been proven useful in healing ulcers and gastric lesions. Its specific properties have proven beneficial in treating respiratory ailments. It is best to purchase raw, unmolested honey to receive the maximum benefits possible from the honey.

Food : If you're a consumer of honey, don't be too sure you have the best honey full of needed nutrients, if your honey is clear and fluid. The absence of your honey's cloudy appearance is proof that the honey has been strained thoroughly through a fine sieve, thus removing from it compounds containing valuable pollen nutrients including vitamins and minerals that body needs for its proper functioning. What you're getting from this type of fancy honey is a sweetener. Processed honey comes in four classifications; Grade A (Choice), Grade B (Standard), Grade C (Standard), Grade D (Substandard).

Honey is about 140 percent sweeter than sugar. Use less amount of it than you would refine white sugar. Darker honeys are generally richer in nutrients than light honeys. The best honey will congeal in a room temperature. It is called uncooked honey when the degree of heat in melting down the honey is less than 104 degrees Fahrenheit. In this state, the component enzymes, vitamins and minerals are preserved. When honey is highly heated its chemistry alters.

Try Taking This Refreshing Honey balm
every evening before bedtime

Ingredients
1 Gallon spring water
8 Table spoonful or bags Balm (Melissa) / Chamomile will do just fine
16 Ounces Raw Dark honey
16 Ounces Fresh ginger roots.

Instructions:
Peel fresh ginger roots
Put ginger roots in blender and process to a fine paste
Remove ginger paste from blender and put in vessel ready to heat with water.
Add gallon of water and stir
Add fresh or dried balm leaves
Put on stove bring to boil under low 80 degrees Fahrenheit temperature
Add honey and stir for 5 minutes to mix
Remove from stove and cover to steep for 20 minutes.
Strain
Bottle and refrigerate
Enjoy as desired before bedtime

Chapter Twelve: Balm

Balm

Also known as: Melissa Officinalis, Lemon Balm, Sweet Balm., Bee Balm, Balm Mint, Blue balm, Cure-All, Dropsy Plant, and Garden Balm. In Genesis 43:11, the patriarch is quoted as instructing his son to take as gifts to "the man "in Egypt among others "...a little balm..." Lemon Balm was believed to be an elixir of youth. It was used as part of a drink to ensure longevity. Modern science maintains the claims for this plant are not farfetched.

The name Melissa is from the Greek word for "bee". Officinalis, translates as 'workshop', which speaks of the compelling attraction the plant has for honey bees. The word Balm is short form for Balsamon, referring to the plant's oily fragrant resin credited with the ability to soothe and calm nerves.

Constituents:

Volatile oil including citronella, polyphenols, tannins, flavonoids. It is carminative, diaphoretic and febrifuge.

Medicinal Uses

Balm is used as an antidepressant, sedative, antiviral, antibacterial, and antispasmodic ointment. It induces mild perspiration and makes a refreshing tea to treat early stages of cold, fever, catarrh, and influenza. Balm is a useful herb, either alone or in combination with others. It is also taken for depression, nervous exhaustion, sleeplessness, menstrual cramps, nausea, and indigestion. It repels mosquitoes. Lemon Balm may be used alone by itself or in combination with other herbs. Used externally, lemon balm may relieve painful gout swellings. Harvest before flowering.

For a relaxing Lemon balm bath, tie up a bunch of fresh or dried lemon balm leaves in a towel or fabric gauze. Place in bathtub. Run hot water over. Enjoy the refreshing lemon-mint health giving aroma.

For treating minor wounds and insect bites, make a hot compress putting 4 crushed tablespoon of lemon balm in a cup of water. Boil for 10 minutes. Soak a clean towel in the solution, and place it on the wound.

For treating herpes simplex, make a poultice of fresh lemon balm. Add a teaspoon of dark, uncooked honey. Apply ointment on herpes lesion. Same lemon balm, mixed with vinegar, and dark uncooked honey applied as ointment on sore, itching groin will speed up healing.

For repelling mosquitoes and other insects, rub crushed fresh lemon balm leaves or balm oil on exposed body parts.

For calming nerves, restful sleep, reducing fever, or easing menstrual cramps, treating anxiety, indigestion and acidity due to eating too much, too quickly or missing meals, bloating, heartburn or stomach pain take lemon balm tea.

Food: Lemon-mint scented, honey sweet balm is used also as flavoring to salad and salad dressing, or garnish in soups, stews, custards, pudding or cooking.

Drink Lemon Balm Tea

It makes a refreshing replacement for carbonated soft drinks.

Ingredients

2 tablespoonful fresh lemon balm leaves
2 tablespoon or 4 bags chamomile
1 pint fresh water
Honey

Instruction:

Boil fresh lemon leaves and chamomile in water for 10-20 minutes
Pour infusion in a cup
Add honey as desired
Drink at bedtime

Lemon Balm –Ginger Drink

Ingredients

1 Gallon spring water

8 Table spoonful or bags Balm (Melissa) / Chamomile will do just fine
16 Ounces Raw Dark honey
16 ounces Fresh ginger roots.
Instruction
Peel off fresh ginger roots
Put ginger roots in blender and blend to paste
Put in vessel and add gallon of water
Stir. Add fresh or dried balm leaves
Put on stove bring to boil under low 80 degrees Fahrenheit temperature
Add honey and stir for 5 minutes to mix
Remove from stove and cover to steep for 20 minutes.
Strain
Bottle infusion and refrigerate
Enjoy as desired before bedtime
Read a chapter of the Word of God, meditate on the Word, and pray! Amen

Chapter Thirteen: Resin

"He was given much incense to mingle with the prayers of all the saints upon the golden alter before the throne...and the smoke of the incense rose with the prayers of the saints from the hand of the angel before God. (Rev. 8: 3-4)

Resin—Boswellia Thurifera

Resins – are aromatic gums obtained by bleeding trees, notably, of the genus Boswellia for use as incense, and for use in perfumes. Resins are insoluble in water. Frankincense is the common name by which the gum resin of Boswellia Thurifera is known. Frankincense, cinnamon and myrrh were three of the most important spices of ancient times. In ancient Israel, frankincense was an important component of incense and used as part of offering to Almighty God, Jehovah: "You shall make an altar on which to offer incense..." God commanded Moses, "Take the finest spices of liquid myrrh...Take sweet spices...with pure frankincense... and make incense...pure and holy. When you make incense according to this composition, you shall not make it for yourself, it shall be regarded by you as holy to the Lord" (Exodus 30:1-37).

About one thousand years after Jacob's sons delivered presents including frankincense to Joseph, "wise men from the East" would arrive in Judea with gifts of frankincense, myrrh and gold to celebrate the birth of the Son of the Most High God, our Lord and Savior Jesus Christ. (Matthew 2:11) This was in fulfillment of Isaiah's prophecy; "they shall bring gold and frankincense and shall proclaim the praise of the LORD" (Is 60:6) .

Frankincense, an almost white resin, was one of the most prized and costly substances in the ancient world. It was worth more than its weight in gold. Frankincense pointed to Christ's role as our high priest who "is able for all time to save those who approach God through him, since he always lives to make intercession for them. For it is fitting that we should have such a high priest, holy, blameless, undefiled, separated from sinners, and exalted above the heavens. (Hebrews 7:25-26)

"Incense which are the prayers of the saints", according to Rev. 5 :8 , was burned in the belief that it carried prayers to God. "He was given much incense to mingle with the prayers of all the saints upon the golden alter before the throne…and the smoke of the incense rose with the prayers of the saints from the hand of the angel before God. (Rev. 8 3-4) Frankincense symbolically draws us to the Throne of Grace.
"…For by grace you have been saved through faith, and this is not your won doing; it is the gift of God-not the result of works, so that no one may boast. For we are what he has made us, created in Christ Jesus for good

works, which God prepared beforehand to be our way of life." Ephesians 2:1-10.

If by this time Jesus Christ is still not part of your life, I wish to suggest to you to do something radical right now. Pause. Reflect on your life. Think about death...about when you die and where you will spend eternity. Eternity is a long time. But eternity has two sides; the happy side with Christ where he is the high priest interceding the Father Almighty God for you and me. There is the other side of eternity, the hurtful side with Satan. Which side of it will you be?

"In my Father's house are many mansions. If it were not so, I would have told you. I am going to prepare a place for you. If I go and prepare a place for you, I will come again, and will receive you to myself; that where I am, you may be there also. Where I go, you know, and you know the way." (John 14:2-4)

Have you ever had a nightmare? Have you ever fallen asleep and dreamt sweet dreams? Nightmare and sweet dreams are very, very poor imitations of the two sides of eternity. Your sweet dreams do not make a smidgen of what it will be like to be with Jesus. And your nightmare is a very poor imitation of Gahena...hell. If so, eternity in hell is a hell of a place to live in. The way to avoid hell is to believe in Jesus Christ now. Come to Jesus right now. Listen to this exhortation: "Take care that none of you may have an evil, unbelieving heart that turns away from the living God...Today, if you hear his voice, do not harden your heart as in the rebellion". (Hebrews 3:12-15) These are the words of a well-known bible teacher, Rev. Dr. David Jeremiah, "This is your time to come to Jesus. Aim at heaven and you will have earth thrown in. Aim at earth and you will get nothing!"

It costs you nothing to come to Jesus. Repent your sins! "If you confess with your mouth Jesus is Lord, and believe in your heart that God raised Him from the dead, you will be saved; for with the heart a person believes, resulting in righteousness, and with the mouth he confesses, resulting in salvation." (Romans 10:9, 10 NASB).

Say these words of prayer. "Our Father in heaven, Almighty God and Creator, I come before your Throne of Mercy in the name of Jesus Christ my Lord and Savior to thank you for loving me, and sending your only Son to die for my sins. Lord Jesus Christ, I am sorry for my sins, I repent and will not turn back. I do believe that you came, you died for me, you were buried, resurrected and ascended to heaven where you are constantly interceding the Father for me. Thank you Jesus, for saving me and for forgiving me. I know I am forgiven. I am free from sin. Satan has no power over me. By the blood of Jesus I am free! Thank you for allowing my prayers to rise before your Throne of Grace like the fragrance of Frankincense.

Boswellia is a genus of trees known for their fragrant resin which has many pharmacological uses particularly as anti-inflammatory. There are four main species of Boswellia, which produce true Frankincense, and each type of resin is available in various grades, namely, Boswellia Sacra (syn. B. carteri, B. thurifera) Boswellia frereana, Boswellia serrata, and Boswellia papyrifera.

Constituents
Resins , Volatile oil , Water-soluble gum , Bassorin , Plant residue .Resins contain boswellic acid and alibanoresin.

Studies showed that boswellic acids deliver anti-inflammatory action identical to action by conventional non-steroidal anti-inflammatory drugs (NSAIDs). Boswellia inhibits pro-inflammatory mediators in the body, such as leukotrienes but unlike NSAIDs, long-term use of boswellia does not appear to cause irritation or ulceration of the stomach, experts say. It was also shown to possess marked cholesterol and triglyceride lowering activity. Boswellia is an astringent. It is also credited with stimulant, expectorant, diuretic, diaphoretic, antipyretic, and antiseptic properties.

Medicinal Uses: Boswellia has been used in treating asthma. It is believed to be effective against rheumatoid arthritis, osteoarthritis, osteoarthritis, back pain, and in reducing inflammatory associated with Crohn's disease and ulcerative colitis. Boswellia also helps control excessively high blood lipids and arteriosclerosis, and protect the liver against bacterial galactosamin-endotoxins. It is reported to be useful in ulcers, tumors, goiter, cystic breast, diarrhea, dysentery, piles, asthma, bronchitis, chronic laryngitis, jaundice, and skin diseases.

Recipe
For chronic bronchitis
4 tablespoon of frankincense
2 tablespoon Sea salt or Epsom salt preferably
Bath towel

Instruction
Draw hot water of desired temperature in bathtub
Add frankincense
Add Epsom salt or Sea salt
Get into the bathtub, relax
Massage your chest with bath towel soaked in the frankincense solution.

For Stress and Muscle Pain
Try the following combination of essential oils in a warm (not hot) bath to ease stress and muscle pain:
1-2 drops Frankincense (Boswellia cateri)
3 drops Lavender (Lavandula angustifolia)
2 drops Petitgrain (Citrus aurantium var. amara)
Instruction
Draw warm water in bathtub
Add essential oils,
Swirl oils in warm water around with foot or hand
Get inside tub
Relax and relax.
Allow yourself 10 to 20 minutes. Do not get the bath water in to your eyes, as the oils will sting.

Myrrh: Chapter Fourteen

Myrrh is a symbol of our own suffering and inevitable death. Many people cannot deal with death, especially when it strikes closer to home. For where death strikes, hysteria reigns.
Commiphora myrrh, Buseraceae
Also known as chervil, cicely, and sweet cicely,
Genesis 43: 11- Genesis 50:26

Myrrh is a bitter tasting aromatic gum resin obtained from several shrubs of the genus Commiphora. Its name derives from the Semitic word *mara, murr or maror,* meaning bitter. Myrrh has been used for generations as part of ingredients in pomanders -- a mixture of aromatic substances enclosed in a sachet, ball, or other container, kept near stored clothes or in a room to impart a pleasant smell. -- cosmetics and other scented preparations, and for embalming. It is part of additives to mouthwashes because the tannins in myrrh help in preventing canker sores and gum diseases.

Myrrh has been used also in the treatment of stomach problems, lung diseases, and applied externally to treat wounds. Myrrh is bacteriostatic; like other resins it does not decay. It is best known for its use as an embalming agent in Bible lands. "...So Joseph died, being a hundred and ten years old; and they embalmed him. And he was put in a coffin." (Gen. 50: 25-26) The bible mentions it over 22 times. Myrrh was used as incense in religious rituals. It featured prominently among the embalming ingredients brought to be used on the dead body of Jesus: "And after this Joseph of Arimathea, being a disciple of Jesus, but secretly of fear of the Jews, besought Pilate that he might take away the body of Jesus; and Pilate gave him leave. He came therefore, and took the body of Jesus. And there came Nicodemus, which at the first came to Jesus by night, and brought a mixture of myrrh and aloes, about a hundred pound weight. Then took the body of Jesus, and wound it in linen clothes with the spices, as the manner of the Jews is to bury." (John 20: 38-40).

Despite its healing abilities, it was its acridity, bitter taste and popularity as an embalming agent that earned myrrh the reputation as a symbol of human pain, suffering, and the Passion of Christ. In the Matthew chapter 2 verse 11 we are told that when the Wise men from the East who came to Judea to celebrate the birth of Jesus arrived in the house of Mary, they fell down, and worshipped him; "and when they had opened their treasures, they presented unto him gifts; gold, and frankincense, and myrrh." The gifts signified kingship for gold, frankincense his divine priesthood, myrrh his painful death and triumph over death. Myrrh is a symbol of our own suffering and inevitable death.

Many people cannot deal with death, especially when it strikes closer to home. For where death strikes, hysteria reigns. Peter too had a big problem dealing with death when Jesus foretold His impending death. Hearing our LORD speak about how he would "undergo great suffering in the hands of the elders and chief priests and scribes, be killed, and on the third day be raised" in Jerusalem, "Peter took him aside and began to rebuke him, saying God forbid it Lord! This must never happen to you." (Matt 16: 21-22)

Most normal people cannot handle death. Peter could not. Another example of people's inability to handle death was demonstrated among the children of Israel when their father died; "… Joseph threw himself on his father's face and wept over him," the scriptures report in Genesis chapter 50 starting from verse 1 to 11; "Joseph commanded the physicians in his service to embalm his father. So the physicians embalmed Israel. They spent forty days in doing this, for that is the time required for embalming. And the Egyptians wept for him seventy days...When they came to the threshing floor of Atad, which is beyond the Jordan, they held there a very great and sorrowful lamentation; and he observed a time of mourning for his father seven days. When the Canaanites saw the mourning...they said, "This is a grievous mourning on the part of the Egyptians"

    I could not handle death when my parents and all my four siblings died either. I was the baby in the family, being the last-born. But I was three thousand miles away in the United States when they died, and I was an illegal alien or an undocumented immigrant – call it what you may . I did not have the funds for my airfare back home because of the kind of wages that I earned; three dollars and thirty-five cents an hour. Even if I had the funds, I could not take the risk of traveling to be denied a reentry visa by the U.S. authorities. That was my plight nearly thirty years ago. This situation is typical even today with many undocumented immigrants.

    I was so devastated and traumatized that I avoided the company of people, and hated making friends. I just could not be trusted with enduring relationships or friendships. I feared such relationships were toxic to me.I lived within a short distance from

DRUG FREE HEALING 11 : Medical Science Supporting Scriptures

four hospitals, Montefiori, North Central, Mercy and Jacoby in the Bronx, New York, but I hated the sight of hospitals. I associated hospitals with morgues and dead bodies, which were reminders to me of my dead parents and siblings. I avoided funerals too. I was miserable. I wanted to die. I contemplated suicide.

My apartment was only a block away from Woodlawn Cemetery separated by Gunhill Road. On one of my depressingly unhappy days, I went out, ambling around the Woodlawn Cemetery. In my hand I carried along a bottle of an over-the-counter sleeping pills. I went around that cemetery looking for a convenient spot to lie and to take my final sleep, but just when I had sighted a convenient location close to the fence, something strangely happened to me. Maybe, I was a coward! I am not going to claim that I had any supernatural experience. The truth is that I forgot why I was walking around the cemetery. I just kept on going. I walked along the northern side of the cemetery from Jerome Avenue on the west, turned toward Webster Avenue on its eastern side, and proceeded southwards towards the Gunhill Road. From there, I turned left on Gunhill Road and kept on walking until I got to White Plains Road.

In the corner of 221st Street and White Plains Road, was an old Movie theater. A fellow compatriot that I had not seen for ten years was standing in front of a store on the street level of the building. He is

Reverend O.B. Alexander Kissi, bishop of New Life Christian Center. Rev. Kissi told me that his church had just bought the landmark building at 3933-3941 White Plains Road, and invited me to take up the position of an administrator for his church. I would ultimately yield to Christ, and work for the church, but not until I had dabbled in other religions.

Sometime back, I had met a Swami who introduced himself as one of the twenty governors of the International Society for Krishna Consciousness, Hare Krishna sect. I took him up on a prior invitation, and sat in as a guest at a meeting with the leadership in the sect's New York headquarters. The discussion they had was concerning death. Naturally, it was of interest to me. However, the information I gathered was so frightening that I decided to distance myself from that organization. From the sect's point of view, any adherent that accidentally killed another human being could be excused, but that courtesy would not be extended to anyone who killed a cow. The individual deserved death.

I sought answers to the meaning of life and death also from Hinduism with the 330 million gods and goddesses, and its doctrine of reincarnation, or transmigration of souls. This is grounded in the belief that the souls of the dead return to occupy another human or animal body, depending upon the good or evil that person did in his or her previous lifetime. If an

individual was evil while alive, according to Hindu beliefs, not only would he or she receive a karmic payback in his life time, but if that person died, he or she faced the possibility of
reincarnating in the body of a beast. This process would continue as the individual strove to perform his or her religious duties of self-denials, yoga, and doing good deeds to earn the privilege of reaching Nirvana which is believed to be an "ideal condition of rest, harmony, stability or joy", according to New American Heritage Dictionary definition.

    Unfortunately, the gods and goddesses do not accord everyone the privilege of reincarnation. They exclude the people in lowest level of the four-tier caste system, namely, the poor, and the "untouchables", usually, black, but favor the first three, priest at the top, followed by military leaders and rulers, and business owners and farmers at the third level down.

    For me, the thought that after I died, I could be reincarnated as a goat or a fish and end up in somebody else's cooking pot, was not a happy thought. So I tried Islam.

    N.J. Dawood's English translation of the Koran was my point of reference. I also read Marmaduke Pickthall' explanatory translation as well as The Koran For Dummies by Sohaib Sultan.

    The Muslim holy book promised the faithful a place in paradise where there "shall be gardens and

vineyards, and high-bosomed virgins for companions." (Sura 37:40-48). But it also disavowed Mohammad's ability to dispense any divine favors: "I have not the power to acquire benefit," said the prophet in Sura 7:125-188. "...I am but a mortal like you." (Sura 18:110), and "I am not your keeper" (Sura 6:104). Those statements shook off any speck of lingering faith I might have had. Worst still were the edicts of hate stated in Sura 5:48-51: ".. Take neither Jews nor Christians for your friends. They are friends with one another. (Sura 5:48-51) And this: "... He that chooses a religion other than Islam, it will not be accepted from him and in the world to come he will surely be among the losers... Say: Unbelievers, I do not worship, nor do you worship, I shall never worship what you worship nor will you ever worship what I worship; you have your own religion, and I have mine" (Sura 109:6) That did it! I had bottled up so much
hate for myself I did not think I had any more room for hate and bigotry.

What I needed was to be set free from my state of depression, and anger and apathy and self-hate. I opened the Holy Bible, the Gospel of Matthew chapter 28 verse 11, and I could almost hear the reassuring voice of Jesus Christ calling: "Come to me all you that are weary and are carrying heavy burdens and I will give you rest." I was surely carrying a heavy burden. I needed rest. Jesus also said, "I am the resurrection and the life. Those who believe in me, even though they die, will live, and everyone who lives and believes in me, will never die."

For me, that clinched it. I cried out, "Lord Jesus, how could I not believe in you? I believe in you, please 'help my unbelief, and thank you for saving me!" I flipped the pages to 1 Corinthians chapter 15 reading verses 1 to 26:

"Now I would remind you, brothers and sisters of the good news that I proclaimed to you, which you in turn received, in which also you stand, through which also you are being saved, if you hold firmly to the message that I proclaimed to you – unless you have come to believe in vain.

"For I handed on to you as of first importance what in turn I had received: that Christ died for our sins in accordance with the scriptures, and that he was buried, and that he was raised on the third day in accordance with the scriptures, and that he appeared to Cephas, then to the twelve.

"Then he appeared to more than five hundred brothers and sisters at one time, most of whom are still alive, though some have died. Then he appeared to James, then to all the apostles. Last of all, as to one untimely born, he appeared also to me... Now if Christ is proclaimed as raised from the dead, how can some of you say there is no resurrection of the dead? If there is no resurrection of the dead, then Christ has not been raised; and if Christ has not been raised, then our proclamation has been in vain and your faith has been in vain.

"We are even found to be misrepresenting God, because we testified of God that he raised Christ – whom he did not raise if it is true that the dead are not raised. For, if the dead are not raised, then Christ has not been raised. If Christ has not been raised, your faith is futile and you are still in your sins. Then those also who have died in Christ have perished. If for this life only we have hoped in Christ, we are of all people most to be pitied. But in fact Christ has been raised from the dead, the first fruits of those who have died. For since death came through a human being, the resurrection of the dead has also come through a human being; for as all die in Adam, so all will be made alive in Christ. But each in his own order: Christ the first fruits, then at his coming those who belong to Christ, then comes the end, when he hands over the kingdom to God the Father, after he has destroyed every ruler and every authority and power. For he must reign until he has put all his enemies under his feet. The last enemy to be destroyed is death.

Myrrh is the sweet-smelling oleo-gum resin that naturally exudes from wounds or cuts in the stems and bark of several species of this shrubby desert tree. This sap forms a thick, pale yellow paste as it seeps out. It then hardens into a mass about the size of a walnut, taking on a reddish-brown color.

Constituents:

The volatile oil contained in the resin consists of sesquiterpenes, triterpenes, and mucilage. It also contains heerabolene, cadinene, elemol, eugenol, cuminaldehyde, numerous furanosesquiterpenes including furanodiene, furanodienone, curzerenone, lindestrene, methoxyfuranodiene and other derivatives. The tannin content gives myrrh its astringent action.

Medicinal Uses:

Myrrh is an effective anti-microbial agent that has been shown to work in two complementary ways. Primarily it stimulates the production of white blood corpuscles (with their anti-pathogenic actions) and secondarily it has a direct anti-microbial effect. Myrrh may be used in a wide range of conditions where an anti-microbial agent is needed. It finds specific use in the treatment of infections in the mouth such as mouth ulcers, gingivitis, pyorrhea, as well as the catarrhal problems of pharyngitis and sinusitis. It may also help with laryngitis and respiratory complaints. Systemically it is of value in the treatment of boils and similar conditions as well as glandular fever and brucellosis. It is often used as part of an approach to the treatment of the common cold. Externally it will be healing and antiseptic for wounds and abrasions. Taken internally in tincture or capsule form, myrrh is a beneficial treatment for loose teeth, gingivitis, and bad breath. The tincture may also be applied directly to a tooth to relieve toothache. It is antifungal, and has been used to treat athlete's foot and candida. Myrrh powder has been endorsed by the German advisory Commission E as a beneficial treatment for mild inflammations in the throat and mouth. Myrrh acts as a broad-spectrum antiseptic and can be applied directly to sores and wounds.

Some research indicates that myrrh is effective in reducing cholesterol levels. It is a tonic remedy taken to relax muscles, increase peristaltic action, and stimulate gastric secretions. The myrrh resin has antimicrobial properties and acts to stimulate macrophage activity in the blood stream.

Myrrh is available in capsule, powder, and tincture form. It is pulverized into powder, and prepared as a tincture. **Myrrh powder is rubbed onto sore gums and often used as an analgesic.**

When mixed with safflowers, it is good for abdominal pain associated with blood stagnation (as in menstrual pain). It is found in combination with other ingredients in dental powders, mouthwash preparations, and toothpaste.

Myrrh is used as fragrance in cosmetics, perfumes, and soaps. **Myrrh has long been used for skin infections, including acne, as well as for muscular pains and in rheumatic plasters.**

Placing a little myrrh in a hot bath and "marinating" for about twenty minutes is an excellent way to relax and to tone the skin at the same time. In Germany, its drying and slightly anesthetizing effect has led to its being used as a treatment for pressure sores caused by prosthetic limbs.

Chapter Fifteen: Pistachio

"Godliness with contentment is great gain…" (1 Tim 6:6) "Whoever comes to me and does not hate father and mother, wife and children, brothers and sisters, yes and even life itself, cannot be my disciple. Whoever does not carry the cross and follow me, cannot be my disciple." (Luke 14: 26-27).
Pistachio . Heb. Botnim (Genesis 43:11). Pistacia Vera

Jacob's sons took along with them pistachios among other gifts to the Prime Minister of Egypt who they did not recognize to be their own brother, Joseph, the very person they had sold into slavery. They took pistachio nuts because they were highly valued in their world. From ancient times, pistachio trees symbolized Almighty God's provision for us. But it also represents a call to believers to be ready to face and endure tribulations. Although pistachios trees are small, measuring twenty to thirty five feet in height, they possess a great ability to withstand long hot summers, defying cold and stormy weathers. Their strength, durability, productivity, and capacity to endure adverse conditions exemplify what God expects from true Christian believers. Pistachios hate excessive dampness or high humidity. Christ himself detests wishy-washy spirituality; "I know that you are neither cold nor hot. How I wish that you were either one or the other, but because you are lukewarm, neither hot or cold, I am going to spit you out of my mouth" (Revelation Chapter 3 Verse 15 and 16).

God calls upon us, believing Christians to endure hardships when they come our way, resist the seduction of sin and defy the stormy weathers of tribulations. For, "the kingdom of God," the scripture says, "is not meat and drink; but righteousness, and peace, and joy in the Holy Ghost". (Romans 14:17).

Our Lord Jesus who himself did not escape the stormy terrains of persecution in this world, cautioned us saying, "…In the world you will face persecution." (John 16:1-33) His disciples who saw him raised from the dead lived in the periods of persecution. Peter, for example, was crucified upside down, according to tradition. Paul was beheaded. Emperor Nero used some early Christians as torches to light his insane gladiatorial shows. Christians were hated, and denounced by family and friends alike.

"Whoever comes to me and does not hate father and mother, wife and children, brothers and sisters, yes and even life itself, cannot be my disciple. Whoever does not carry the cross and follow me, cannot be my disciple." (Luke 14: 26-27).

When we make a decision to follow Jesus, we must be aware that our fathers, mothers, brothers and sisters may desert us because of who we have become. Our friends may scorn us, you and I may lose our jobs, our livelihoods, our health, or we may become homeless. But "the call of God is without repentance" We must be resolute in our faith, and continually seek the presence of the Holy Spirit. We must acquire the habit of praying always, asking for the grace of God upon us so that we are not cast away from his presence. For, "If God is for us, who can be against us? "

There will come times when we may be ridiculed for staying in the word, even so, we must stay in the word. When people talk about us and against us because they cannot stand our staying in the word, stay in the word. Let us stay constantly in the Word and be hearers not of the word only, but most of all we must also be doers of the word.

Let us pray the enabling of the Holy Spirit so that we too, like the Apostle Paul, can proclaim firmly; "…Neither death nor life, nor angels nor rulers, nor things present nor things to come, nor powers, nor height nor depth, nor anything else in all creation, will be able to separate us from the love of God in Christ Jesus our Lord. (Romans 8: 32-39)

Paul who wrote nearly two-thirds of the New Testament recounts his own encounters for the benefit of every believing Christian in 2 Corinthians 11: 24-27... "Five times I received from the Jews the forty lashes minus one. Three times I was beaten with rods, once I was stoned, three times I was shipwrecked, I spent a night and a day in the open sea, and I have been constantly on the move. I have been in danger from Gentiles; danger in the city, in danger in the country, in danger at sea; and in danger from false brothers. I have labored and toiled and have often gone without sleep; I have known hunger and thirst and have often gone without food; I have been cold and naked."

Let us pray, that God grants us strength to flourish in our faith in Christ in spite of rocky times as we learn the lesson of the pistachio tree knowing that Godliness with contentment is great gain.

Pistachio:

The pistachio is a broad, bushy, deciduous tree which grows slowly to a height and spread of only 25-30 feet. Under favorable conditions pistachio trees live and produce for centuries. Pistachio plants have been used to promote good health. The leaves and nuts have been used to promote fertility, and as aphrodisiacs. They are especially rich in phytosterols, which are directly associated with lowering cholesterol levels, and may offer protection from certain types of cancer. High cholesterol, a major risk factor associated with heart disease, affects nearly 100 million adults. Lowering high cholesterol through a healthy diet and exercise can significantly lower heart disease risk. While it is well accepted that diets high in saturated fats are linked to increased incidence of heart disease, more recent evidence shows a link between monounsaturated fatty acids and decreased heart disease risk."

In July 2003, the FDA approved a qualified health claim that can appear on packages, stating: *"Scientific evidence suggest but does not prove that eating 1.5 oz. per day of most nuts, such as pistachios, as part of a diet low in saturated fat and cholesterol, may reduce the risk of heart disease."* For thousands of years pistachio leaves and nuts have been used to promote fertility, and as aphrodisiacs. The amino acid, arginine in pistachios helps to lower cholesterol levels, enhancing blood flow by boosting nitric oxide, a compound that relaxes blood. It can help trigger erection of the penis in the same way, because the relaxation increases blood flow . The drugs for treating erectile dysfunction Viagra, Levitra and Cialis are designed to increase nitric oxide's effect.

In 1998 three Americans (Robert F. Furchgott, PhD, Louis J. Ignarro, PhD, and Ferid Murad, MD, PhD) were awarded the Nobel Prize for their independent discoveries concerning "nitric oxide" as a signaling molecule in the cardiovascular system, according to CNN news report .

Since the discovery that Nitric oxide (NO) is able to induce vasodilatation, a large number of other roles have been attributed to Nitric oxide (NO) including credit for the effectiveness and potency of such known drugs for treating erectile dysfunction as Viagra, Levitra and Cialis. Experts also credit pistachio nuts with sedative action attributable to the presence of arginine.

Like the drug Viagra, L-arginine enhances the action of nitric oxide, which relaxes muscles surrounding blood vessels supplying the penis. As a result, blood vessels in the penis dilate, increasing blood flow, which helps maintain erections. The difference in how they work is that Viagra blocks an enzyme called PDE5 that destroys nitric oxide and L-arginine is used to make nitric oxide, writes Cathy Wong, ND, CNS, a licensed naturopathic doctor and certified nutrition specialist with the American College of Nutrition.

"A 1994 study found that some men with erectile dysfunction, after taking 2800mg arginine every day for two weeks, experienced improved erections, and were able to achieve better vaginal penetration."

This report was published in a book entitled **New Medicine – Complete Family Health Guide –** co-edited by Dr. Kenneth R. Pelletier, and Dr. David Peters. The former is a Clinical Professor of Medicine,

DRUG FREE HEALING 11 : Medical Science Supporting Scriptures

Department of Medicine, at the University of Arizona School of Medicine and Chairman, American Health Association. Dr Pelletier is also a medical and business consultant to the US Department of Health and Human Services, the World Health Organization, and Fortune 500 companies. Professor Peters is a leading practitioner in the field of integrated medicine. He is the Clinical Director of the School of Integrated Health at the University of Westminster, and a board member of the Prince of Wales Foundation for Integrated Health.

New Medicine, the book that both eminent medical authorities co-edited, also stated that in 1999, a larger double-blind, placebo-controlled study showed that a third of men with confirmed erectile dysfunction benefited from taking 5,000mg of arginine each day for six weeks. They reported improvement and satisfaction in their sexual performance.

In a 1998 study of men with mild to moderate erectile dysfunction, a formulation with a principal constituent of 2,800mg of arginine helped many of the participants. It improved their ability to maintain an erection during sexual intercourse and enhanced their satisfaction in their sex lives.

In general, at least some men with erectile dysfunction may be helped by taking 2,800-5,000mg of arginine . " Unlike Viagra, L-arginine must be taken daily.

Pistachios are good source of dietary fiber with over 10% of the Daily Value in a one-ounce serving. A comprehensive USDA analysis of the phytochemical content of fruits, vegetables and tree nuts had been completed and the values of various phytochemicals in foods maintained and updated on USDA's Nutrient Data Laboratory Web site, and reproduced on the next page.

Constituent

Gum, resin, oil, monosaturated fat, magnesium, copper, amino acid, beta-sitosterol. Pistachios contain predominantly monounsaturated fat, and 1.5 grams of saturated fat per one-ounce serving. They also contain magnesium, copper and potassium, amino acid (arginine) and beta-sitosterol, and significant amounts of phytochemical compounds like lutein,
and gamma-tocopherol as well as compounds like cyaniding, epicatechin, quercetin and proanthocyanidin.

Medicinal Uses

Pistachios have been used in treating abdominal, chest pains, constipation, and dysentery, and to aid the circulation. They are also used in cases of, gynecopathy, pruritus, and rheumatism. They help purify the blood, and tone the liver and kidneys. Pistachio root powder dissolved in pistachios oil has been used against children's cough, to promote fertility, and as aphrodisiacs. The gum and mastics are helpful in preventing periodontal disease and relieve toothache. The shells have been used in dyeing and tanning.

Food

The greenish kernels are invaluable flavorings for confectionery, ice cream, cakes, and pies. Chopped or as paste, pistachios make delicious salad thickener and stuffing. One ounce serving, of pistachios contains 13 grams of monounsaturated fat and zero cholesterol making more than 10% of the Dietary Value of fiber, vitamin B6, thiamine, magnesium, phosphorous, copper and also 2 mg. vitamin C, 66IU vitamin A, magnesium 44.9mg, folic acid 16.5mcg, iron 1.9 mg., calcium 38.3 mg, and 5.8 g protein.

The potassium content of one ounce of pistachios is equal to that of one orange. Two ounces of pistachios contains more potassium than one medium banana. The health benefits of pistachios are best when the nuts are eaten raw as some of the nutrients reduce when the nuts are roasted. For example the component of vitamin C goes down to 19.8 mg, iron .9 mg, magnesium 36.9 mg. and 275 mg. potassium.

Eating daily one-ounce serving of pistachios equals 49 nuts – more per serving than any other snack nut. You can get more dietary fiber from a serving of pistachios than a ½ cup of broccoli or spinach. A serving of pistachios has as much thiamin as a ½ cup serving of enriched cooked rice.

One serving of pistachios has as much potassium as half a large banana.

To promote fertility and enhance sexual performance (Genesis Chapter 9 verse 1)

Ingredients

2 quart spring water
12 tablespoonful fresh shoots or grated dried pistachios leaves
8 tablespoon crushed oat straw
16 ounces raw dark honey
4 Ounces fresh ginger roots

Instructions:

Peel fresh ginger roots
Put ginger roots in blender and process to a fine paste
Remove ginger paste from blender and put in vessel ready to heat with water
Add water and stir
Add fresh or dried pistachios leaves
Add crushed oat straw
Put on stove bring to boil under low 80 degrees Fahrenheit temperature for 30 minutes. Add honey and stir for 5 minutes to mix
Remove from stove and cover to steep for 20 minutes. Strain
Bottle infusion and refrigerate. Drink one glass in the morning and before bedtime daily.
Dietary value, per 100 gram edible portion

DRUG FREE HEALING 11 : Medical Science Supporting Scriptures

* Percent of recommended daily allowance set by FDS, assuming a 154 lb male adult. 2700 calories per day.

If you want to store a large quantity of nuts, it is best to put them in heavy-duty freezer bags and freeze them. When kept frozen, pistachio nuts will remain fresh for several months. If they lose their natural crispness, you can restore by placing them on a baking sheet and heating in an oven at a temperature of 250 to 300 degrees Fahrenheit for 5 to 8 minutes.

Chapter Sixteen: Almonds

"The word of the LORD came to me, saying, Jeremiah, what do you see?" And I said, I see a branch of an almond tree. Then the LORD said to me, you have seen well, for I am watching." (Jer.1:11)

Almonds; Prunus dulcis, Prunus Amygdalius
Genesis Chapter 43:11

Almonds were the last in the list of the best fruit trees of the land of Canaan that the patriarch Jacob instructed his sons to take along with them as gifts to the leader of Egypt. According to author, Diane Omsted, "shelled almonds and raisins combined, were early symbols of good luck for Jews. Omsted also wrote; "In Greece almonds in uneven numbers of three, five or seven are offered to guests for good fortune and happiness at christenings, weddings and the ordination of priests." Other authorities hold that, almonds, known as *shaked* in Hebrew, meaning a 'hasty awakening,' or 'to watch for,' is a symbolic reminder to the descendants of Jacob of their ancestors' hasty redemption from slavery in Egypt, and also an exhortation to all believers to be vigilant, and watchful against the persistent tricks of the adversary, the Devil.

But based upon the following scriptures, Exodus 7: 8-11, Numbers 16; 1-50, Numbers 17: 8-11, Jeremiah chapter 1:11 and Jeremiah 2:7-19, I beg to submit that almonds represent the leadership of the Christian church of today, and a warning of God's coming judgment against those who are grieving the Holy Spirit and disobeying God. The message of almonds is this: "…The time is come that judgment must begin at the house of God." (1 Peter 4:17)

We know from Num. 17: 8 that Aaron's stick represent the tribe of Levi, and by extension some of the church leadership. We also know from the same text that Aaron's staff was almond. "The next day Moses went in to the Tent, he saw that Aaron's stick, representing the tribe of Levi, had sprouted. It had budded, blossom, and produced ripe almonds." This was the same stick that Aaron used to perform a wonder before Pharaoh. Ex. 7:8-11: "The Lord said to Moses and Aaron. 'When Pharaoh says to you, Perform a wonder,' then you shall say to Aaron, 'take your staff and throw it down before Pharaoh and it will become a snake. So Moses and Aaron went to Pharaoh and did as the LORD have commanded; Aaron threw down his staff before Pharaoh and his officials, and it became a snake."

We know also that Aaron was not the only one among leaders of Israel to lead with a staff. "The LORD said to Moses, "Tell the people of Israel to give you twelve sticks, one from the leader of each tribe." (Ex. 17:1) "So Moses spoke to the Israelites, and each of their leaders gave him a stick, one for each tribe, twelve in all, and Aaron's stick was put with them. Moses then put all the sticks in the Tent in front of the LORD'S Covenant Box."

Of the twelve sticks placed in the presence of the LORD'S Covenant Box, only one blossomed – Aaron's.

" The next day, when Moses went into the Tent he saw that Aaron's stick, representing the tribe of Levi had sprouted. It had budded, blossomed, and produced ripe almonds. Moses took all the sticks and showed them to the Israelites. They saw what had happened, and each leader took his own stick back. The LORD said to Moses, "Put Aaron's stick back in front of the covenant box. It is to be kept as a warning to the rebel Israelites that they will die unless complaining stops. Moses did so as the LORD commanded."

We are further told by Jeremiah in his book chapter 1 verse 11, "The word of the LORD came to me, saying, Jeremiah, what do you see?" And I said, I see a branch of an almond tree. Then the LORD said to me, you have seen well, for I am watching over my word to perform it." In Jeremiah 2: 7-19, God said: "I brought you into a plentiful land to eat its fruits and its good things. But when you entered, you defiled my land, and made my heritage an abomination. The priests did not say, "Where is the LORD?" Those who handle the law did not know me; the rulers transgressed against me; the prophets prophesied by Baal, and went after things that do not profit... Know and see that it is evil and bitter for you to forsake the LORD your GOD."

Like the leaders of the tribes of Israel whose sticks had nothing to show in the presence of the Just and Holy God, some preachers in the Christian church of today, will soon face the LORD'S judgment. Despite their big names, their staff of authority will not sprout almonds because they have given up the gospel of the LORD for the gospel of "money, money is coming!" Some have perverted the authority of our Creator and God Almighty, and are following the desires of their flesh and the gospel of politically correctness because we are living in the "time when men will not put up with sound doctrine. Instead, to suit their own desires, they will gather around them a great number of teachers to say what their itching ears want to hear. They will turn their ears away from the truth and turn aside to myths." (2 Timothy 4:1-8) But the word of God clearly says this: "Do you not know that wrongdoers will not inherit the kingdom of God? Do not be deceived! Fornicators, idolaters, adulterers, male prostitutes, sodomites, thieves, the greedy, drunkards, revilers, robbers, - none of these will inherit the kingdom of God." (1 Corinthians 6:9-10) They are like the church in Sardis to whom our Lord Jesus Christ has this to say:

"This is the message from the one who has seven spirits of God and the seven stars. I know what you are doing; I know that you have the reputation of being alive, even though you are dead! So wake up, and strengthen what you still have before it dies completely. For I find what you have done is not yet perfect in the sight of God. Remember, then, what you were taught and what you heard; obey it and turn from your sins. If you do not wake up, I will come upon you like a thief, and you will not even know the time when I will come." (Rev. 3:1-3)

To bible believing churches where the word of God is preached, taught and lived, Jesus offers these sweet almonds of hope; "But a few of you there in Sardis have kept your clothes clean. You will walk with me, clothed in white, because you are worthy to do so. Those who win the victory will be clothed like this in white, and I will not remove their names from the book of the living. In the presence of my Father and his angels I will declare openly that they belong to me. If you have ears, then, listen to what the Spirit says to the church!" (Revelation 3: 4-6)

Two Varieties of Almonds

There are two varieties of almonds; sweet almonds and bitter almonds. Genetically both are the same. The Sweet Almonds are valuable as food; they are used in dishes and confectionary being rich in nutrients. They are used also medicinally. But eating bitter almond nuts can be deadly, about one twentieth of a gram is considered lethal for an adult. Bitter almonds contain 3% to 5% amygdalin, a so-called *cyanogenic glycoside* composed of mandelic nitrile and gentobiose as well prunasin which converts into hydrocyanic acid during digestion or when in contact with liquid.

Constituents: Demulcent. Almonds contain about 50% of fatty oil, glycerides 80%, oleic acid 15% , 5% palmitic acid. Almond oil is a clear, pale yellow, odorless liquid. Almond oil has properties similar to those of olive oil. Therefore, almond oil may be substituted for olive oil. Almonds are rich in Vitamin E, and Calcium. Bitter almonds contain 3% to 5% amygdalin, a so-called cyanogenic glycoside. Lesley Bremness says, "Most need treatment before they are safe to use."

Medicinal Uses: Almonds are a natural "wate-on" for the convalescent and underweight. They are believed to possess healing properties; as a result, some doctors recommend almonds to their patients to take daily. "Studies showed that patients adding 3 ounces, that is, 84 grams of almonds to their daily low fat diet had an average of 10 per cent drop in LDL cholesterol in three weeks", says Miriam Polunim, author, **"Healing Foods".** One-ounce daily intake of almonds equal twice average daily intake of vitamin E. One and three quarters an ounce, that is fifty grams of almonds equal ten percent of the daily calcium requirement per adult.

Almonds are applied in bronchial cases. They are used n treating acute inflammatory disorders, and given for heartburn as well. For external application choose Sweet Almonds oil. The sap of some species contains a chemical that makes the sap suitable for use as soap.

Food: Soaked, crushed and strained Sweet Almonds make nutritious milk substitute for the lactose intolerant. Juice may be collected from the flower and stalk of almond. It's refreshing drink is rich in vitamins E and C. Sweet almonds may be made into flour for bread, cakes or cookies for those on low carbohydrate diets, or for diabetes mellitus patients. Its flowers and flower buds are edible. Cooked flowers may be included in daily diet. The fixed oil may be pressed from both Bitter and Sweet Almonds. Unblanched almonds are better than blanched.

Green Beans with Almonds and Thyme Recipe

2 lbs of Green beans, trimmed
¼ cup of Olive Oil
2 Tbsp chopped fresh thyme
1 Tbsp Dijon mustard
1 teaspoon garlic salt
1/3 cup slivered almonds, toasted

Cook green beans in a large pot of boiling salted water until just crisp-tender, about 5 minutes. Use a strainer, transfer beans in to a large bowl of iced water. Allow to cool. Drain well. If preferable, make the beans a day earlier and store in refrigerator until needed, then steam the beans for 5 minutes and proceed directly to the skillet.

Melt ¼ cup of butter in a heavy large skillet over medium high heat.

Whip in 1 Tbsp of fresh thyme, 1 Tbsp of mustard and 1 teaspoon of garlic salt into butter. Add beans to skillet and toss until heated through, about 4 minutes.

Transfer to serving bowl. Sprinkle with toasted almonds and remaining 1 tbsp of thyme.

Almond Milk : This is nutrient-rich drink which can be used as an alternative to or in combination with dairy milk.

Ingredients

½ Cup of unsalted chopped Almonds

1 Cup water.

1 teaspoonful dark honey, or pure malt syrup

Instruction

Almonds in a blender or food processor

Blend to paste.

Add water

Strain

Add dark honey, or pure malt syrup.

Store in a jar.

Refrigerate and use when desired.

Almond milk can be served as a drink or with cereal. The leftover pulp can be used in cooking, such as in grain and vegetable dishes or in baking.

Chapter Seventeen: Barley

"You have profaned me among my people for handfuls of barley and for pieces of bread, putting to death persons who should not die and keeping alive persons who should not live, by your lies to my people, who listens to lies...". (Ezekiel chapter 13 verse 19, Judges Chapter 7 verse 13)

Barley, Hordeum vulgare
Read from Exodus chapter 1 to chapter 9 verses 27 through 32.
Mk 4:3-8

"Then Pharaoh summoned Moses and Aaron, and said to them, 'This time I have sinned; the Lord is in the right, and I and my people are wrong. Pray to the Lord! Enough of God's thunder and hail! I will let you go; you need to stay no longer. Moses said to him, 'As soon as I have gone out of the city, I will stretch out my hands to the Lord; the thunder will cease, and there will be no more hail, so that you may know that the earth is the Lord's. But as for you and your officials, I know that you do not yet fear the Lord GOD". Now the flax and the barley were ruined, for the barley was in the ear and the flax was in bud. But the wheat and spelt were not ruined for they are late in coming up." (Exodus 9:27-32)

God spoke to Moses. Does God still speak to us? This report by an anonymous writer was reproduced in March 1-14, 2000 issue of CITIZENS & Immigrants

Journal in New York published by the author of this book.

"A young man had been to Wednesday night Bible Study. The pastor had shared about listening and obeying the Lord's voice. The young man could not help but wonder, "Does God still speak to us?" After service he went out with some friends for coffee and pie and they discussed the message. Several different ones talked about how God had led them in different ways.

"It was about ten o'clock when the young man started driving home. Sitting in his car, he just began to pray. "God, if you still speak to people, speak to me. I will listen. I will do my best to obey." As he drove down the main street of his town, he had the strangest thought to stop and buy a gallon of milk. He shook his head and said aloud," God is that you?" He did not get a reply and started on toward home. Again the thought, buy a gallon of milk. The young man thought of God, and how little Samuel ran to Eli. "Okay, God, in case that is you, I will buy the milk." It did not seem too hard a test of obedience. He could always use the milk. He stopped and purchased the gallon of milk and started toward home. As he passed Seventh Street, he again felt the urge, turn down that street. "This is crazy," he thought, and drove past the intersection. Again, he felt that he should turn down Seventh Street. At the next intersection, he turned back and headed down Seventh. Half jokingly, he said out aloud, "Okay

God, I will." He drove several blocks when suddenly, he felt like he should stop. He pulled over to the curb and looked dark like the people were already in bed. Again, he sensed something, "Go and give the milk to the people in the house across the street."

"The young man looked at the house. It was dark and it looked like the people were either gone or they were already asleep. He started to open the door and then sat back in the car seat. "Lord, this is insane. These people are asleep and if I wake them up, they are going to be mad and I will look stupid." Again, he felt he should go and give the milk. Finally, he opened the door, "Okay God, if it is you, I will go to the door and I will give them the milk. If you want me to look like a crazy person, okay, I want to be obedient. I guess that will count for something, but if they don't answer right away, I am out of here."

He walked across the street and rang the bell. He could hear some noise inside. A man's voice yelled out. "What do you want?" Then the door opened before the young man could get away. The man was standing there in his jeans and T-shirt. He looked like he just got out bed. He had a strange look in his face and he did not seem too to have some stranger standing on his doorstep.

"What is it?"

The young man thrust out the gallon of milk. "Here, I brought this to you." The man took the milk and rushed down a hallway speaking loudly in Spanish. Then from down the hall came woman carrying the milk toward the kitchen. The man was following her holding the baby. The baby was crying. The man had tears streaming down his face. He began speaking and half crying. "We were just praying. We had some bills this month and we ran out of money. We didn't have any milk. Are you an Angel? "The young man reached into his wallet and pulled all the money he had on him and put it in the man's hand. He turned and walked back toward his car and tears were streaming down his face. He knew that God still answers prayers. God still speaks to us by his Word, "the first fruit of the first fruits," Jesus Christ our Lord and Savior.

  Barley and flax are few of the fruits that bud much earlier than other fruits. They are the first of the first fruits. God commanded that the first fruit was given as an offering to him. (Leviticus 23:10-14) The first of the first fruits of the early barley harvest, offered the first day of the week, Sunday morning, symbolized the dedication of the whole year's crops. It was a picture of Jesus Christ as the first of the first fruits of the spiritual harvest, even as he appeared before God the father on the first day of the week, Sunday morning.

  Barley (Hebrew – *"Se'orah"*, "hairy", an allusion to the length of the awns) was cultivated through Bible Lands as provender for horses and asses (1 Kings 4:28), and also as a staple food among the poor, working men, and the people at large during times of distress. The grain was either roasted (Leviticus 2:14; 2 Kings 4:43) or milled, kneaded and baked or cake. Barley, being the commonest grain, it was considered as having no value.

"You have profaned me among my people for handfuls of barley and for pieces of bread, putting to death persons who should not die and keeping alive persons who should not live, by your lies to my people, who listens to lies...". (Ezekiel chapter 13 verse 19, Judges Chapter 7 verse 13) "When Gideon arrived there was a man telling a dream to his comrade; and he said, "I had a dream, and in it a cake of barley bread tumbled into the camp of the Midian, and came to the tent", (Judges chapter 7 verse 13) and." So I bought her for fifteen shekels of silver and a homer of barley. (Hosea chapter 3 verse, 2).Another important use of barley is for malt. Malt is used in beer, liquor, non-intoxicating malt drinks as well as malted milk and flavorings in a variety of foods. Malt is produced by germinating moistened barley steeping or soaking the barley in water for two days. When it begins to sprout to absorb moisture and begin germination. The wet grain is moved to a damp and dark enclosure for four days where the sprouts are allowed to grow longer. The barley is transferred into an oven for drying. The finished product is called malt.

Barley is rich in vitamins B and E, thiamin, manganese, iron and phosphorous. It is a great source of protein when it is hulled; that is, with the bran unremoved from the grain. Unfortunately, the commonly consumed barley, Pearl Barley, has the most of the nutrients removed. Both wheat and barley are grown for bread, the staple food. Wheat makes better dough, but needs good soil and water. There are also many kinds of barley products. Barley flakes resembling rolled oats are grains flattened through processing. Grits are toasted. Cracked barley grains are like tapioca. Hulled barley, also known as Groats, Pot or Scotch barley is the whole brown grain with its inedible outer husks removed. Because it is only the inedible spikelet that is removed leaving the bran, hulled barley is the most nutritious form of the grain. It has all of its nutrients, including the rich dietary fiber, vitamins and minerals unlike pearled which loses most of its nutrients during processing.

The barley grains are scoured six times during milling to completely remove their double outer hull, called the spikelet, and their bran layer. The thorough milling shortens the grain's cooking time considerably. Quick barley is instant pearled barley. It cooks much faster than pearled because it is precooked by steaming. It is no less nutritious than regular pearled barley. Barley flakes, grits or hulled can be consumed as hot cereal or when added to baked dishes. Whole barley, (hulled, pearled, quick, or pot barley can be cooked much the same way like rice: in boiling water and served hot as a side dish or cold in a salad. It can be cooked along with other ingredients in a soup or stew. Malt and brewer's yeast are barley extracts.

In Bible Lands where barley consumption is a staple, studies showed that heart diseases rates are low. Barley helps in lowering blood- cholesterol level. It is believed to help heal stomach ulcers, soothe the digestive tract and liver, prevent tooth decay, and loss of hair. Dianne Onsted says, "Sprouted barley treats indigestion from starchy food stagnation, strengthens weak digestion, and tonifies the stomach. Barley by-products such as brewer's yeast and malt drinks help the convalescent. Barley help patients regain lost weight.

Constituents

Barley is an excellent source of soluble fiber, and effective in lowering cholesterol levels. It is rich in vitamin B, thiamin, manganese, iron and phosphorous. It is a mucilage. Barley is the most alkaline of the cereals. Pearl barley is 80% starch, 8%-19% proteins and cellulose with other constituents making up the rest (enzymes, thiamine , riboflavin, pyridoxine, niacin, chlorine, phosphorous, and iron). It contains the alkaloid hordenine which is a diuretic and mildly relaxing (chest). The stem juice contains chorophyllins and antioxidant activity. Sprouts contain amylase, dextrin, phospholipid, maltose, glucose and vitamin B.

Medicinal Uses

Sweet, warming, demulcent, bodybuilding, tissue healing, expectorant, abortifacient, febrifuge, stomachic, tonic, vulnerary, soothes irritated tissues, stimulates appetite, digestive aid, and suppresses lactation (not given to nursing mothers). Barley has been used internally for indigestion, especially in babies, and for candida albicans infections. It has also been used as a remedy for excessive lactation, hepatitis, coughs, and debility. Barley water for poor appetite, and recurring diarrhea in children. Malt extract has been used for weak digestion.

Cooked poultice is used as a healing agent applied to sores. Barley grain sprouts infusion is used in treating bronchitis. It has been used in facial masks. Barley has been used to treat urinary cystitis particularly in females. The recipe consists of boiling the herb till it is soft and straining the liquid, then flavoring it with fresh lemon juice and cinnamon powder. Sometimes it is also prepared in combination with corn silk or couch grass and taken orally to treat urinary stones, infections or irritations. Water distilled from the fresh green barley has been used externally when there is a film over the eyes or for pain by saturating white bread in the water, squeezing gently and applying to eyes. Its sodium content keeps calcium in solution making it useful for arthritis and rheumatism. Seeds have been used as a poultice for burns and wounds. Whole plant is anti-tumor. The cooked barley has been used externally on tumors and as part of a nutritious diet for maintenance and sugar balance (especially for hypoglycemia and diabetes).

Malt sugar extract containing maltose is demulcent, nutritive and antispasmodic. It has been used to moisten lungs, stop coughs and treat weak digestion.

Food:Barley Feta Toss - This Greek inspired salad is filled with lively Mediterranean flavors.

Ingredients
1 cup pearl barley
3 cups water
Salt as desired
1/3 cup olive oil
2 tablespoons fresh lemon juice
2 tablespoons red wine
1 tablespoon vinegar
½ teaspoon dried oregano
¼ cup fine chopped onion
¼ cup minced fresh parsley
2 medium tomatoes, diced
1 small green or red bell pepper, diced
½ cup crumbled feta cheese
Lettuce leaves, washed and chilled

Instruction

Place barley, water and 1 teaspoon salt in saucepan
Bring to boil
Cover, reduce heat to low and cook 45 minutes or until barley is tender and liquid is absorbed
Combine olive oil, lemon juice, vinegar, oregano and salt
Pour over hot cooked barley
Cool to room temperature
Gently stir in onions, parsley, tomatoes, bell pepper and cheese
Serve salad chilled or at room temperature on lettuce lined plates
Garnish each serving with tomato wedges or a lemon slice, if desired; Make 6 servings

Barley Broth for the convalescent
Ingredients
1 cup of barley
3 cups of water
1 bulb onion paste
3 cloves garlic paste
¼ oz ginger paste
2 medium size tomatoes diced
6 cups of water

Instruction
Put barley in water
Bring to boil until barley is soft
Add onion, garlic, ginger paste and tomatoes
Bring to boil for 10 minutes

Let stand for 15 minutes
Ready to serve as needed
Cooking times vary with the form. Times specified above apply to boiling the barley in or cooking as soup. With flaked barley, about 30 minutes; grits, add to boiling water and let stand two to three minutes; hulled barley, about 1 hour and 40 minutes; pot barley (Scotch barley), 1 hour; pearled (pearl) barley, 45 minutes; quick barley, 10 to 12 minutes, then cover and let stand for 5 minutes.

Per serving: 266 calories, 5g protein, 15g fat, 30g carbohydrate, 8mg cholesterol, 6g fiber, 558mg sodium

Nutritional Fact
Serving size: 1 cup cooked pearl barley
Calories – 193
Protein – 3.5 grams
Fat – 0.7 gram
Cholesterol – 0
Carbohydrate – 44.3 grams
Dietary Fiber – 9 grams
Calcium – 17mg
Iron – 2mg
Magnesium – 35mg
Phosphorus – 85mg
Potassium – 145mg
Sodium – 5mg
Zinc – 5mg
Niacin – 3.2mg

Folic Acid – 26mcg
*Source: USDA Agricultural Handbook No. 8-20 Composition of Foods

Barley Tonic Water

½ lb barley
¼ lb lemon balm
2 quart water
8 oz dark uncooked honey

Instruction

Wash barley
Wash Lemon balm
Strain
Soak barley in water
Boil for 20 minutes
Remove from stove
Allow to settle
Strain
Add honey
Take as desired daily

Malt drink - health restorative tonic

Ingredients
1 lb barley
1 gallon water
16 ounces uncooked dark honey

Instruction

Rinse the barley in cool water
Soak in cold in a large bowl and cover the bowl
Allow to soak for about 12 hours

The barley will soak up a considerable amount of water
Strain the barley and cover to prevent from drying up
Place in a dark location away from light
Sprinkle cold water on barley three times daily until sprouts begin to show
Spread in tray and dry in oven under low temperature
Put in food processor and blend until finely mixed
Put in a gallon of water and stir until well mixed
Bring to boil for 45 minutes
Add honey over low temperature
Stir until well mixed
Remove from stove and allow cooling
Refrigerate
Serve one glassful after meals daily

COSMETIC Skin Freshener:
An astringent skin freshener to cleanse and soften normal skin:
3 tablespoon barley
3 cups water
Simmer for 30 minutes. Strain and cool. Keep refrigerated
Apply to face when needed. Rinse off face.

Chapter Eighteen: Flaxseed

"He shall put on the holy linen coat, and shall have the linen breeches on his body, be girded with the linen girdle, and wear the linen turban; these are the holy garments" (Ezekiel 4:9)

FLAX also known as Linseed
Linum usitatissimum. Usitatissimum
Suggested readings: Exodus chapters 1 to chapter 11, Ezekiel Chapter 9,
Daniel Chapter 23, Revelation Chapter 19, Luke 24, Matthew 24

"...Now the flax and the barley were ruined, for the barley was in the ear and the flax was in bud. But the wheat and spelt were not ruined for they are late in coming up." (Exodus 9:27-32)

Flax was the most important plant fiber in Bible times because it was used to make linen. All clothing was made either of linen or wool, observed biblical ethno-botanist, Lytton John Musselman.

While its production has declined in recent years due to the superiority of cotton that is more easily handled by machines, flax remains one of the most important fiber plants in the world because of the long, strong fibers found in the outer layer of the stem.

The scientific name for flax is Linum usitatissimum. Usitatissimum means "most useful", and appears to underscore its usefulness both as food and fiber for clothing. Linen is the name of its fiber product.

Linen had several uses in biblical times. The most obvious was clothing. But other uses were for wicks for lamps as told about in Matthew 12:2, and as measuring line in 2 kings Chapter 21 verse 13 made out of linen (flax). Our English word line is from the Latin word for flax. Words such a linear, lineage, are also derived from the same root. One use of flax that is not mentioned in the Bible is eating the seeds. Flax seeds, barley, and wheat are among the oldest known foods. Linseed oil is pressed from the seeds of flax.

The Scriptures teach explicitly the significance of linen when used as clothing; it is the righteousness or righteous acts of saints. Put another way; it represents personal holiness and suggests that the person clothed in linen is in a condition suitable to approach God. In fact, one of the synonyms for a priest is one who "wears the linen ephod." Ezekiel 4:9 states, "He shall put on the holy linen coat, and shall have the linen breeches on his body, be girded with the linen girdle, and wear the linen turban; these are the holy garments" and Revelation 19 verse 8 states that fine linen is the righteous deeds of the saints.

Flax, like barley is an early budding crop. It is identified with the first fruit of the first fruits, and like barley, flax too was ruined in the bud during the hailstorm and thunder that plagued Egypt because of Pharaoh's sin of disobedience against God Almighty.

DRUG FREE HEALING 11 : Medical Science Supporting Scriptures

I believe God designed that event as a prefigure of the soon coming End Time as it parallels the life of God's own first fruit, our Lord Jesus Christ cut in his prime. It also symbolizes the standing of believers with our Lord when he comes to judge the world.

Apostle Paul could not have been clearer when he affirmed in Romans chapter 6 verses 3 to 5, "Do you not know that all of us who have been baptized into Christ were baptized into his death? We were buried therefore with him by baptism into death, so that as Christ was raised from the dead by the glory of the Father, we too might walk in newness of life. For if we have been united with him in a death like his, we shall certainly be united with him in a resurrection like his. "

Flax is grown both for seed and for fiber. Various parts of the plant have been used to make fabric, dye, paper, medicines, fishing nets and soap. The seeds produce a vegetable oil known as linseed oil or flaxseed oil. It is one of the oldest commercial oils and solvents. Processed flax seed oil has been used centuries as a drying oil in painting and varnishing. Flax seeds are edible. Cold pressed linseed oil is suitable for human consumption. It is one of the most concentrated plant sources of the omega-3 alpha-linolenic acid. Its use as a nutritional supplement is increasing.

Flax seeds come in two basic varieties; brown and yellow (also referred to as golden). Although brown flax can be consumed and has been consumed for thousands of years, it is better known as an ingredient in paints, fiber and cattle feed. Brown and yellow flax have similar nutritional values and equal amounts of omega-3 fatty acids. The exception is a type of yellow flax called solin which is very low in omega-3 and has a completely different oil profile. Of late, there has been a massive resurgence of interest in flax among nutritionists, the health conscious public, food processors, and chefs alike.

The reason for the increasing interest in flaxseed is its apparent benefits for a host of medical conditions, says Roberta Lee, MD, medical director of the Center for Health and Healing at Beth Israel Deaconess Medical Center in New York. In a report reviewed by Michael Smith, MD for WebMD, Carol Sorgen wrote; "Flaxseed is very high in omega-3 essential fatty acids." Sorgen then quoted Lee as saying; " It is the omega 3s – "good" fats – that researchers are looking at in terms of their possible effects on lowering cholesterol, stabilizing blood sugar, lowering the risk of breast, prostate, and colon cancers, and reducing the inflammation of arthritis, as well as the inflammation that accompanies certain illnesses such as Parkinson's disease and asthma. "

In addition to the omega-3s, the remaining two components of flaxseed – lignans and fiber – are being studied for their health benefits as well, says Diane

Morris, PhD, RD, spokesperson for the Flax Council of Canada. Lignans act as both phytoestrogens and antioxidants, while the fiber contained in the flaxseed is of both the soluble and insoluble type. "Flax is an interesting mixture of nutrients and other components," adds Morris.

Researchers from the University of Toronto found that flaxseed may boost conventional treatment for breast cancer. In the study, reported in the American Institute for Cancer Research Newsletter in 1998, postmenopausal women with breast cancer ate either a plain muffin or a muffin containing 25 grams of flaxseed oil every day for approximately five-and-a-half weeks. Of the 29 out of the 39 women who ate both muffins, researchers found reductions in the growth of their tumors. These results were encouraging, says Morris, but she adds, "It's just one study." The favorable results of that study, however, are leading to others. At the John Wayne Cancer Institute in Santa Monica, California, for example, investigators are also looking into the effect of essential fatty acids on breast cancer, says Rachel Beller, MS, RD, director of the Brander Nutritional Oncology Counseling and Research Program. But here, too, says Beller, 'It's too soon to have any conclusive findings."

In addition to research on breast cancer, Morris says, other studies are looking at heart disease, blood pressure, diabetes, menopause, osteoporosis, and inflammatory bowel disease, to name just a few. Yet another study has found that omega-3 fatty acids, and by extension, flaxseed, can reduce the risk of macular degeneration – an eye disease that destroys vision by damaging nerve cells in the eye. The results of a Harvard study, published in August 2001 in the Archives of Ophthalmology, showed that people with a high intake of omega-6 (vegetable oils) were more likely to develop macular degeneration, while those with a combination of lower omega-6 intake and high omega-3 intake were less likely to have the disease.

"Flaxseed is the best source of omega-3 fatty acids," says Lylas G. Mogk, MD, director of the Henry Ford Visual Rehabilitation and Research Center in Detroit, chairman of the Vision Rehabilitation Committee of the American Academy of Ophthalmology, and co-author of Macular Degeneration: **"The Complete Guide to Saving and Maximizing Your Sight."**

Flaxseed is also good for combating dry eyes, a very common problem, says Mogk, probably because of poor omega-3 intake. "Dry eyes are usually the result of an insufficient outer oil layer in the tear film, so the water in the tears doesn't have anything to keep it from evaporating," she says. Omega-3 fatty acids help the oil glands produce the proper consistency of oil so it will flow from the oil glands and coat the surface of the eye. Mogk recommends that her patients take a tablespoon a day of flaxseed oil. "I think all adults should do this," she says, "and most certainly those at high risk for macular degeneration which includes those between the ages 65 and 74, those who have a family member with the disease, women, and whites.

Flaxseed is available in supermarkets and health food stores and comes in whole seeds, ground seeds, or oil. Most nutrition experts recommend the ground seeds, which have "all the goodies," say Morris – fiber, the lignans, and the essential fatty acids. Whole seeds will pass through your system undigested, she says, while the oil lacks the fiber, which, if nothing else, will help alleviate any problems of constipation. Some patients with diverticulosis, however, find the ground flaxseed too irritating; for those people, says Lee, the flaxseed oil is a better choice.

Medicinal Use

Consuming one to two tablespoons of ground flax seed (from a coffee or spice grinder) or one teaspoon of fresh linseed oil daily is a possible alternative to oily fish or fish oil supplements (also high in Omega-3 fatty acids) for vegetarians/vegans. For those who are concerned about high levels of heavy metals such as mercury in fish, although quality cod liver oil supplements are certified free of heavy metals, eating flax seed is a safe alternative.

Food: One tablespoon of ground flax seeds and three tablespoons of water may serve as a replacement for one egg in baking by binding the other ingredients together.

Ground flaxseeds can also be mixed in oatmeal, yogurt, water, or any other food item where a nutty flavor is appropriate. Flaxseed oil is most commonly consumed with salads or in capsules. Flax seed owes its nutritional benefits to lignans and omega-3 essential fatty acids. Lignans benefit the heart and possess anti-cancer properties. Omega-3s, often in short supply in populations with low-fish diets, promote heart health by reducing cholesterol, blood pressure and plaque formation in arteries. In addition, flaxseed oil is often recommended as a galactagogue, that is, it helps increase the flow of breast milk in nursing mothers.

Studies showed that people have a very hard time absorbing the Omega-3 from flaxseed oil compared to oily fish. Flax seed sprouts are edible, with a slightly spicy flavor. Texas nutritionist Natalie Elliott offers these additional suggestions for adding flax to our diet:

Sprinkle ground flax on cereal, yogurt, or salads.
Mix flax into meatloaf or meatballs.
Add ground flax to pancake, muffin, or cookie batter, or other baked goods such as pie crust. Coat fish or homemade chicken nuggets in ground flaxseed and oven fry.
Try one of her favorites;
"Nat's Flax Snacks":

Toss salads with flax oil and vinegar.
1 cup Karo corn syrup
1 cup brown sugar
1 cup smooth peanut butter – Natural peanut butter
1 cup ground flax
1 teaspoon vanilla
6 cups of Rice Krispies

Instruction
Mix the first five ingredients in a saucepot over low heat until melted and smooth.
Add Rice Krispies to the pot and stir.
Pour contents into a buttered 9"x 13" pan.
Press down to flatten.
Stir, cool and cut into 8 bars.

Flax Bran Muffins
Vegetable cooking spray
1 cup multigrain wheat flour
1½ teaspoons baking powder
½ teaspoon baking soda
1¼ teaspoons cinnamon
¼ cup butter
2 eggs
¼ cup molasses
1 cup skim milk
1½ cup bran
1/3 cup flax seed

Instruction

Spray muffin tins with cooking spray.
In a medium size bowl, sift all-purpose flour, baking powder, baking soda, and salt together.
Add cinnamon, and set aside.
In a large bowl, cream butter, no sugar, add eggs.
Add molasses, and beat together well.
Add milk and next three ingredients, mixing well.
Stir in flour mixture, and mix all together just until moistened.
Fill prepared muffin tins 2/3 full.
Bake at 400 degree for about 17 minutes or until lightly browned.
Yield: 18 muffins

Whole-Grain Flax Bread

Ingredients

1 ¼ cups ground flax seed (Vita Flax)
5 cups warm water
4 tablespoons softened raw honey
2 ½ tablespoons instant yeast
1 cup oatmeal
4 cups unbleached flour
½ cup whey powder
8 cups stone-ground whole-wheat flour (approximately)

Instruction

Combine water, honey with yeast.
Let it sit for 3 to 4 minutes.
In a separate bowl, mix the oatmeal, unbleached flour, ground flaxseed, whey powder, .

DRUG FREE HEALING 11 : Medical Science Supporting Scriptures

Add these dry ingredients to the yeast mixture and mix well.
Beat for 5 minutes by hand, then add the whole-wheat flour and mix until dough is quite stiff.
(If using a bread-kneading machine, add the whole-wheat flour and mix on high speed for minutes.)
Knead.
Let rise 15 minutes.
Punch down and let rise another 15 minutes.
Punch down and shape into loaves.
Let the bread rise until doubled in size.
Bake loaves at 35o degree for 40 to 45 minutes.
Makes 2 loaves.

Chapter Nineteen: Hyssop

"Purge me with hyssop, and I shall be clean; wash me, and I shall be whiter than snow." (Ps. 51:7)

Hyssop officinalis
Hyssop , Hebrew: Ezob
Exodus 12:22-23

"Then Moses called all the elder of Israel and said to them, "Go, select lambs for your families, and slaughter the Passover lamb. Take a bunch of hyssop, dip it in the blood that is in the basin, and touch the lintel and the two doorposts with the blood in the basin. None of you shall go outside the door of your house until morning. For the LORD will pass through to strike down the Egyptians; when he sees the blood on the lintel and on the two doorposts, the LORD will pass over that door and will not allow the destroyer to enter your houses to strike you down."

Lintel is the horizontal joining of two vertical doorposts, presenting a picture of the cross. In the Gospel of John 19:29, we are told; "Now there was set a vessel full of vinegar: and they filled a sponge with vinegar, and put it upon hyssop, and put it to his mouth."

Except in John 19:29, eleven of the twelve references to hyssop were about purification, which goes without saying that hyssop symbolized spiritual cleansing, though we may disregard the fact that the act was more of the flesh than of the spirit; "things which are a mere shadow of what is to come; but the substance belongs to Christ."

Paul explains, "For if the sprinkling of defiled persons with the blood of goats and bulls and the ashes of a heifer sanctifies for the purification of the flesh, how much more shall the blood of Christ, who through the eternal Spirit offered Himself without blemish to God, purify your conscience from the dead works to serve the living God?" (Hebrews 9: 13-14).

Christians are cleansed through Christ by his shed blood so that we might be reconciled to God. "All this is from God, who reconciled us to himself through Christ, and has given us the ministry of reconciliation; that is, in Christ, God was reconciling the world to himself, not counting their trespasses against them, and entrusting the message of reconciliation to us. So we are ambassadors for Christ." (1 Corinthians chapter 5 verses 18-20). He has sanctified us, cleansed us, and purified us; set us apart as his ambassadors for divine worship and service. "All authority in heaven and on earth has been given to me. Go therefore and make disciples of all nations, baptizing them in the name of the Father and of the Son and of the Holy Spirit, and teaching them to obey everything that I have commanded you. And remember, I am with you always, to the end of the age" (Matthew 28: 18-20).

Do not let the enemy talk you out of obeying the Master's call on your life. Don't let anyone tell you that you are not ready; that you are not qualified to proclaim the Gospel. Remember that whatever mission, whatever plan God has for you, God has set you apart so that you can fulfill that calling. He has told you alone. Hyssop is taken as a cleansing tonic, but Christ is the only cleansing agent in heaven and n earth that can give you everlasting life, from God the Father. By Him and through Him all healing agents are made.

Hyssop: The genus name Hyssop consists of ten to twelve species. The most popular is Hyssop Officinalis which belongs to the family Labiates, and is a semi-evergreen, perennial shrub with opposite leaves and spikes of purple-blue, two-lipped, late-summer flowers. The flowers appear from July to October in groups of three to seven in the upper axils, and the fruit are brown nut lets. Hyssop has a woody base with linear leaves up to one inch long and can grow up to two feet tall. The stems are square, very branched, and covered in downy hair. Hyssop's aroma is similar to camphor or mint, and the flavor is a cross between rosemary and savory. Hyssop is a decorative and long-lasting herb that has been cultivated since ancient times used for purifying temples and cleansing lepers because the leaves contain antiseptic, antiviral oil, and for a variety of medicinal, culinary, and economical uses.

Constituents

Its active constituents include volatile oil, flavonoids, tannins and bitter substance (marrubin). It also has astringent, carminative, diaphoretic properties. It promotes menstrual flow (emmenagogue). Hyssop is an expectorant. It is a pectoral, stimulant, stomachic, tonic, and vasodilator .

Medicinal Uses

The leaves containing antiseptic and antiviral properties have a slightly bitter, mint flavor. Hyssop tea is a remedy for the common cold and for controlling bacterial plant diseases. It is taken internally for respiratory problems such as bronchitis, especially where there is an excessive mucous production, for digestive disorders and as a cleansing tonic. It is also taken to eliminate flatulence. The oil is used in perfumes for skin conditions and to treat herpes simplex virus that causes cold sores. Hyssop is used to treat cuts, burns, and bruises. A poultice made from the fresh herb is used to heal wounds. Pregnant women should avoid taking hyssop. Other uses include essential oil, fungicide, pot-pourri, repellant. Hyssop may be taken as a tea or tincture. The tea is prepared by infusing 2-3 teaspoons of herb in one cup (250 ml) of hot water for ten to fifteen minutes. Three cups can be taken per day. One teaspoon (5 grams) of hyssop herb steeped in 1 cup (250 ml) hot water in a closed vessel for 15-20 minutes, and taken in sips over a period of 2-3 hours, may help calm colic. Alternatively, 1- 4 ml of tincture can be taken three times a day. If hyssop is being used to help soothe sore throat, gargle with the tea or tincture before swallowing. The essential oil should never be used at a level higher than 1-2 drops internally per day, though more can be used topically on unbroken skin

Herbal Recipes- Hyssop Syrup

Ingredients

1 liter water
100 grams fresh hyssop leaves
16 oz dark honey

Instruction

Pour 1 liter of boiling water over 100 g fresh syrup
Cover and leave to infuse for 15 minutes.
 Strain
Add uncooked dark honey while warm
Stir and bring to syrup consistency
Leave to cool, bottle and store

Take 4-6 dessertspoons (15 ml) a day

For sore throats, cough and helps shortness of breath.

Ingredients

2 tablespoons or 1/3 of a cup dried or fresh flowering tops chopped hyssop
½ pint water
1 teaspoon crushed aniseed
1 gram ginger root paste
¼ teaspoon black pepper
8 oz uncooked dark honey

Instructions

Put all ingredients except honey in water and stir.
Put on stove and bring to boil slowly under less than 100 degrees F heat.
Add honey and stir.
Cover and simmer for 20 minutes.
Strain and allow to cool.

Food

The leaves have a slightly bitter, mint flavor, including young shoot tips – raw are used in seasoning vegetable dishes, casseroles, sauces, pickles, salads, and meat dishes.

Recipe

Hyssop Salad with Potato Cake and Goat's Cheese

Ingredients

½ kilo potatoes, unpeeled
675 grams chevre or goat's cheese

Salt and white pepper to taste

¾ cup olive oil

1 cup arugula, well cleaned and with thick stems discarded

2 cups mixed lettuces, well cleaned and torn into convenient pieces

½ cup fresh hyssop (can substitute fresh basil leaves)

1 tablespoon dried za'atar mixture

½ cup black olives, pitted and halved

Instruction

Cook the potatoes until tender.

Drain

Peel potatoes and slice thinly.

Mix goats' cheese and season with pepper.

Apply salt if needed.

Place 1 tablespoon of oil in a small baking dish and spread half of the goats' cheese on the bottom of the baking dish.

Lay potato slices and spread goats' cheese.

Glaze the baking dish with oil.

Place baking dish in an oven preheated 175 degrees Celsius until the cheese is lightly golden (about 20 – 25 minutes).

Let cool slightly.

To serve, toss the arugula, lettuces, hyssop and olives together with olive oil and lemon juice to taste.

Season to taste.

DRUG FREE HEALING 11 : Medical Science Supporting Scriptures

CHAPTER TWENTY: PALM TREES

"The righteous flourish like palm trees...They are planted in the house of the Lord; they flourish in the house of God. In old age, they still produce fruit; they are always green and full of sap."
Palm Tree
Text : Exodus chapters 14 and 15
Suggested additional readings:
John 12: 1-13
Psalm 19: 1-4
Psalm 92: 12-14
Rev 6: 1-17, Rev 7 :1-17, Luke 10

Background:According to Exodus chapters 14 and 15, God led the Israelites to cross the Red Sea on dry ground, having parted it to form a vertical wall of water on both left and right sides of them as they walked through. He commanded Moses to lift his staff and stretch it over the sea to cause the water to part enabling the Israelites also known as Hebrews to walk through safely. As the pursuing army of the Egyptians closed in on the Hebrews, the seawater flowed back into place behind the Hebrews, and drowned Pharaoh's army. The bible further stated that the Hebrews wandered around the desert, thirsted for three days without ever finding water. When they arrived at a place where they found water, that water tasted too bitter to drink. They complained to Moses, and Moses called on God Almighty for His provision. God told Moses to throw a piece of wood into the bitter water. When Moses acted as God told him to do, the bitter water miraculously turned into sweet drinkable water.

Exodus 15: 25-27, then stated:" There, Almighty God made for them a statute and an ordinance, and there He put them to the test. He said, "If you will listen carefully to the voice of the Lord your God, and do what is right in His sight and give heed to his commandments and keep all his statutes, I will not bring upon you any of the diseases that I brought upon the Egyptians; for I am the LORD who heals you." Then they came to Elim, where there were twelve springs of water and seventy palm trees; and they camped there by the water."

I believe God led the children of Israel to this location to enable them to have a fore view of the Messianic Age, and God's purpose for the emerging nation; that through them all other nations would be blessed. The Israelites camped beside "twelve springs of waters and 70 palm trees," following three days of wandering in the wilderness. The number twelve we know is symbolic of the nation of Israel. In 1 Kings 18: 31, we are told that "Elijah took twelve stones, according to the number of the tribes of the sons of Jacob, to whom the word of the LORD came saying, "Israel shall be your name." As pillars for the foundation of the Church, our Lord Himself selected 12 Apostles.

The number 70 signifies the elders of the Church. Back in the days of Moses, Moses had seventy elders. (Ex. 24: 1). Our LORD Jesus Christ appointed "seventy others, and sent them on ahead of Him, two by two into every nation where He Himself was about to come…" (Luke 10:1). They wandered in the wilderness for three days without water, thirsty, like Jonah being in the belly of the fish three days and three nights, - a picture of Christ's crucifixion, internment and resurrection from the dead. Our Lord Himself interpreted the story of Jonah in the belly of the fish for three days as a sign of the miracle of his own death, burial and resurrection. (Matt 12:40). The number three therefore represents Christ death , burial and resurrection.

We, Christian believers have also been crucified with Christ. (Gal. 2:20). Apostle Paul wrote; "Know ye not, that so many of us as were baptized into Jesus Christ were baptized into his death? Therefore we are buried with him by baptism into death: that like as Christ was raised up from the dead by the glory of the Father, even so we also should walk in newness of life." (Romans 6:3-4.)The Spring of Waters coming from twelve sources in Elim is a picture of our Lord Jesus Christ Himself. A commentary in **Halley's Bible Handbook** states this: "They signify Heaven's River of

Water of Life which is a picture of the benign influences of Christ coming out of Jerusalem and flowing forth in ever widening, ever deepening stream to the whole wide world, blessing the nation with their life-giving qualities, and into eternities of Heaven."

Palms feature significantly in bible imagery. They signify success, victory, peace, joy and righteous acts. Bible references to palms occur more than twenty-four times. King David linked the palm tree with the character of the righteous in psalm 92 verses 12 to 14. He wrote, "The righteous flourish like palm trees...They are planted in the house of the Lord; they flourish in the house of God. In old age, they still produce fruit; they are always green and full of sap."

Christians celebrate Palm Sunday at the beginning of the Holy Week; the Sunday preceding Resurrection Sunday. Palm Sunday recalls the triumphal entry of our Lord Jesus Christ into Jerusalem as he rode on a donkey's colt, and was met by a great crowd spreading their clothes and palm branches in front of Him, shouting, "Hosanna! Blessed is the one who comes in the name of the LORD, the King of Israel." (John 12:12-13). Palm Sunday celebrations involve church attendance during which palm fronds are blessed and distributed to congregants amidst singing of joyful songs culminating into a victory procession.

In Christian martyrs were usually depicted in art holding palms representing the victory of spirit over flesh. Palms also represent heaven, evidenced by ancient art often depicting Jesus in heaven among palms. During the era of the persecution of Christians, graves marked with palm frond or its picture were indication of a martyr occupant. Palm branches are also considered as a symbol of the Church. Palm trees are symbolic representation of the Church in the coming Messianic Age. The significance of palm branches as representing the redeemed in Christ in end time prophecies is demonstrated in Rev. 7: 1-17:"…After this I looked, and there was a great multitude that no one could count, from every nation, from all tribe and peoples and languages, standing before the throne and before the Lamb robed in white, with palm branches in their hands…"

Palm Tree : Of all the trees and shrubs Almighty God planted on this earth, the palm tree is unique. It is a plant that is ceaselessly worshipping God. With more than 200 genera and over 2,600 species, palms differ from other trees in many ways, and vary greatly in size, flowers, leaves and fruits. Most palms grow straight and tall to a height of 100 feet. Most palms, with a few exceptions, have a single unbranched stem that does not increase in girth. The leaves of some palms are like large fans or palms of human hands. Others are like huge feathers growing in clusters around the shoulder of the tree, and extending upwards like giant arms uplifted high to the sky praising the King of Glory, Jehovah God. In bad weather when other plants of lesser fiber easily succumb under the pressure of the turbulent wind, or are swept away by the ferocious current of a violent rainstorm, most palms remain firmly grounded. Come storm or hurricane they remain relentless in their worship-like poses, bowing and lifting their flailing arms acknowledging the sovereignty of Almighty God our Creator. God wants us to be like the palm tree through our faith in Christ Jesus.

Coconut Palm, Cocos Nucifera

Palm trees have more than 800 uses. Most valued of all palm trees is the coconut, Cocos Nucifera. At any one time a coconut palm has 12 different crops of nuts on it, from opening flower to ripe nut. "Coconuts play a unique role in the diets of mankind because they are the source of important physiologically functional components," wrote Dr.

DRUG FREE HEALING 11 : Medical Science Supporting Scriptures

Mary G. Enig, author and researcher at Coconut Research Center, Colorado Springs, Colorado, U.S.A. "These physiologically functional components are found in the fat part of whole coconut, in the fat part of desiccated coconut, and in the extracted coconut oil. Lauric acid, the major fatty acid from the fat of the coconut, has long been recognized for the unique properties that it lends to nonfood uses in the soaps and cosmetics industry. More recently, lauric acid has been recognized for its unique properties in food use, which are related to its antiviral, antibacterial, and antiprotozoal functions. Now, capric acid, another of coconut's fatty acids has been added to the list of coconut's antimicrobial components. These fatty acids are found in the largest amounts only in traditional lauric fats, especially from coconut. Also, recently published research has shown that natural coconut fat in the diet leads to a normalization of body lipids, protects against alcohol damage to the liver, and improves the immune system's anti-inflammatory response. Clearly, there has been increasing recognition of health-supporting functions of the fatty acids found in coconut. Recent reports from the U.S. Food and Drug Administration about required labeling of the trans fatty acids will put coconut oil in a more competitive position and may help return to its use by the baking and snack food industry where it has continued to be recognized for its functionality. Now it can be recognized for another kind of functionality: the improvement of the health of mankind."

Constituents

One of its major constituents is octanoic acid. This octanoic acid has antifungal activity against candida and most of the dermatophytes. A dermatophyte is a parasitic fungus upon the skin. Octanoic acid is also known as caprylic acid. .

Medicinal Use: Coconut water is produced by a 5 month old nut. Coconut water is sterile until the coconut is opened (unless the coconut is spoiled). In World War II, fresh juice from immature coconut was used in emergencies intravenously in the absence of sterile glucose solution.

Coconut roots are used as mouthwash, and dysentery. Coconuts have been used in treating tumors. They promote antidotal activity. They are reportedly also aphrodisiac, antiseptic and used as a mild laxative. Coconuts have been used in treating a wide range of health issues from abscesses to fever and venereal diseases.

Food: At the top of the tree is the growing point, a bundle of tightly packed, yellow-white, cabbage-like leaves, which, if damaged, causes entire tree to die. The undamaged heart makes a tasty salad. A clump of unopened flowers may be bound tightly together, bent over and its tip bruised. Soon it begins to 'weep' a steady dripping of sweet juice, up to a gallon per day. It contains 16-30 mg ascorbic acid/100 g. The cloudy brown liquid is boiled down to syrup, called coconut molasses, and when crystallized it turns into a rich dark sugar, almost like maple sugar. Sometimes it is mixed with grated coconut for candy. When it is left standing, it ferments quickly into toddy with alcohol content up to 8%. After a few weeks, it becomes vinegar. If nut is allowed to germinate, its cavity fills with spongy mass called 'bread' which is eaten raw or toasted in shell over fire. Sprouting seeds may be eaten like celery. Pith of stem contains starch which may be extracted and used as flour.

The white, fleshy immature part of the seed is edible. It is like custard in flavor and consistency. It is eaten or scraped and squeezed through cloth to yield a 'cream' or 'milk' used on various foods fresh or dried. It can be cooked with rice. It is also cooked with taro leaves or game. It is used in ice cream and as cream in tea or coffee, cakes, pies, candies, in curries and sweets dried, desiccated, and shredded. **Other uses :** When nuts are cut open and dried, meat becomes copra, which is processed for oil, rich in glycerin and used to make soaps, shampoos, shaving creams, toothpaste lotions, lubricants, hydraulic fluid, paints, synthetic rubber and plastics. The oil is also used in lamps. Coconut shell flour is used in industry as filler in plastics. Boiled toddy, known as jaggery with lime makes a good cement. Fresh inner coconut husk can also be rubbed on the lens of snorkeling goggles to prevent fogging during use.

The Date Palm
Phoenix dactylifera

The Date Palm is cultivated extensively. It has high sugar, protein, low fats contents. It is used medicinally..

Constituents: W.H. Barreveld, in the 1993 Bulletin of the Food and Agriculture Organization of the United Nations entitled Date Palm Products, states that when dates are mature; they contain reasonable amounts of vitamins A, B1, B2 and niacin. Although there are no significant amounts of other vitamins, dates are good source of calcium, iron, chlorine, copper, magnesium, sulphur, phosphorous, and potassium.

Medicinal uses

Dates are regarded as aphrodisiac. They are also used as a demulcent. A demulcent is meant to relieve the irritation of the inflamed mucous membrane. " Dates are used in the treatment of a variety of ailments including anemia, asthma, bronchitis, cancer, catarrh, chest, gonorrhea and vaginitis.

Food: Fruits are preserved by drying or pressing them together into large cakes. Dry or soft dates are eaten out-of-hand, or may be seeded and stuffed with fillings such as almonds, candied orange, lemon peel, and marzipan. Dates may be chopped and used in a range of sweet and savory dishes, such as puddings, bread, cakes and other dessert items. Dates may be processed into cubes, paste, spread, date syrup or "honey" called dibs, powder (date sugar), or vinegar. Young date leaves may be cooked and eaten as vegetable. The finely ground seeds may be mixed with flour to make bread. The flowers of the date palm are edible. Traditionally the female flowers are the most available for sale and weigh 300-400 grams. The flower buds are used in salad or pounded with dried fish to make condiments for bread. Other products include date honey, made from juice of fresh fruit -- date sugar. Date sap is often made into fermented beverage. Date palm flour can be made from pith of tree, and oil from the seeds.

	Inorganic constituents of dates (mg/ 100 g dry weight)	
Element	Halawy	Sayer
Potassium	716.0	657.0
Sodium	37.0	38.0
Calcium	65.0	97.0
Magnesium	71.0	79.0
Phosphorus	84.0	63.0
Iron	3.7	3.1
Aluminum	5.1	--
Copper	0.2	0.2
Sulfur	52.0	59.0
Manganese	3.3	4.6
Silicon	66.0	66.0
Chlorine	27.0	31.0

DRUG FREE HEALING 11 : Medical Science Supporting Scriptures

Saw Palmetto, Serenoa repens

Saw Palmetto (Serenoa.repens) are ornamental palms with fan-shaped leaves. They are common in Florida. Saw Palmettos are touted as containing medicinal properties benign to male and female reproductive functions. The plant's cream-colored flowers with vanilla-like fragrance, blossom in the summer. The dark blue fruits are harvested from September throughout the autumn, even until January.

Constituents: Steroidal saponins (beta-sitosterol). Saponins are glycosides of Steroid alkaloids, (steroids with a nitrogen function) or triterpenes are found in the plant's skins where they form a waxy protective coating.. Saponins are believed to be useful in the human diet for controlling cholesterol, but some in plants, including those produced by the soapberry, are poisonous if swallowed, and can cause skin rash in many people. Any markedly toxic saponin is known as a "sapotoxin". Other active constituents of Saw Palmetto are fatty acids, caprylic acid, polysaccharides (complex carbohydrate), zinc, and volatile oils. The liposterolic (fat-soluble) extract of saw palmetto provides concentrated amounts of free fatty acids and sterols.

One study with a saw palmetto extract suggests that it reduces the amount of dihydrotestosterone (DHT) (an active form of testosterone) binding in the part of the prostate surrounding the urethra - the tube carrying urine from the bladder. Test tube studies also suggest that saw palmetto weakly inhibits the action of 5-alpha-reductase, the enzyme responsible for converting testosterone to DHT. In test tubes, saw palmetto also inhibits the actions of growth factors and inflammatory substances that may contribute to BPH). Contrary to some opinions, saw palmetto does not have an estrogen-like effect in men's bodies.

Medicinal Use : Saw palmetto is used as a mild diuretic and urinary antiseptic. It is also as a tonic . Saw palmetto is to treat asthma, sore throats, colds, bronchitis, whooping cough, excessive sinus mucus conditions and other upper respiratory problems . It gained clinical reputation in the early part of this century as an expectorant and as a remedy for chronic cystitis. Recent interests in saw palmetto have been linked with the finding that sitosterols may act on steroid receptors. Remedies made from the berries gained a reputation for treating symptoms related to BPH. A lipido/sterolic extract (Permixon), using n-hexane to extract serenoa repens, has long been available in Europe and used in vitro and in vivo studies in humans and animals. The liposterolic (fat-soluble) extract of saw palmetto provides concentrated amounts of free fatty acids and sterols.

The prostate gland—the solid, chestnut-shaped organ that forms part of the male reproductive system—surrounds the first part of the urethra and is situated immediately under the bladder and in front of the rectum. It produces secretions that form part of the seminal fluid secreted into the urethra when sperm move through, i.e., during sexual climax. Prostate enlargement/maturation is initiated by androgen hormones at puberty and stops at about age 20. The enlargement continues later in a man's life but rarely causes a problem before age 40. At age 60, about 50% of males experience some symptoms of BPH. Over 90% of males in their 70s experience symptoms.

The following symptoms suggest a prostate problem: more frequent urination, especially during the night, a hesitant, interrupted, weak urine stream, urgency, and leaking or dribbling. Additional symptoms include lower back pain, diminished libido and discomfort during intercourse. Surgery represents a final solution for BPH patients.

In the U.S., 350,000 surgical procedures are performed annually while an additional 1.6 million patients undergo pharmacological treatment. The phytopharmaceutical therapy of BPH includes different plant extract capsules of seeds, roots, leaves and berries that are currently available in the U.S. and are widely used in Europe for symptomatic relief. The most popular among these herbal remedies is saw palmetto. It is the fruit that is the medicinal part of the plant.

Research indicates that the plant is known for its sedative, warming, tonic abilities. In other words, the berries of the Saw Palmetto Plant have the power to act as a calming sedative to the nervous system, yet as a stimulant to the physical system, most especially in the urinary-reproductive system.

They have a pungent flavor and a sweet aroma, and are believed to affect the endocrine system. They act as an antiseptic and a diuretic in the urinary tract. Saw Palmetto is also known for its capacity as an expectorant and, reputation as an aphrodisiac.

Men's health

Saw Palmetto Berries have become known as a Specific Herb for male problems such as impotence, lack of libido, energy, and benign prostate conditions. Research in Germany confirms the effectiveness of this herb in the treatment of enlarged prostate problems. Dr. Andrew Weil, stated in his book, **"Spontaneous Healing"** that Saw Palmetto is one of two plants now recognized as holistic complementary treatment for enlarged prostate problems. He claims it can be used indefinitely. Saw Palmetto is now considered the herb of choice for toning, nourishing, and empowering the male reproductive system, boosting the male sex hormones, aiding in the relief of enlarged prostate problems, and helping with urinary tract infections.

For strengthening the reproductive system, David Hoffman, in **"The Herbal Handbook"** suggests combining it with Damiana, a diuretic and a genitourinary tract stimulant widely regarded as an aphrodisiac, and Kola .

      According to Nutritionist Dr. Mary Enig, "Over the last decade, double-blind clinical trials have proven that 320 mg per day of the liposterolic extract of saw palmetto berries is a safe and effective treatment for BPH. A recent review of studies, published in the Journal of the American Medical Association, concluded that saw palmetto extract was comparable to finasteride in the treating BPH without side effects, such as loss of libido. The clinical effectiveness of saw palmetto has been shown in trials lasting six months to three years.

      A three-year trial in Germany found that taking 160 mg of saw palmetto extract twice daily reduced nighttime urination in 73% of patients and improved urinary flow rates significantly. One trial using a combination of saw palmetto extract (320 mg per day) and nettle root extract (240 mg per day) improved urine flow, decreased nighttime urination, over a one-year treatment period"

Women's Reproductive Health

      Saw Palmetto, however, is not an herb for men alone. It is also a galactagogue, which means it helps the body produce milk for nursing mothers, and acts as a fertility aid for women. Saw palmetto may also be useful in treating the following conditions: hirsutism -- an excessive growth of dark, coarse body and facial hair in women, and polycystic ovarian disease -- multiple ovarian cysts that lead to menstruation problems.

The dosage of Saw Palmetto Berries

For an adult, 1/2 to 1 teaspoon of the crushed berries infused in 1 cup of water for 5 minutes should be taken 2 to 3 times a day. On other hand, 20-40 drops of Saw Palmetto Berry Tincture (1-2 ml.) in water, 3 times a day. Many herbal companies manufacture capsules for male conditions that contain Saw Palmetto berries as one of the main ingredients, and these are available in many health food stores.

Chapter Twenty One : Coriander

Then the LORD said to Moses, "Behold, I will rain bread from heaven for you..."

"..Now the house of Israel called its name manna; it was like coriander seed, white, and the taste of it was like wafers made with honey."

Coriander: Coriandrum sativum
Ex. 16: 1-4, 13-15 and 31-32

"They set out from Elim, and all the congregation of the people of Israel came to the wilderness of Sin, which is between Elim and Sinai, on the fifteenth day of the second month after they had departed from the land of Egypt. And the whole congregation of the people of Israel murmured against Moses and Aaron in the wilderness, and said to them; "Would that we had died by the hand of the LORD in the land of Egypt, when we sat by the fleshpots and ate bread to the full; for you have brought us out into this wilderness to kill this whole assembly with hunger."

Then the LORD said to Moses, "Behold, I will rain bread from heaven for you; and the people shall go out and gather a day's portion every day, that I may prove them, whether they will walk in my law or not. .. In the evening quails came up and covered the camp; and in the morning dew lay round about the camp. And when the dew had gone up, there was on the face of the wilderness a fine, flake-like thing, fine as hoarfrost on the ground. When the people of Israel saw it, they said to one another, "What is it?" For, they did not know what it was. And Moses said to them, "It is the bread which the LORD has given you to eat. . . Now the house of Israel called its name manna; it was like coriander seed, white, and the taste of it was like wafers made with honey."

Six weeks into their freedom from bondage as they wandered in the wilderness of Sin halfway between Elim and Mount Sinai, the children of Israel began complaining. They had set their minds back to the past, and craved for Egyptian fleshpot of meat and bread instead of putting their trust in the Word of God and looking ahead toward the Promised Land of Milk and Honey. The wilderness of Sin was named after Hadramawt moon god Sin. Hadramawt, an ancient South Arabian kingdom occupied what are now southern and southeastern Yemen and present-day Sultanate of Oman (Muscat and Oman). Hadramawt maintained its political independence until late in the 3rd century AD, when it was conquered by the kingdom of Saba.

Other nations in the region worshipped the moon god among their pantheons under many different names. The Sabeans called it al Maqah. To the Mineans, it was known as al-Wadd and the Qatabanians worshipped the moon god as al-Amm. Among the Aws and the Khazraj tribes of al-Hijaz highlands of the western border of Arabia which stood parallel to the Red Sea and whose people were those who rallied to support the prophet Muhammed during his fateful hijirah, the moon-god was known as al-Lah and al-Ilah. According to Dr. Phillip Hitti, Professor Emeritus of Semitic Literature, Princeton University, New Jersey, al-Lah entered Arabia through Syriac word Hallah which was in turn a carry-over from Mesopotamia from where it originated.

The more closer you get into the presence of God the more intense are satanic activities of diversion against you. Rev. Dr. Chuck Swindoll, chancellor of Dallas Theological Seminary, in one of his inimitable radio bible expositions once made this observation; "Whenever anything or anyone is worshipped, Satan is pleased. Whenever anything or anyone rather God takes the center of our attention, Satan is pleased. Satan does not care who it is or what it is that takes the center of our focus. His goal is to keep us from serving God."

Satan's plan for the children of Israel was to cause them to turn away from God because of hunger in the hope of thwarting Almighty God's salvation plan for humanity. Satan reasoned that without Israel, there would be no Messiah. But Almighty God in whom there is no limit to His grace, rained down bread from heaven upon His children.

For forty years as they journeyed to the Promised Land, God fed the children of Israel with bread from heaven which they called "manna", not just to fill the physical body but as a foretaste of food for the spirit. Our Lord Jesus Christ regarded Manna as a shadow of himself. "...The bread of God is that which comes down from heaven and gives life to the world...I am the bread of life, he who comes to me shall not hunger, and he who believes in me shall never thirst." (John 6:31-40).

The bible said, the children of Israel described manna as tasting like "coriander seed, white, and the taste of it was like wafers made with honey."

There are far too many of us, Christians who are not satisfied with what we have in Christ Jesus -- our salvation. Like the children of Israel, we are going around looking for religious experiences that are like the "taste of coriander seed- wafers made with honey" from our past. Christ is our true Coriander.

Coriander foliage   Dried seeds   Coriander roots

Coriander-Cilantro-

Coriander is the name given the seeds of the plant. The name derives from the Greek word *Koris* for "smelly bug". The leaves are called Cilantro, in Spanish. The leaves, flowers and seeds are used both medicinally and for food.

Coriander (*Coriandrum sativum*), is an annual herb in the family Apiaceae. It is a soft, hairless, foetid plant growing to 50 cm tall. The leaves are variable in shape, broadly lobed at the base of the plant, and slender and feathery higher on the flowering stems. The leaves are variously referred to as coriander leaves, cilantro (in the United States, from the Spanish name for the plant), dhania (in the Indian subcontinent, and increasingly, in Britain) They are also known as Chinese parsley or Mexican parsley. The leaves have a very different taste from the seeds, similar to parsley but "juicier" and with citrus-like overtones.

  The seeds are round like tiny balls. They lose their disagreeable scent on drying and become fragrant. The longer they are kept, the more fragrant they become. They are used in condiments. They form the major ingredient in curry powder. The flowers are borne in small umbels, white or very pale pink, asymmetrical, with the petals pointing away from the centre of the umbel longer (5-6 mm) than those pointing to the middle of the umbel (only 1-3 mm long).The fruit is a globular dry schizocarp 3-5 mm diameter. All parts of the plant are edible, but the fresh leaves and the dried seeds are the most commonly used in cooking. The young leaves can easily be mistaken for parsley in appearance. But it has a distinctly different taste. Cilantro, that is, coriander leaves have zesty flavor. Coriander is a natural insecticide.

---Constituents---

  Coriander promotes antispasmodic and analgesic actions. It contains flavonoids, phenolic acids, and alpha-pinene. Coriander fruit contains about 1 per cent of volatile oil, which is the active ingredient. The oil is pale yellow or colorless. It has the odor of coriander, and a mild aromatic taste. The fruit yields about 5 per cent of ash and contains also malic acid, tannin and some fatty matter. It also contains antioxidant properties and vitamin C. Its main properties consist of substances that prevent fat from turning rancid. ; it kills meat-spoiling bacteria, fungi and insect larvae, as well as microorganism that cause infections in wounds. Coriander is believed to possess aphrodisiac property as well.

Food

Chopped coriander leaves are also used as garnish on cooked curry dishes. As heat diminishes their flavor quickly, coriander leaves are often used raw or added to the dish right before serving. Coriander roots are also used in a variety of cuisine.

Medicinal Uses

Coriander is used to treat minor digestive problems and pain. Coriander is used as a remedy for bloating, cramps, and flatulence. It also soothes nervous tension and alleviates muscle spasms. Coriander has been used in lotion to treat rheumatic pain. It is a stimulant and carminative. The fruit powder, fluid extract and oil are chiefly used medicinally as flavoring to disguise the taste of active purgatives. It is an ingredient of the following compound preparations: confection, syrup and tincture of senna.

Researchers have found that coriander can assist with clearing the body of lead, aluminum, and mercury.

Coriander has been used as a relief for anxiety and insomnia. Coriander essential oil exhibits antibacterial action against <u>E. Coli</u>. The seeds have been used in the preparation of herbal <u>diuretic</u> by boiling equal amounts of coriander seeds with <u>cumin</u> seeds. The extract is then cooled and taken. Chew the seeds to aid digestion, and sweeten breath after eating garlic.

Dosage:

Coriander essential oils can be used externally to treat rheumatic pain. Leaves can be ingested to sooth digestion, and seeds can be pulverized into a paste to be used on skin or in the mouth for odor relief.

An infusion of 2 teaspoons dried seeds in 250 mL (1 cup) of water can be taken once a day for digestive relief.

Chapter Twenty Two: Cucumber

Now the rabble that was among them had a strong craving; and the people of Israel also wept again, and said, "O that we had meat to eat! We remember the fish we ate in Egypt for nothing, the cucumber,
Cucumber – Cucumis sativo
Number 11:1-6

"And the people complained in the hearing of the LORD about their misfortunes; and when the LORD heard it, his anger was kindled, and the fire of the LORD burned among them, and consumed some outlying parts of the camp. Then the people cried to Moses; and Moses prayed to the LORD and the fire abated...Now the rabble that was among them had a strong craving; and the people of Israel also wept again, and said, "O that we had meat to eat! We remember the fish we ate in Egypt for nothing, the cucumber, the melons, the leeks, the onions and the garlic; but now our strength is dried up, and there is nothing at all but this manna to look at."

While I was studying this scriptural text, the secular media came out with a mid-term election perennial shocker, which involved one of the top Conservative religious leaders of America. Until the scandal broke out, Ted Haggard was pastor of a mega-church with a congregation of 14,000. He was also the head of the National Evangelical Association which boasted a membership of 30 million. Rev. Ted Haggard was additionally, one of the spiritual advisors to the 43rd President of the United States of America, George W. Bush.

When the media broke the allegations of the reverend Ted Haggard's homosexual trysts with a male prostitute, frankly, I thought it was an election-year attempt to destroy a good man, and believed Rev Haggard's denials of ever knowing his accuser, Mike Jones, let alone having a three-year homosexual relations with that male prostitute. However, after two days of his initial denials, the Reverend did not only reverse himself to admit knowing his accuser who he alleged, had once sold him the drug meth , but Haggard also confessed in a letter read in his church that he is a

DRUG FREE HEALING 11 : Medical Science Supporting Scriptures

"Liar and a Deceiver' . He made this declaration while admitting he had committed a "sexual immorality".

I do not think I am the only one who grieved and groaned upon hearing this report. I whispered to myself in pain, "Why? What did he do that for?" Reverend Ted Haggard, who relentlessly preached God's message of judgment against aberrant life styles, was a married man with children and a vocal anti-gay advocate. He was also a spiritual adviser to the currently the most powerful man on earth, President Bush. So why did he do what he did? The explanation Rev. Haggard gave for his moral failures was that he "was tempted". In other words, he had a strong craving for whatever it was that he did which brought him down. Each one of us has an inherent base nature that blinds us to our blessings and induces in us a craving for what we do not have instead of counting our blessings for what we have. In this way, we are no different from the children of Israel who complained and nagged about the things that they did not have despite their many blessings. The bible said, "The rabble that was among them had a strong craving…"

The American Heritage Dictionary defines rabble as "…the lower class of people, a mob." I would say our lower nature. Each one of us has within us a rabble, that is, our sinful nature. Each one of us is capable of yielding to the strong craving of the rabble within us. "Therefore, "the bible warns, " let any one who thinks that he stands take heed lest he fall." (1 Cor. 10: 12) Sometimes God allows us to experience hardships to test our obedience to Him, which is, to believe in His Son our Lord Jesus Christ, and be thankful even for the little we may have instead of turn our eyes upon what we do not have.

Ted Haggard blamed "temptation" for his perversion. But we have assurances by the Word of God that "No temptation has overtaken you that is not common to man. God is faithful, and he will not let you be tempted beyond your strength, but with the temptation will also provide the way of escape, that you may be able to endure it." (1 Cor. 10: 13).

Almighty God, our heavenly Father has made provision for our salvation through the blood of His only Son our Lord Jesus Christ. The time for repentance is short while the day of grace still lasts. Soon and very soon there will be no more opportunity to plead the blood of Jesus for our sin because there will be an end of grace.

God has made a solemn commitment in Revelation 22: 11 that there will come an end of God's grace when everyone will experience a spiritual suspended animation, the lost will be lost forever, and the saved will be saved forever. "Let the evildoer still do evil, and the filthy still be filthy, and the righteous still do right, and the holy still be holy."

While we have the chance, let us not be like the rebellious Israelites on their way from Egypt to Canaan. Let us show contentment with everything that the Lord gives knowing that He that provided Israelite manna for forty years, the Creator of the heavens and earth, and the vegetation, the One who gave us life and health, is able to supply our needs for onions, leeks, garlic, melons, cinnamon, pomegranates, aloes, mustard, yes, cucumber as well.

Cucumber: *Cucumis sativus*

Sometimes called a cuke, Cucumber is in the gourd family Cucurbitaceous, which includes squash, and in the same genus as the muskmelon. The plant is widely cultivated today. The cucumber plant has large leaves that form a canopy over the fruit. The vine is grown on the ground or on trellises, often in greenhouses. The fruit is roughly cylindrical, elongated, with tapered ends, and may be as large as 60 cm long and 10 cm in diameter.

Constituents

Cucumber is upwards of 96 per cent water in its composition. Fresh cucumber is a good source of vitamin C, vitamin K, vitamin A, vitamin B6, and potassium. Cucumber also provides some dietary fiber, thiamin, folate, pantothenic acid, magnesium, phosphorus, potassium, copper, and manganese.

Food

Cucumbers are grown to be eaten fresh (called *slicers*) and those intended for pickling (called *picklers*) are similar. The fruit is commonly harvested while still green. They are eaten as vegetable, raw, cooked, or made into pickled cucumbers. Slicers are generally longer, smoother, more uniform in color, and have tougher skin. Picklers are generally shorter and thicker.

Pickling cucumbers

Medicinal Uses

Cucumber *seeds* promote diuretic action. They are used also as a taeniacide; a substance for killing tapeworms when one or two ounces of the seeds are taken after being blended into paste and mixed with honey . They also promote emetic action when mixed with water and taken while fasting. Emetic, is any medicinal agent used to induce vomiting. The most common purpose of an emetic is to force a person to disgorge some ingested poison.

As a cosmetic, Cucumber is excellent for rubbing over the skin to keep it soft . It is cooling, healing and soothing to an irritated skin, whether caused by sun, or the effects of a cutaneous eruption.

Cutaneous eruption primarily involves the skin and is contracted mainly by those who handle contaminated hides, wool, or carcasses. The bacteria enter through a cut or other opening in the skin, and a dark, itchy bump that resembles an insect bite appears. The bump then develops into an open sore with a black area in the center. Cucumber juice is used as a cooling and beautifying agent for the skin. Cucumber soap is used by many women.

DRUG FREE HEALING 11 : Medical Science Supporting Scriptures

Chapter Twenty Three : Onion
Did the children of Israel sin because they craved for onions et al which they claimed they " ate for nothing" in Egypt?

Onion *Allium cepa*
Number 11:1-6
Ezek. 47: 12

"…Now the rabble that was among them had a strong craving; and the people of Israel also wept again, and said, "O that we had meat to eat! We remember the fish we ate in Egypt for nothing, the cucumber, the melons, the leeks, the onions and the garlic; but now our strength is dried up, and there is nothing at all but this manna to look at…" (Num.11:4-6)

Did the children of Israel sin because they craved onions et al which they claimed they " ate for nothing"? No. They sinned because apart from being unthankful for God's provisions for them, they made anything else but God the center of their focus. That is idolatry. God Himself has made these provisions, stating, "Every moving thing that lives shall be food for you; and as I gave you the green plants, I give you everything." (Gen. 9: 3). He also said, "There will grow all kinds of trees for food…Their fruit will be for food, and their leaves for healing." (Ezek. 47: 12).

If you give more time to your personal pursuits than you do to God, that is idolatry. If you spend much more time on the computer rather than to the things of

God, it is idolatry. If you spend much more efforts and time on pleasure than on the things of God, you are an idolater. The children of Israel did not sin because they had a craving for onions among other types of food. God made onions and other vegetation for our good. Making onions the center of their focus, they were idolizing onions as they saw the Egyptians did. But God said, "My glory I will not give to another..." (Is.48:11) The Egyptians regarded onion as a sacred symbol of the universe. Onions were an object of worship for them.

Onion

Onions belong to the lily family, Amaryllidaceae, and the genus, Allium. Alliums are perennial herbs with bulbous, onion-scented underground stems. This genus includes garlic, chives, shallots, leeks, and even a non-edible species grown solely for its showy flower. The common garden onions are in the species, *Allium cepa.*

There are five ways to classify onions -- basic use, flavor, color, shape of the bulb, and day length. The four basic types of onions are "storage onions", "fresh onions", "pearl or mini onions", and "green onions". The major differences between "storage" and "fresh" is that "storage onions" have a darker color with thicker skins, more pungent flavor, and are usable for many months of the year since they are better keepers. "Fresh onions" have lighter color with thin skin, milder, sweeter flavor. They are best eaten fresh because they are not good keepers. There are three onion flavors -- sweet, mild, and pungent. The color of onions can be white, yellow, or red. The bulb shape is globular or round, flattened, or torpedo shaped. Onions release a powerful vapor when cut that affects the nerves in the nose and eyes. Holding them under running water while peeling or putting them in the freezer for 1/2 hour before chopping may help you avoid the tears while cutting. The root end of the onion contains more of the irritating compound.

Constituents

Onions are low in calories yet they add abundant flavor to a wide variety of foods. With only 30 calories per serving, onions are sodium, fat, and cholesterol free . They provide dietary fiber, vitamin C, vitamin B6, potassium, and other key nutrients. Research shows that onions may help guard against many chronic diseases, as they are anti-viral. That is probably because onions contain generous amounts of a flavonoid called quercetin. Other sources are tea and apples, but research shows that absorption of quercetin from onions is twice that from tea and more than three times that from apples.

Studies have shown that quercetin protects against cataracts, cardiovascular disease, and cancer. Onions also contain a variety of other naturally occurring chemicals known as organosulfur compounds that have been linked to lowering blood pressure and cholesterol levels.

Food: Onions are edible with a distinctive strong flavor and pungent aroma, which is mellowed and sweetened by heat. Used worldwide for cooking purposes, they come in a wide variety of forms and colors. Eating onions regularly helps prevent general diseases. Onions are available in fresh, frozen, canned, and dehydrated forms. Onions can be used, usually chopped or sliced, in almost every type of food, including cooked foods and fresh salads, and as a spicy garnish

Medicinal Uses.

Curry and onions might do much more than spice up a meal. They also could help prevent colon cancer, according to a recent Los Angeles Times medical report by Shari Roan. A new study published in the August 2006 issue of Clinical Gastroenterology and Hepatology, found that a pill containing large doses of curcumin, a chemical found in curry and tumeric, and quercetin, an antioxidant in onions, helped prevent precanceroous polyps in several people at high risk for colon cancer.

Five people with an inherited disease called familial adenomatous polyposis, which often leads to colon cancer, took the pill for six months. The average number of polyps the patients developed dropped by more than 60 percent, and the average size of the polyps was reduced by 50 percent, said Francis M. Giardiello, senior author of the study and a gastroenterologist at the Cancer Center at John Hopkins University.

Onions are used in the treatment of colds, coughs, flu, asthma, parasites, wounds, blisters, boils, heart disease, contaminated blood and kidney infections. They are used to promote anti-inflammatory action. Onions possess anticholesterol properties. They help lower the "bad" cholesterol LDL. Onions contain the chemical quercetin which stimulates antioxidant action. Products containing onion extract mederma are used in the treatment of topical scars.

People with heart problems have been encouraged to eat onions because they help reduce blood pressure, diminish the stickiness of platelets. Quercetin has inhibited breast cancer cells in a test tube. It is believed that quercetin neutralizes free radicals and protects the body's cell membranes. For heavy chest congestion or bronchitis an onion poultice provides relief. When you have a cold, eat a lot of fresh onions.

Chapter Twenty Four: Leeks Allium porrum -

The leek The leek is a vegetable belonging with onion and garlic, to the *Alliaceae* family. Also in this species are two very different vegetables: The elephant garlic (*Allium ampeloprasum* var. *ampeloprasum*) grown for its bulbs, and kurrat grown for its leaves. Rather than forming a bulb as onion, the leek produces a long cylinder of bundled leaf sheaths which are generally blanched by pushing soil around them (trenching). It is in flower from July to August. The flowers are hermaphrodite, that is they have both male and female organs. They are pollinated by bees, and insects.

Constituents
Anthelmintic, antiasthmatic, anticholesterolemic, antiseptic, antispasmodic, cholagogue, diaphoretic, diuretic, expectorant, febrifuge, stimulant, stings, stomachic, tonic, vasodilator.

Medicinal Uses : Leeks, like its cousin garlic, have been used in treating a wide range of ailments, including ringworm, candida and vaginitis. Leeks have been used to promote fungicidal, antiseptic, tonic and parasiticidal activity.

Other Uses: The juice of leek and the entire plant are used as insect and mole repellent.

Food: Its flowers, leaves and root are edible. The leaves and long white blanched stem are eaten cooked. They can also be cut into thin slices and added to salads, producing a mild onion flavoring with a delightful sweetness. The bulb is consumed raw or cooked but frequently used as garnish.

Chapter Twenty Five : Garlic
Garlic –Allium Sativo

Now, for a status report on my health. I am eleven months into writing this testimony, and twenty seven months since I took up daily consumption of raw garlic as a health requirement. It followed Dr Hemstreet's consent to allow me to use for only three months some bible herbs in treating my complex sickness under his supervision. He had said that I could go ahead provided it was combined with a regimen of balanced diet and daily walking exercises. I had since become a garlic aficionado. I chewed three cloves of raw garlic one hour before breakfast and one hour before my evening meal every day and have continued to live on garlic since then. I chew raw garlic when I feel I am about to catch a cold. I chew garlic when I have a scratchy throat, and I chew garlic after leaving a place full of people sneezing and coughing.

If you had a habit of chewing raw garlic as much as I have been doing, I am sure that you would be the first to admit that its hot, spicy, harsh, tang could be quite intolerable. You might want to lessen the irritating effect by ingesting a dessert spoonful of garlic paste diluted with half a teaspoon of raw honey, or swallow little chunks of it with a glass of water. Any process of ingesting you may choose, regardless, the effect of raw garlic inside your system is the same. You feel it moving down your organs as it "exerts its effects throughout the digestive, respiratory and urinary systems, disinfecting as it goes enhancing immunity and remedying coughs and colds, stomach and bowel infections, " writes, Dr. Anne McIntyre, author **The Medicinal Garden – How To Grow and Use Your Own Medicinal Herbs** and former director, National Institute of Medicinal Herbalists. "Garlic is a wonderful medicine for the heart and circulation," she adds, "lowering raised blood pressure and harmful cholesterol levels and reducing the tendency to blood clotting..." For any patient as deadly sick as I had been, and looking for a speedy recovery, eleven months of undergoing any medical treatment was eternity.

However, having endured the punishment of eating raw garlic for so long a time, I was eager to keep my appointment with Dr. Hemstreet not just to give him my health status report, I wanted to let him know my gratitude that Almighty God allowed him to be my primary care provider. To show him my physical improvement, I latched my hands together at my rear, then, stretched my arms from my rear-end and painlessly pulled them as far up as I could, attempting to get them over my head. I told Dr Hemstreet, " My shoulders are no more hurting !" It was not just my shoulders; the persistent pain that engulfed my entire body completely disappeared. I told him also that I no longer felt the shortness of breath that had plagued my life for so long, and that I could breathe normally. "I think I have completely recovered," I said enthusiastically. "I thank God for you, doctor". He replied that the glory be given to God." When I told Dr. Hemstreet that I believed that I had been healed from the sleep apnea disorder as well, he examined my air passageway thoroughly. After that, he ordered that I saw an independent ENT specialist, for a second opinion. Two months later, I was in the presence of one of America's top Christian endocrinologists, Dr. Carolyn Hall. Like her other professional colleagues to whom I had been previously referred, she too was thorough in her examination of my condition. The procedure involved inserting an instrument called tracheoscope through my nose into my throat to look in. She then concluded there was no obstructive tissue present. Meaning? I am healed of that terrible sleep apnea too!

The bible is 6000 years ahead of modern medical science. It knew then what modern medical science has now found out, that the antibiotic compounds produced by garlic may offer another option for treating antibiotic resistant diseases. Garlic yields alliin and allicin - sulfur-containing compounds that act against a range of bacteria and fungi.

Allicin is antibiotic against bacteria such as staphylococcus and salmonella. Garlic derived compounds are now used as antibiotic for chickens and cattle and as pesticides that eliminate mosquito larvae, nematode worms, and parasites such as lice and intestinal worms." Michael Castleman , a prolific author with as many as fifteen titles on herb and health issues to his name, states in his book; **"The Healing Herbs – The Ultimate Guide To The Curative Power Of Nature's Medicines :**"No standard medication can match garlic when it comes to acting on so many cardiovascular risk factors at the same time. Some drugs lower cholesterol level. Others rein in blood pressure. Still others reduce the likelihood of the blood clots that trigger heart attacks and most strokes. But garlic does all of the things, thanks to allicin and another chemical called ajoene." Dr Castleman further states that two groups of researchers – one Australian and the other American – have published analyses of a selection of garlic cholesterol studies. The Australians reviewed 16 trials involving 952 people with high cholesterol. They concluded that a daily dose of either 10 fresh cloves or 1 gram of a dried high-allicin preparation can reduce total cholesterol levels by 12 percent. Meanwhile, the American team reviewed five vigorous trials involving 365 people. They concluded that a daily dose of either one fresh clove or 1 gram of a dried high-allicin preparation can lower total cholesterol level by 9 percent. In yet another study, researchers in Humboldt University in Berlin concluded that garlic can also treat heart condition. Arterial blockages recede by 3 percent. Demographic studies suggest that garlic is responsible for the low incidence of arteriosclerosis in areas of Italy and Spain where consumption of the bulb is heavy. Studies of 7 AIDS patients who took a clove of garlic a day for 3 months showed that they experienced increased immune activity, 2 of the 7 saw chronic herpes sore clear up during treatment, while 2 others with chronic diarrhea – a common AIDS symptom reported improvement. Use of garlic by diabetic patients helps in the reduction of blood sugar levels. Garlic contains several potent antioxidants. The chemicals in garlic can help reduce serum cholesterol, hypertension, blood clotting, blood sugar, bowel parasites, respiratory and other infections, and the aging process itself. It enhances anticancer activity.

-**Constituents**---Volatile oil, mucilage, germanium, glucokinins, vitamins, antiseptic, antibiotic. antifungal, anthelmintic, antiasthmatic, anticholesterolemic, antiseptic, ntispasmodic, cholagogue, diaphoretic, diuretic, expectorant, febrifuge, stimulant, stomachic, tonic, vasodilator.

Medicinal Uses: Garlic is used as a diaphoretic, diuretic, expectorant, and stimulant, stomachic and as an antiseptic. When garlic is chewed, chopped, bruised or crushed, a complex chemical activity is unleashed resulting into the release of allcin in garlic - a powerful antibiotic that kills the bacteria that causes TB (mycobactererium tuberculosis), food poisoning salmonella, women's bladder infection and vaginal yeast infection. Garlic is also used in the treatment of meningitis trichophyton mentagrophytes (fungi that cause athlete's foot). It prevents or treats heart disease, high blood pressure, high cholesterol, and cancer, earache, and nail infections. The syrup of garlic is an invaluable medicine for fending off the flu virus, asthma, hoarseness, coughs, and most other disorders of the lungs. Constant use of helps regulate sugar level in diabetic patients. It is used externally to treat or prevent insect bites.**Expectorant for chronic bronchitis, antibacterial mucus-cutting syrup**

Recipe

Ingredients

2 Lb fresh bulb of garlic

8oz dark honey

2 medium size fresh lemon ½ glass water

Instruction

Crush garlic into a fine paste. Squeeze juice from lemon. Boil water until there is half the original quantity left. Mix honey with boiled water. Add garlic paste, stir vigorously. Add juice of lemon, and stir. Add vinegar. Stir until it has a syrupy blend. Bottle it and allow to stand 24 hours to mature. Refrigerate.

Note: To increase quantity double or triple ingredients.

Dose:

Shake bottle well before using

Take two teaspoonful three times daily before meals. Half the dosage is administered to children under 12 years.

Liver flush

Ingredients

4 bulbs garlic

3 medium size grapefruit

2 medium size lemon

1 pound ginger root

4 ounces dark honey

¼ pound olive oil

Instruction

Clean ginger thoroughly, then peel root. Crush ginger into a fine paste. Crush garlic into a fine paste. Add garlic and ginger paste and stir till well blended. Press juice out of garlic and ginger mix.

Press juice out of lemon and grapefruit. Mix garlic and ginger juice with lemon and grapefruit juice, stir. Add olive oil to mixture, stir. Add honey, stir until it turns into a creamy blend. Take a tea cup of it first thing in the morning before breakfast. Don't eat for at least an hour or two. Follow the flush with two cups of hyssop or mint tea.

To enhance anticancer activity

Ingredients.

1 lb. dark honey
1 lb. Garlic,
1/4 lb. onions,
3/4 lb. ginger,
3/4 lb. dried mustard-seed,
1 lb vinegar,

Instruction

Blend thoroughly washed garlic, onions and ginger into a fine paste. Soak mustard seed in vinegar, then blend. Add honey to garlic, ginger and onion pastes with mustard seed and vinegar.

Bottle. Take one dessertspoonful every morning and evening one hour before meals.

To treat nail infection

Ingredients
1 bulb garlic
¼-ounce olive oil
Instruction
Make paste of garlic.
Mix with olive oil
Allow 4 days
Apply mixture to affected nail and bandage.

To treat nail infection and Ear mites
Ingredients
2 bulbs garlic
¼ olive oil
Instruction
Press juice from garlic
Thoroughly mix with olive oil
Dose
Use 3-4 drops twice daily.

Chapter Twenty Six : Cinnamon
Cinnamon
Rev.18: 1- 14. (Ex. 30:23). Pro 7:17; Sol 4:14

"After this I saw another angel coming down from heaven. He had great authority, and the earth was illuminated by his splendor. With a mighty voice he shouted: "Fallen! Fallen is Babylon the Great! She has become a home for demons and a haunt for every evil spirit, a haunt for every unclean and detestable bird. For all the nations have drunk the maddening wine of her adulteries. The kings of the earth committed adultery with her, and the merchants of the earth grew rich from her excessive luxuries." Then I heard another voice from heaven say: "Come out of her, my people, so that you will not share in her sins, so that you will not receive any of her plagues; for her sins are piled up to heaven, and God has remembered her crimes. Give back to her as she has given; pay her back double for what she has done. Mix her a double portion from her own cup. Give her as much torture and grief as the glory and luxury she gave herself. In her heart she boasts, 'I sit as queen; I am not a widow, and I will never mourn.' Therefore, in one day her plagues will overtake her: death, mourning and famine. She will be consumed by fire, for mighty is the Lord God who judges her. "When the kings of the earth who committed adultery with her and shared her luxury see the smoke of her burning, they will weep and mourn over her. Terrified at her torment, they will stand far off and cry: "'Woe! Woe, O great city, O Babylon, city of power! In one hour your doom has come!'

"The merchants of the earth will weep and mourn over her because no one buys their cargoes any more — cargoes of gold, silver, precious stones and pearls; fine linen, purple, silk and scarlet cloth; every sort of citron wood, and articles of every kind made of ivory, costly wood, bronze, iron and marble; cargoes of cinnamon and spice, of incense, myrrh and frankincense, of wine and olive oil, of fine flour and wheat; cattle and sheep; horses and carriages; and bodies and souls of men. They will say, 'The fruit you longed for is gone from you. All your riches and splendor have vanished, never to be recovered'"

Cinnamon Hebrew: kinamon , the Cinnamomum zeylanicum of botanists, is a tree of the Laurel family.

Constituents: Volatile oil, tannins, mucilage, gum, sugars, coumarins.

Medicinal Uses

Bark and twigs used as carminative, promote sweating, antispasmodic, antiseptic, tonic, uterine stimulant. Bark decoction is used to alleviate chronic diarrhea, or weakened kidney. Twig decoction is taken for colds, stomach chills, and as a circulatory stimulant in combination with ginger. Tincture of up to 5 ml diluted in a little hot water for colds. Powder or capsules are taken for cold condition affecting the kidneys and digestion.

In the August 2000 issue of the *New Scientist* Journal researchers at the U.S. Department of Agriculture's Human Nutrition Research Center in Beltsville, Maryland, looked at the effects of common foods on blood sugars. They concluded that taking a teaspoon of cinnamon a day can help lower glucose or even prevent the onset of diabetes, writes, Elizabeth

Mueller. The discovery was made accidentally by Richard Anderson, one of the researchers at the time of this discovery. "We were looking at the effects of common foods on blood sugar," he told New Scientist. One was the American favorite, apple pie, which is usually spiced with cinnamon. "We expected it to be bad. But it helped," Dr Anderson told Debora MacKenzie in the New Scientist Journal. Dr. Anderson and the other researchers found that cinnamon rekindled the ability of fat cells in diabetics to respond to insulin and greatly increased glucose removal. They found that a substance in cinnamon called MHCP is the main reason for its beneficial results. "All you need is a teaspoon of cinnamon a day to help lower your glucose or even prevent the onset of diabetes. You can even soak a cinnamon stick in a cup of tea. It is as simple as that."

American scientists have claimed that a teaspoon of cinnamon a day may help prevent the onset of diabetes. The common spice could help millions of sufferers of Type II, non-insulin dependent diabetes. This condition usually develops in middle-age and prematurely kills 100 million people around the world every year. Type II diabetes causes cells to lose their ability to respond to insulin, the hormone that tells the body to remove excess glucose in the bloodstream. If glucose builds up in the blood, tiredness, weight-loss and blurred vision are some of the resulting symptoms. In extreme cases this can lead to blindness, heart disease and premature death. Data from the Agricultural Research Unit in Maryland first published in the **New Scientist** in August 2000 reported by Debora MacKenzie, implicated a substance in cinnamon called MHCP as the main reason for its beneficial results. When mice were given MHCP, their glucose levels fell dramatically and tests on humans have begun this year. The researchers are so confident that cinnamon will have the same dramatic effect of reducing insulin tolerance in humans they recommend that type II diabetics should take a quarter to one full teaspoon of cinnamon per day.

Many Type II diabetics have already found a new feeling of well-being and improvement in health by using this simple cinnamon supplementation in their diet. Cinnamon has long been known as an "energizing" spice, and it is likely that increasing the intake of this common and cheaply available food will benefit even non-diabetics, if used as a daily energizing tonic. The insulin resistance that leads to type II diabetes develops relatively slowly as the body ages and even those who have not yet experienced severe symptoms may have some degree of elevated insulin resistance.

Cinnamon is also a rich source of magnesium, which is essential for maintaining bone density, electrolyte balance, certain enzyme functions and many other crucial biochemical processes. Magnesium is also linked to the more dramatic forms of diabetes that occur earlier in life. Much research has been carried out to establish a metabolic defect in diabetics that prevents the absorption of magnesium. As cinnamon provides a readily available source of MHCP, magnesium and possibly other beneficial substances it seems like a very cost-effective way of offsetting future health problems related to glucose/insulin imbalances as we grow older. Cinnamon can be bought inexpensively in a convenient powdered form at almost any food store, and taking it couldn't be easier: just use up to a teaspoon a day in milkshakes or fruit juice.

    I personally take a half-teaspoon daily in this way every morning and can confirm a distinct energy benefit. Diabetics should always inform their doctor before taking cinnamon as it may affect medication requirements. Just half a teaspoon of cinnamon a day significantly reduces blood sugar levels in diabetics, a new study has found. The effect, which can be produced even by soaking a cinnamon stick in your tea, could also benefit millions of non-diabetics who have blood sugar problem but are unaware of it. Sugars and starches in food are broken down into glucose, which then circulates in the blood. The hormone insulin makes cells take in the glucose, to be used for energy or made into fat. But people with Type 1 diabetes do not produce enough insulin. Those with Type 2 diabetes produce it, but have lost sensitivity to it. Even apparently healthy people, especially if they are overweight, sedentary or over 25, lose sensitivity to insulin. Having too much glucose in the blood can cause serious long-term damage to eyes, kidneys, nerves and other organs. The active ingredient in cinnamon turned out to be a water-soluble polyphenol compound called MHCP. In test tube experiments, MHCP mimics insulin, activates its receptor, and works synergistically with insulin in cells. To see if it would work in people, Alam Khan, who was a postdoctoral fellow in Anderson's lab, organized a study in Pakistan. Volunteers with Type 2 diabetes were given one, three or six grams of cinnamon powder a day, in capsules after meals. All responded within weeks, with blood sugar levels that were on average 20 per cent lower than a control group. Some even achieved normal blood sugar levels. Not surprisingly, blood sugar started creeping up again after the diabetics stopped taking cinnamon. The cinnamon has additional benefits. In the volunteers, it lowered blood levels of fats and "bad" cholesterol, which are also partly controlled by insulin. And in test tube experiments it neutralized free radicals, damaging chemicals which are elevated in diabetics. "I don't recommend eating more cinnamon buns, or even more apple pie - there's too much fat and sugar," says Anderson. "The key is to add cinnamon to what you would eat normally." The active ingredient is not in cinnamon oils. But powdered spice can be added to toast, cereal, juice or coffee. Anderson's teams were awarded patents related to MHCP in 2002. But the chemical is easily obtained. He notes that one of his colleagues tried soaking a cinnamon stick in tea. "He isn't diabetic - but it lowered his blood sugar," Anderson says. The group now plans to test even lower doses of cinnamon in the US, and look at long-term blood sugar management with the spice.

****

"The sayings of wise men are like sharp sticks that shepherds use to guide sheep, and collected proverbs are as lasting as firmly driven nails. They all have been given by God, the one Shepherd of us all" (Eccl. 12:11)
****

DRUG FREE HEALING 11 : Medical Science Supporting Scriptures

PART TWO

DRUG FREE HEALING 11 : Medical Science Supporting Scriptures

Twenty Seven: Treating Loneliness

On February 20, 2014, media queen Oprah Winfrey announced on CNN a campaign she had launched against loneliness, and named it , "Just Say Hello" because she believed if people would "Just Say Hello" to one another, loneliness would die away. Partnering with her in the campaign are her long-time best friend, "CBS This Morning" Co-Anchor Gayle King, and CNN's chief medical correspondent and practicing neurosurgeon Dr. Sanjay Gupta.

Researchers have said that loneliness can cut off a lifespan by ten years.

In a report by Stephanie Pappas, a New Orleans blogger for "LiveScience", research suggests loneliness can do great harm to the body's immune system. The new study by the Society for Personality and Social Psychology, according to Pappas, revealed that

> people who are lonely experience more reactivation of latent viruses in their systems than the well-connected. Lonely people are also more likely than others to produce inflammatory compounds in response to stress, a factor implicated in heart disease and other chronic disorders, said study researcher Lisa Jaremka, a postdoctoral fellow at the Institute for Behavioral Medicine Research at Ohio State

University College of Medicine. Jaremka and her colleagues were interested in immune links to loneliness because feeling socially disconnected is associated with poor health and chronic disease. They recruited 200 female breast cancer survivors, average age 51, and 134 overweight, middle-age adults with no major health problems. In the first study, the researchers analyzed the blood of the breast cancer survivors for antibodies against cytomegalo virus, a herpes virus. These common viruses can remain dormant and symptomless inside the body. Even when active, they may not cause symptoms, but they do trigger the immune system to produce antibodies or protective proteins that help the immune system hunt down the rogue viruses. Higher antibody levels indicate higher levels of activated virus .In a second study, the researchers measured inflammatory proteins called cytokines in 144 of the breast cancer survivors as well as the healthy though overweight middle-age adults. The participants gave a blood sample and then were subjected to the stress of having to give an impromptu speech and do mental math in front of a panel of people in white lab coats. To up the anxiety, the panel gave the participants no encouragement.

No matter what they say and no matter what jokes they crack, no matter how much they smile, the panel just stares at them, basically. (Pappas, 2013)

In a 2003 article on loneliness, Dr. Sanjay Gupta wrote:

People who feel lonely tend to experience more nighttime sleep disruptions than those who don't. Researchers found that the link between sleep disruptions and loneliness persisted even after marital status and family size were taken into account, suggesting that loneliness depends on how people perceive their social situation rather than the situation itself. The 95 participants in the study all had strong social connections and were part of a close-knit, rural South Dakota community. Yet, researchers found, even small differences in their degrees of loneliness were reflected in their sleep. (Gupta,2014)

Our parents taught us when we were young not to talk to strangers. In turn, we programed our children not to talk to strangers. They too taught their children, "Don't Talk To Strangers." So when Oprah says to us, "Just Say Hallo!", we have mixed feelings.

DRUG FREE HEALING 11 : Medical Science Supporting Scriptures

In American small towns where everybody knows everybody, people "Just Say Hello" naturally anyhow. If just saying "hello" is the cure for loneliness, we should all pack up our luggage and relocate to small towns. Not so. Tampa, Florida, is not our description of a small town. Even for its size and growing population nearing half a million, there's no shortage of people able and ready to "Just Say Hello" to someone they are only meeting for the first time. It is in the DNA of Tampa. For example, Temple Terrace chiropractor, Dr. Mike Stangherlin, on his days off work, strolls down the Mall across the from his clinic at 8834 N 56th Street with his wife both pausing , just to say "hello" to people they are only meeting for the first time.

Because being friendly to others is written in the DNA of Tampa, Hartline bus operators, Bridget Williams, and Tito Goicochea, among other Hartline's conscientious employees make it their daily routine to "Just Say Hello" and "Have A Good Day" with a smile to their patrons entering and exiting the buses they operate; why, Small Business couple, Onyema and Lovelyn Anozie endlessly attend to the needs of their customers and why Physician Orlando Rangel and his team of nurses at 4160 N Armenia Avenue, Tampa, treat patients with such empathy you would think patients and health professionals are all members of the same family. Despite the friendliness of people in Tampa, and friendly cities like Tampa, there exists also an unavoidable truth that small towns, or big cities of America, do have their share of loneliness and lonely people where there is absence of interaction – and touching. Lonely people, like the rest of us, need to be talked with, to be touched, to be hugged, and to be loved."Just Say Hello" is not enough.

Chapter Twenty Eight : Believing

2 Chronicles 7:14, "If My people who are called by My name will humble themselves, and pray and seek My face, and turn from their wicked ways, then I will hear from heaven, and will forgive their sin and heal their land."

Scientists have concluded that church attendance is correlated with increased longevity, or better health. California – based researcher, New York Times bestselling author, and gynecologist, Dr. Lissa Rankin states declares:

> some combination of positive belief and the element of nurturing care of right healers can help turn off stress responses and activate the body's natural self repair mechanisms in your body...Alleviation of loneliness is preventive medicine... Scientific evidence suggests loneliness is a stronger risk factor for illness than smoking or failure to exercise. Alleviating loneliness is medicine for the soul....In order to

be optimally healthy you need a healthy feeling of spiritual connection, a healthy relationship, a healthy environment, a healthy relationship with your money, ...a healthy mind... a healthy sex life. You may not think that your relationships, or your spiritual life, or your financial life affect the health of your body, but the scientific literature proves that they do. The body is the physical manifestation of the sum of your life's experiences... It is the outward reflection of your precious inner life.(Rankin, L 2013).

Dr. Rankin's well-studied scientifically proven conclusions confirm the unchanging message of the Scripture that Jehovah is the God who heals us. *"I am the God that healeth you, I am the LORD your healer, I speak one word,and heal your disease, I am the God, your healer,"*(Ex.15:26) A growing school of practicing physicians and healthcare professionals are discovering that that patients are best served when therapy is directed at not only the physiological symptoms but emotional and Spiritual conditions as well. It prompted primary care provider and author, Dr. Christopher Hobbs to declare ; "As a primary care provider , I see many patients who aren't well served by today's modern healthcare system – people who are often encouraged to depend on drugs and medical procedure to fix symptoms and conditions without and without any mention of the personal power they possess to create and maintain health." (Hobbs, 1985) Rankin (2013)asserts, "You can pray, or attend religious services... Gifts giving activate the body's relaxation response mechanisms which bolster the bodies natural self repair mechanisms"

These are not quotes from the pulpit by a preacher Reverend Doctor......Name him, or, Her. They are utterances based on results of analytical scientific studies. Rankin (2013) further states, "In order to be optimally healthy you need a healthy feeling of spiritual connection, a healthy relationship."

What modern medical science calls "a healthy feeling of spiritual connection, a healthy relationship," (Rankin, L 2013), is simply obeying what our Lord Jesus Christ names The Greatest Commandment in the Gospel of Matthew 22: 37 -40 ; "Love the LORD your GOD with all your heart, with all your soul, and with all your mind...Love your neighbor as yourself." If anyone is looking to have "a healthy feeling of spiritual connection" (Rankin, L, 2013) the person needs to strive to love God with all of his or her heart and all of her and his mind and all of his or her soul; to surrender to Him, knowing that whatever is the outcome of his of her life, it is Jehovah God is in control . So, she or he will say, "It is well with my soul." He or she must treat his or her body as the temple of God . Somebody said, observe the Ten plus

Two Commandments and live a long fulfilled healthy life.

Chapter Twenty-Nine: Loving

Having "a healthy relationship... a healthy environment" (Rankin, L 2013) is calls for doing as Jesus commands concerning relation with our neighbors, "Love your neighbor as you love yourself" (Mark 12:31). But one may ask, "how are you able to love somebody else if you are incapable of love for yourself"? So, you must know who you are. You must know your relationship with Jesus Christ. You must know who God says you are in Him. You must know in whose image and likeness God made you. (Genesis 1:26)

"No one has ever seen God. The One and Only Son-- the One who is at the Father's side-- He has revealed Him." (John 1:18) Our Lord Jesus Christ is the Only One who has seen Jehovah God. His actions show us God's Divine nature. "The Son is the image of the invisible God, the firstborn over all creation." (Colossians 1:15) "If anyone loves me, he will keep my word. Then my Father will love him, and we will go to him and make our home within him". (John 14:23)

You are part of the Trinity. God is in you. Christ is in you. The Holy Spirit is in you. Respect your body.

Quit poisoning your body with unnecessary junk which is the fad of the day. "Studies have shown that certain chemicals, including drugs, food additives, tobacco smoke and air pollution can cause irritated, tight muscles, leading to subluxations," (Stangherlin, M (2009)"The Chiropractic Way To Health – The Ultimate Self-Help Guide For Chiropractic Patients" P23).

Your neighbor near you is made in the image of God. So you must see Christ in your neighbor. When we are loving our neighbor, or are in love, or extending acts of kindness or generosity, and compassion toward somebody selflessly, and when you bring Jehovah into the mix, miracles happen. Miracles happen in healing the sick, and making the lonely full because love is involved. Miracles happen in the lives of those who are extending acts of love. Miracles happen to those to whom love is being given . Love works wonders.

"How is it possible for love, which is essentially spiritual, to have a transforming effect on the human body, which is corporeal and the natural object of scientific intervention?" Asks Donald De Marco PhD. (2009), professor emeritus of philosophy at St. Jerome's University Ontario and adjunct professor at Holy Apostles College and Seminary in Cromwell, Connecticut. "The answer to this timeless question," he writes, "lies in the integral wholeness of the human person...Love operates as the desire to help others return, as much as possible, to the original state of wholeness...Disease, depression, sin, and alienation are all impediments that compromise wholeness...."(DeMarco D 2009, "Love and Healing").To rid ourselves of loneliness, we must have a lot of love to give. This is NOT sexual, lustful, love. but compassionate, Christian non-judgmental love that never gives up. This is the love that shows up when every one else is down or gone; the love that reveals God in action, and appears real to the one who is rejected, dejected and lonely on the receiving end of love. God is Love.

> Jesus, the Son of God, gave central importance to love and healing during his earthly ministry. Of the 3,779 verses in the four Gospels, 727, or nearly one fifth, are related specifically to the healing of physical and mental illnesses and to the resurrection of the dead. In most cases, Jesus combined the speaking words with touching. His practice of touching began a tradition which survives in the present in the "laying on of hands". (DeMarco, 2009)

So to those who are willing, ready, and able, and are called in ways we cannot tell to help the lonely out of their misery, let us take a pledge of transparency; "Abstain from all appearances of evil."(1

Thessalonians 5:22). Satan was able to pull away a third of the angelic population from the presence of God following his rebellion. Be warned. "Be alert, be on the watch! Your enemy, the Devil, roams around like a roaring lion, looking for someone to devour." (1 Peter 5:8).

If you go visiting the lonely person, do not go alone. Remember, that as early as in Genesis, God saw all things that they were good. The one thing God said was not good is this creature called **alone.** Take with you on your visit at least one other person of the same gender as the person you are visiting. Remember , that if Adam had not left Eve **alone**, the Devil would not have stood a chance, and this Earth would still have been a paradise, with no sickness or disease, no loneliness, and no death.

Do some grocery shopping to take along with you. Yes. You will be surprised to know that everybody eats. Get some nutrient rich groceries. Get some broccoli sprouts, some kale, cucumber, garlic, grapes, and nuts . Get tomatoes, onions, beans, lentils, and flax seeds . No French fries. No sodas. No sugar. No salt. No animal products. No oil. Let what you don't take with you speak volumes. Bring along some music cds, and dvds of hymns and gospel songs. They are therapeutic. Christian hymns and gospel music can be effective tool in changing lives, healing the Spirit, body and the emotions –it is useful tool in stress reduction, and the alleviation of loneliness.

Somebody wrote this, " More and more today, music is being used as a complementary healing modality...Music transforms the experience of illness or death. It connects one person with another even when s/he may not be able to interact. It calms, relaxes ,and creates a comforting environment"(Anonymous).

Chapter Thirty: Hymns Singing

Studies say different types of music affect people in different ways. "Some songs stir up nostalgia, some deep emotion, and some melancholy. Some songs stimulate the imagination, while others mirth and joy. Some songs are celebratory, some devotional, and some praises, some meditational, some prayers and some worship." (Moody Bible Handbook P231)

Some songs produce a feeling of calmness for the sick, or dying, some, a sense of relaxation and comfort to one stressed down. Some songs can speed up the healing process, relieve anxiety, and renew the spirit, soul and body....Moses sang, and taught people to sing.(Ex 15). Israel sang songs along the journey to the Promised Land.(Deuteronomy 32 Deborah and Barak sang praises to God. (Num. 21:17, Judges 5) David sang with all his heart.(Ps.104:33). Hezekiah's Singers Sang the Words of David. Jesus and the Disciples sang at the Last Supper. (Matt. 26:30) Paul and Silas sang in prison. (Acts 16: 25) The morning stars sang together, and all the Sons of God shouted for joy.(Job 38:7) In Heaven 10,000 times 10,000 Angels sing and the whole redeemed creation joins in the chorus." (Rev 5:11-13) (Moody Bible Handbook P231)

When we go out to help the helpless and lonely, let us remember we're with them to give them our helping hands. We are not to attempt to shove our spirituality or Godliness down anyone's throat.

Jesus warns us, "Listen! I am sending you out just like sheep among wolves. You must be as cautious as snakes and as gentle as doves." (Matthew 10:16) Let the pastors do the work of their calling. Jesus our Lord and Savior has called us to the Ministry of Mercy and Helps, and to proclaim the Gospel ; He has given us the gift of healing ; to lay our hands on the sick and they shall recover. (Mark 16:15-18) Leave the Shepherd's work to those that the Lord has chosen to be Pastors of his flock.

On your first visitation, do not go about throwing tracts around. The Lord himself will present plenty of opportunities through your acts of kindness and compassion. When such an occasion begins to open up usually around your third visit when the protective shield of loneliness begins thawing down, and the one you are visiting decides to confide his/her personal issues, that is the time you ask in a non-threatening manner if you can BOTH take it to the Lord in prayer.

Play some worship CDs softly. With some people, the ice breaker comes as early as the first visit. But with some others, it happens around the fourth or the fifth visitation. When the timing is right, you will know it. Whether it is on the first day or the fifth, be careful that you ask permission in a non-threatening way if it will be all right to study the word together. Explain how beneficial it is to have the knowledge of Scripture and be able to apply it appropriately when saying prayers. "Preach the word, be ready in season, and out of season."(2 Timothy 4:2).

Perhaps, so you can learn as the Holy Spirit teaches, go with us now, as we go to visit one 65 year-old woman, Priscilla, who shut herself down completely from the community for five years since her husband of 43 years died. The Scripture we chose is Paul's Letter to the Philippians Chapter 4 verses 1 to 9 for our studies in seven visitations of 30 minutes' duration.

Chapter Thirty- One: Scripture Studying

Day 1. We began with prayer after singing hymns. We read the first three verses of Philippians 4.

> So, then, my brothers, and sisters, how dear you are to me and how I miss you! How happy you make me, and how proud I am of you! - this, dear brothers and sisters, is how you should stand firm in your life in the Lord.

Verse 1: We set out to (a) Identify to whom the letter was written (b) By whom? (c) From where was it written? (d) Why it was written? (e)Backgrounds of the writer/recipients ? (f)How does the letter apply to our own individual circumstances?(g) What is God saying to us ? At the end , we asked questions and answered questions. If we did not have an answer, we said so, and gave each one of us a home work to study for our next meeting. It was also an opportunity for inviting our host to church. We would say, "Let's go and ask Pastor, or we will pray about it," We always asked for God's direction, and his favor for the spirit of wisdom and of revelation in the knowledge of Him through His word as we studied. Amen.

DRUG FREE HEALING 11 : Medical Science Supporting Scriptures

Let's begin. Paul wrote this letter from prison to the first church he established in Europe, in Macedonia. Acts 16 contains an eyewitness account by the physician Luke, who is also the writer of the gospel by the same name. Dr. Luke gives us background information. Luke informs us that Paul and his companions, including Silas, were on their way to pray, possibly in the house of the two women Paul mentioned in his letter - Euodia and Syntyche . It turned out that there was a young girl who worked as a fortuneteller and made money for her masters. She habitually followed Paul's party on their way to prayers, shouting, "These men are servants of the Most High God! They announce to you how you can be saved" (Acts 16:17).

So one day as they walked the street to church, the girl followed them again , shouting as usual. Paul turned around to face the girl. Looking at the girl sternly, Paul said in a commanding tone, "In the name of Jesus come out of her!" The scripture said, "The spirit came out of her at once." (Acts 16:18)

Paul's action enraged the girl's handlers because the girl could not make money for them any more. So they trumped up charges against Paul and Silas , and had them put in prison. While in prison with their hands and legs chained, Paul and Silas, started to pray and sing to God all through the night while other prisoners listened to them and the guard soundly slept. The Bible said, suddenly, there was a violent earthquake, resulting in the chains falling off all the prisoners and the prison gates opening up ajar. The awakened guard was so frightened that the prisoners had escaped that he pulled his sword from its sheath and was about to fall on it when Paul restrained him, shouting at the top of his voice, "Don't harm yourself! We're all here." When he had finished lighting up the prison, the guard rushed to his prisoners and fell at the foot of Paul and Silas, "Sirs, what must I do to be saved?"(Acts 16:30)

"Believe in the Lord Jesus, and you will be saved – you and your family" (Acts 16:30).This was the prison from where Paul wrote the letter to the Philippians. Church historians date this event at around 51 AD.

Verse 1 says "'So, then, my brothers, how dear you are to me and how I miss you...How happy you make me, and how proud I am of you! --this, dear brothers and sisters, is how you should stand firm in your life in the Lord."

Can we imagine ourselves thrown into such a stressful prison condition while working for the Lord? Yet Paul maintains a cheerful attitude, and thinks of the well-being of his fellow Christians. We must follow his leadership by example. Paul emulates Jesus Christ. His letter to the Corinthians (1 Corinthians 11:1) unequivocally states so, "Follow me as I follow the example of Christ." We find Paul in prison, in Rome, but he is unperturbed by his surroundings. He is, instead, congratulating the congregation . Those people must be doing something really right! He is writing to thank them for the gift they sent him in his troubles and need. We have this information from previous chapters. He praises them for standing firm in their life in the Lord.

Hard times will come to us believers. We must help one another. We must stand with one another. We must be understanding of one another's problems, and appreciate each other's burdens. Just because we are Christians does not mean trying times will not come our way. We must endure. The words of the old hymn says , "Have we trials and temptations? Is there trouble anywhere? We should never be discouraged. Take it to the Lord in prayer."

Day 2,Verse 2 reads; "Euodia and Syntyche, please, I beg you, try to agree as sisters in the Lord."

We have the tendency of focusing on our own troubles, and have no time for the problems of other people, even though they may be our closest relatives, or friends or believing brothers and sisters. But here, we see that Paul is appealing to Euodia and Syntyche to settle their differences. Euodia and Syntyshe were in the leadership of the church in Philippi, and were having some personal disagreements.

Clearly in our own personal lives, there are times of vehement disagreement among Christian brothers and sisters. The Bible does not gloss over such embarrassing occasions. Paul had a confrontation himself with Peter over whether Jews should eat with Gentiles.(Galatians 2:11-14). He had a dispute also with Barnabas, his Encourager, over Mark, resulting in Barnabas' breaking away from Paul and taking Mark along with him on Barbabas' successive missionary journeys. Yes, the same Mark who later wrote the gospel named after him.(Acts 15:35-40)

Was the dispute between Paul and Mark finally resolved, and what was their relationship subsequently? Read the Acts for your home work. As Paul counsels Euodia and Sytynche, we must learn to disagree and agree as brothers and sisters in the Lord. Our union in Christ must override any inclination to bear grudges. Argue when it is called for, and know when to settle your differences. We must not let the sun go down while we are angry, the Bible warns us, and not to give the devil a foothold. This guideline applies to all our relationships.

Day 3 Verse 3 says;

And you too, my faithful partner, I want you to help these women; for they have worked hard with me to spread the gospel, together with Clement and all my other fellow workers, whose names are in God's book of the living.

Who is the "you too my faithful partner? The faithful partner is the Pastor of the Philippian church, Luke. You say, "But Dr, Luke is with Paul as his amanuensis."

Previous chapters, specifically, the first chapter, informs us that Paul is in Rome, and Timothy is with him. Philippi is a city in the Roman province of Macedonia where Luke is pastor. Paul speaks of Euodia and Sytynche as having worked hard with him to spread the gospel. Recall that the Philippian Church is the first church Paul established in Europe ten years before the letter. He equates the work of the women with the labors of Clement and other unnamed "fellow workers, whose names are in God's book of the living." It must be mentioned that Clement became bishop of Rome, 91-100 AD. Clement suffered martyrdom in the third year of Trajan, who was Roman emperor from 98 AD until his death 117 AD.

When we have differences among ourselves as fellow Ministers of Christ, we must be aware that we all are fallible. We make mistakes. The same people upon whom we relied previously as faithful servants of the Lord Jesus will disappoint you and me. They will go wrong on you. Not they may...but they will. When you need them, they will not be around. People change. People have their own personal moments too. No matter our personal attachments and loyalties, we must be as a pastor is required to be, a shepherd, though we are not pastors, we are ambassadors for Christ Jesus. We must be peace makers—no partialities. For God is no respecter of persons.

Day 4 Verse 4 says;

"Rejoice in the Lord always; and again I say... Rejoice."

The Good News Bible Today's English Version has it like this , "May you always be joyful in your union with the Lord. I say it again: Rejoice."

Paul is urging the congregation to be joyful. Prison is not a picnic location anywhere at any age. Being a Roman prisoner persecuted for Christ was torturous yet here was Paul gushing with joy urging the church to "Rejoice again I say , Rejoice!" It should be an example to us Christians to have joyful temperament at all times. We say we are lonely. We're depressed. We must find joy in every situation. The word of God is our best source of joy. Rejoice in the Lord. Again, I say, Rejoice! Rejoice because for us, Christians, our troubles have a term limit. They end with the end of this physical body. Beyond it, we have joy with Christ Jesus. Therefore, Rejoice . Again , I say, Rejoice!

"**Day 5 Verse 5** says ; "Show a gentle attitude towards everyone. The Lord is coming soon."

Paul believed, and he proclaimed, "The Lord is coming soon!" Not two thousand years later. He is coming soon. Why? Let's go for a moment to Philippians 3 verses 1 through 6 to find out the basis for his conviction.

> Be joyful in your union with the Lord. I don't mind repeating what I have written before, and you will be safer if I do so. Watch out for those who do evil things, those dogs, those men who insist on cutting the body. It is we, not they, who have received the true circumcision, for we worship God by means of his Spirit and rejoice in our union with Christ Jesus. We do not put any trust in external ceremonies. I could, of course, put my trust in such things. If anyone thinks he can trust external ceremonies, I have even more reason to feel that way. I was circumcised when I was a week old. I am an Israelite by birth, of the tribe of Benjamin, a pure-blooded Hebrew. As far as keeping the Jewish Law is concerned, I was a Pharisee, and I was so zealous that I persecuted the church."

Coming from such a background, Paul, like all Jews of his ilk, was taught from Samuel, through King David, King Solomon, Isaiah, Jeremiah, Ezekiel Daniel and the other Prophets to expect the coming of the Messiah.

Jesus came to his own people; His own people did not know him. They crucified him. Paul too aided in the killing and persecution of Christians But he finally came to the knowledge that Jesus was the Christ of the prophesies. He became aware by the power of the Holy Spirit that our Lord will come back again. And so predicted His Second Coming in 11 Thessalonians 2, ten years earlier that the Lord would not come until after the spread of apostasy. But apostasy was fast taking hold in some of Paul's churches. The presence of apostasy in his time, and the unendingly ruthless persecution of Christians combining with his own imprisonment were factors assuring him of the Lord's Coming – reasons enough to fill him with such overflowing joy. So as Christians, no matter the cost, no matter the pain, "Show a gentle attitude toward everyone."

Day 6 Verses 6-7 say; "Don't worry about anything, but in all your prayers ask God for what you need, always asking him with a thankful heart."

Many of us have memorized King James' Version of this verse, "Be careful for nothing; but in

DRUG FREE HEALING 11 : Medical Science Supporting Scriptures

everything by prayer and supplication with thanksgiving let your requests be known unto God."

He says, you, brother, you, sister. don't you worry about anything that overwhelms you. Just have no concern about anything.... Anything or anyone bothering you? Don't worry. Relationship problems? Don't worry. Are you lonely? Don't worry. Financial problems? Don't worry. Health problems? He is not urging you to ignore the situation. He's not saying, "Don't worry, be happy." Paul recommends God's prescription. "But in everything by prayer and supplication with thanksgiving let your requests be known unto God." The Good News Bible Today's English Version says, "but in all your prayers ask God what you need, always asking with a thankful heart." (Philippians 4:6) We must not go about praying like this. "O God please give me a job so I can pay my bills before I can go to church." And do not offer a prayer like this , "Please God let my girl friend come back to me because the Bible says to ask you God, and you will give me my heart's desire." James 4: 3 says that "when you ask, you do not receive it, because your motives are bad; you ask for things to use for your own pleasures."

Jesus said we must not use a lot of meaningless words, as the worshipers of idols do, who think that their gods will hear them because their prayers are long. Prayer is not repetitive chanting like a mantra of what has been dubbed The Lord's Prayer, but is The Lord's Model Prayer in response to a request by one of the disciples to teach them to pray.(Matthew 6:9),

"After this manner therefore ye pray." Pray like this. This is how to pray. "Our Father who art in heaven" Identify the Subject of your prayer, and the destination of your prayer. Acknowledge his Godness. His Sovereignty and Omnipotence. He is in heaven. He is Omnipresent. He is Omniscient.

"Hallowed be thy name." He is Holy. Honor His Holy name. We dishonor God's Holy name by our actions, by the things we say, by the many vain ways we recklessly and wildly bandy about his name with gross extravagance. "Thy Kingdom come. Thy will be done on earth, as it is in heaven." We have an expectation that our Lord Jesus Christ will return to establish God's Kingdom on earth where death will be banished, and there will be joy and peace and love as it is in heaven. Jesus came to establish God's Kingdom. He led by example obeying God's will himself so that we too will follow his example. He said in many ways in John 5, 8, 14, and 15 the following,

> If you love me obey my commandment...Very truly I tell you, the Son can do nothing by himself; he can do only what he sees his Father doing, because whatever the Father does the Son also does." God's will is being done on earth. It

is not everyone that is doing God's will on earth as it is in heaven.

There are some people who have chosen to be atheists. It is their God-given right of choice. There are also some people who have not yet accepted the Lord as their personal Savior so they choose not to obey God's Will, but for Christians, as we come before God in prayer, we are making a commitment and declaring with our mouth to seek God's face , to do his will, to belong to Team Jesus. When you belong to Team Jesus, you are anxious for nothing. You do not worry about anything. You come to Jehovah God in prayer trusting him for your supplies. It is at this point in the Model Prayer that our Lord addresses our daily need. "Give us this day our daily bread." There are some false teachings going on. Such false teachers existed in Paul's days also.

I attended a church service on December 31, 2008 where the preacher told the congregation, "If you asked Jesus this year for a thousand dollars, ask him for a million dollars in 2009." His wife told of how she went to a bank to request a loan for a car but she had bad credit. Her husband also had a bad credit l,and both had no collateral. She said , she lied on the credit application and prayed for God to blindfold the bank authorities for the loan to be approved. She told the church that the bank loan was approved so she bought a

BMW car for herself, and a Mercedes Benz for the husband.

Do you think Jehovah God would ever condone such foolishness? Three months into the New Year, the mortgage holder on the church building foreclosed on the church and the couple disappeared. God will never act against his nature. He will never endorse a lying act in his name. Our Lord Jesus did not teach covetousness, greed, or personal aggrandizement. Christianity is not about God's material provisions for you or me. Jesus teaches that he will provide for your needs. It is not the prerequisite.

> This is why I tell you: do not be worried about the food and drink you need in order to stay alive, or about clothes for your body. After all, isn't life worth more than food? And isn't the body worth more than clothes? Look at the birds; they do not plant seeds, gather a harvest and put it in barns; yet your Father in heaven takes care of them! Aren't you worth more than birds? Can any of you lie a bit longer by worrying about it?....So do not start worrying: 'Where will my food come from? Or my drink? Or my clothes? (These are the things the pagans are always concerned about.) Your Father in heaven knows that you need all things. Instead, be concerned above everything else with the

Kingdom of God and what He requires of you, and He will provide you will all these other things. So do not worry about tomorrow; it will have enough worries of its own. There is no need to add to the troubles each day brings. (Matthew 6: 25-3)

Day 7 Verse 8-9 say;"Finally, brethren, whatsoever things are true, whatsoever things are honest, whatsoever things are just, whatsoever things are pure, whatsoever things that are lovely, whatsoever things are of good report if there be any virtue, and if there be any praise, think on these things."

The term "Think" in this case. means **meditate on these things.** Here's Paul's secret. He is teaching you and me the secret of relaxation and health through meditation on the word of God and telling you to do as he does. We call it Biblical Meditation.

Verse 9; "Those things, which you have both learned, and received, and heard, and seen in me, do: and the God of peace shall be with you." Oh. Hallelujah. Glory to God!

Chapter Thirty-Two: Keep On Meditating

` The bible urges us to fill our minds with those things that are good and that deserve praise; things that are true, noble, right, pure lovely, and honorable because these "positive thoughts activate the body's relaxation response" (Benson,2014) to elicit the body's God equipped self-repair mechanism.

Galatians 5:22 tells us:"The Spirit produces love ,joy ,peace ,patience, kindness, goodness ,faithfulness, humility and self-control" which our medical science researchers call "relaxation response activators," (Benson, 2014) Scripture calls **Fruit of the Spirit**. Pure science proving God!

Friends, listen. This will shock you. Apostle Paul , reveals a mystery which only now has been accepted as a proven scientific truth by the medical science community; drugs don't cure. God heals our diseases , and meditation is a component of holistic biblical healing to which Jesus Christ, the Son of God gave a central importance during his earthly ministry. Our Lord Jesus often broke away from his disciples for meditation and prayer. This is science.

Researchers at the National Center for Complementary and Integrative Health (NCCIH) following clinical studies have concluded that prayer and meditation are beneficial for healing. "Scientists have concluded that church attendance is correlated with increased longevity, or better health, a finding by Harvard professor Anne Harrington, a leading researcher of Health and Spirituality. In separate studies, a Harvard cardiologist, Dr. Herbert Benson celebrated for his pioneering research on meditation asserts that Prayer Works! This is the scientific conclusion at the National Center for Complementary and Integrative Health :

> The healing powers of strong religious faith helps explain why the human species is so incorrigibly religious in the first place, that just maybe human beings are religious because they're wired to be religious. They're wired for God as people began to say and the reason--the most important reason they're wired for God is because it's good for their health to be wired for God. Believing in God is good for your health because after all over millions of years we didn't have modern medicine, we didn't have antibiotics, all we had was, you know, to protect us against the ravages of disease

really was whatever we were able to sort of do with roots and herbs and our belief in God or whatever kind of higher power. (Harrington A (2014, Online lecture CE)

In the 1960s Harvard Professor, Herbert Benson, MD, now Professor Emeritus at Harvard Medical School, following pioneering studies, established the efficacy of meditation for healthcare through his research. The studies by Dr. Benson and his colleagues showed that meditation acts as an antidote to stress. Under stress, the nervous system activates the "fight-or-flight" response. The activity of the sympathetic portion of the nervous system increases, causing an increased heart beat, increased respiratory rate, elevation of blood pressure, and increase in oxygen consumption. This fight-or-flight response has an important survival function by allowing an organism to run quickly to escape an attack or to fight off an attacker. But if activated repeatedly, as happens for many people in modern societies, the effects are harmful. Many researchers believe that the current epidemic of hypertension, heart disease and depression in the Western world is a direct result. Meditation decreases the heart rate, decreases the respiratory rate, decreases blood pressure, decreases oxygen consumption, and decreases muscle tension.

Not only did my research and those of my colleagues reveal that 25% of people feel more spiritual as the result of the Relaxation Response, but it showed that those same people have fewer medical symptoms than do those who reported no increase in spirituality. It became clear that a person's religious convictions or life philosophy enhanced the average effects of the Relaxation Response in three ways. (Benson, H, (1975) "Relaxation Response")

1. People who chose an appropriate focus, that which drew upon their deepest philosophic or religious convictions, were more apt to adhere to the Relaxation Response routine, looking forward to it and enjoying it.

2. Affirmative beliefs of any kind brought forth remembered wellness. Reviving top down, nerve cell firing patterns in the brain that were associated with wellness.

3. When present, faith in an eternal or life transcending force seemed to make the fullest use of remembered wellness because it is a supremely soothing belief, disconnecting unhealthy logic and worries"(Benson, H, (1975).

Do you wonder then, how it was that Apostle Paul was able to endure his sufferings and remained calm, regardless, and overflowed with such joy? He writes,

> Five times I was given thirty nine lashes by the Jews; three times I was whipped by the Romans; and once I was stoned. I have been in three shipwrecks, and once I spent twenty-four hours in the water. In my many travels I have been in danger from floods and from robbers, in danger from fellow Jews and from Gentiles; there have been dangers in the cities, dangers in the wilds, dangers on the high seas, and dangers from false friends. There has been work and toil; often I have gone without sleep; I have been hungry and thirsty; I have often been without food, shelter, or clothing. And not to mention other things, every day I am under pressure of my concern for all churches. When someone is weak, then I feel weak too; when someone is led into sin, I am filed with distress. (2 Corinthians 11:5-29)

Paul lived by the Spirit. We must live by the Spirit. It is the way to rid ourselves of loneliness.

> Those who live as the Spirit tells them to, have their minds controlled by what the Spirit wants. To be controlled by human nature results in death: **to be controlled by the Spirit results in life and peace.** (Romans 8:5-6).

DRUG FREE HEALING 11 : Medical Science Supporting Scriptures

What the Spirit wants of us is to obey God. To love the Lord our God with all our heart, with all our soul and with all our strength, with all our mind; and love our neighbor as we love ourselves. If those in the secular can, by repetitively chanting, under controlled rhythmic breathing, experience health restorative effects of meditation, how can it not be so with believers of the True God , The Pantocrator? How won't Christ Jesus do for us, his servants who he calls his friends, exceedingly abundantly above all that we ask or think when we keep the guidelines Jehovah Almighty God gave us for meditation and fasting?

God's command to Joshua, applies to us as well.

This book of the Law shall not depart out of your mouth; you shall meditate on it night and day, so that you may be careful to act in accordance with all that is written in it. For then you shall make your way prosperous, and then you shall be successful.(Joshua 1:8).

The book of the Law at the time of Joshua was Deuteronomy. We have Christ Jesus who is the fulfillment of the Law and the Prophets. We must keep the commands of our Lord Jesus Christ, even as he gave them through his servant Paul also.

"Whatsoever things are true , whatsoever things are honest, whatsoever things are lovely, whatsoever thing are just, whatsoever things are pure, whatsoever things are of good report; if there be any virtue, and if there be any praise, think on these things." (Philippians 4:8).

When we put our minds on the awesomeness of Jehovah Almighty God, continuously thinking about his Love, and how we too as his children can emulate his Love, our minds will have little space for "anger, grudge, malice, jealousy,, gossip, foolish talking, jesting, and lusting " (Ephesians 4:31). We ourselves become nothing, as our human Spirit reaches out to align with the Holy Spirit. We hunger and thirst for his word. This is Biblical Meditation. We must set aside an hour for devotion and reading the Scripture. Regurgitate the Scripture. As we reflect on the Scripture, we must breathe in to our stomach deeply and fully the breath of life while examining the Scripture in our thoughts. Genesis 2:7 says ,

> Then the LORD God formed the man from the dust of the ground. He breathed the breath of life into the man's nostrils, and the man became a living person.

I challenge you if you make this your daily routine for twelve weeks, and continue to make it your habit, spend an hour studying the scripture, reflecting on the word studied while breathing fully, deeply into your stomach, and holding in the oxygen breathed into your system for thirty seconds and releasing it slowly, you will notice a difference with your blood pressure. You will lower your blood pressure. The word is in our heart. The word guides us. Counsels us. We reexamine the Word with a wholehearted reverential committed mindset to live by it. We may fall from time to time. We may stray away but we must repent and walk with the Lord.

> Because he loves me," says the Lord, "I will rescue him;
>
> I will protect him, for he acknowledges my name.
> He will call on me, and I will answer him;
> I will be with him in trouble,
> I will deliver him and honor him.
> With long life I will satisfy him
>
> and show him my salvation.(Psalm 91:14-16)

Our Lord Jesus made this promise; "I am telling you the truth: whoever believes in me will do what I do –yes, he will do even greater things because I am going to the Father....I will do whatever you ask for in my name, so that the Father's glory will be shown through the Son"(John 14:12-13).

Because of the certainty we have in the promise of Jesus, a Christian can conquer the ravages of loneliness, and more; slow down aging. You are the reflection of our Lord Jesus Christ. Because he lives you can have no fears for tomorrow. Encourage the sufferer of loneliness to shout for joy and bless the Lord deep in the soul with every fiber of his or her being. Rejoice with the writer of this Psalm 103:1-5 .

> Shout aloud ,
> Bless the Lord O my soul. And all within me, bless his holy name.
> Bless the Lord, O my soul, and do not forget all his benefits, who forgives all your iniquities,
> who heals all your diseases,
> who redeems your life from the Pit,
> who crowns you with steadfast love and mercy,
> who satisfies you with good as long as you live,
> so that your youth is renewed like the eagle's.

Jesus died so that our sins are forgiven when we believe in him. Love him when we say we believe in hm. If we love him, we must keep his commandments.

Chapter Thirty-Two : Forgiving

One of the greatest pillars of prayers is to have a forgiving heart. Jesus taught that if we are about to offer our gift to Jehovah God at the alter and remember that our brother or sister has something against us, we must leave our gift "there in front of the altar, go at once and make peace" with him or her and then come back and offer our gift to God.(Matthew 5:24-25)

Lack of forgiveness blocks up the channel for prayers. Unforgiveness is a grave retardant to physical, emotional or Spiritual healing. Jesus said, "When you forgive, your Father in heaven will also forgive you. If you do not forgive, your Father will not forgive you." (Matthew 6:14)

It is very hard to forgive a wrong. It is equally as hard for the unforgiving to have a chronic sickness to heal. People who cannot forgive a wrong cannot relate with others. Loneliness is their habitation. Their social life is zero. If they are with family members at all, they have little or no connectivity. They hold lingering malice and strife. Pride prevents them from getting down from their high unforgiving horse .Pride is the Devil's stock in trade. "God resists the proud and gives grace to the humble"(1 Peter 5:5).

When we remain unforgiving, the mere mention of the name of the person who wronged us or the wrong they caused us gets us back in a fit of anger resulting in a successive rush of cortisol and epinephrine poisonous hormones that make us fall sick.

Studies show that one of the keys to longevity and good health is to forgive past transgressions. In a ten-year study, Dr. Everett Worthington, Professor of Psychology at Virginia Commonwealth University, and along with a team of researchers, concluded that unforgiveness, defined as "a combination of delayed negative emotions (i.e., resentment, bitterness, hostility, hatred, anger, and fear) toward a transgressor, is linked to a variety of health issues and can be a deadly virus if we leave it untreated."

Professor Worthington (2010) views forgiveness as two types which he calls "Decisional and Emotional. The former "involves deciding to forgive a personal offense and letting go of angry and resentful thoughts and feelings toward the person who has wronged you. "Emotional forgiveness"(Worthington, 2010) involves replacing the negative emotions with positive feelings like compassion, sympathy, and empathy.

Research shows that emotional forgiveness is where most health benefits lie.

This type of forgiveness can reduce our stressful reaction to a transgression—and stress has been shown to lead to a suppressed immune system and an increased risk for cardiovascular issues. Emotional forgiveness also keeps us from ruminating over the wrong that was done to us, and rumination can be harmful, too. It has been associated with a number of mental health problems, including obsessive-compulsive disorder, anxiety, and depression. Decisional forgiveness is more important in repairing and reconciling relationships.(Worthington, 2010)

At Hope College in Holland, Michigan, researchers measured heart rates, sweat rates and other responses of subjects asked to remember past slights. "Their blood pressure increases, their heart rate increases, and their muscle tensions are also higher," said professor Charlotte van Oyen Witvliet(1999). This suggests their stress responses are greater during their unforgiving than forgiving conditions" (CNN medical report). Research suggests that religious belief in a concerned GOD can improve response to medical treatment for depression, a study at Rush University Medical Center, Chicago, concluded, according to the Journal of Clinical Psychology of February 24, 2010.

The claims that God lives within us are not frivolous. When God said , "Let us make man in our image," (Genesis 1:26) and proceeded to make you and me, he did not make us without equipping our bodies with markers of himself within us. Your body is the manifestation of the complex operations of the Unseen realm of God. Your body's physiological constitution is the physical representation of the Unseen Spiritual world of God . – Your brain, your heart, your lung are symbolic representation of The Trinity. The three in one body: God the Father, God the Son, God the Holy Spirit operating together as One. Not three Gods.

Is H20 any different in molecular composition when it is up there as rain cloud than it is when falling down as rain water , snow, sleet, or when it is meandering on land as brook, or a river; or land-logged as a lake or surging and falling as sea water? Is H2 O any different from water when it is evaporating as vapor or steam?

God cannot be mocked'

Your body is a complex network of nerves coming from the brain exiting through the skull. There are 12 pairs of cranial nerves attached to the brain exiting the skull and performing specific functions to keep you alive, and your body in perfect health. Obtaining optimal health requires optimal brain/nerves function. Your skull encases your brain like a crown as it sits on a throne of "24 spinal bones stacked on top of each other like ABC blocks...to allow us to bend and twist the 24 spinal bones move." (Stangherlin , 2009, *The* Chiropractic Way To Health, p.20) Your spinal cord siting inside your spine, extends from your brain to your lower back. Nerves branch off from the cord and blaze millions of trails into your body, not stopping until they end right beneath your skin. Your nervous system keeps your body running.....Restoring better brain/body communications permits a more normal expression of health," (Stangherlin, 2009) Stangherlin asserts, "Your body works together as a whole...The heart works with the lungs, the lungs work with the spleen, and the spleen works with the liver" (Stangherlin,2009)

Chapter Thirty Four
Connecting With Jehovah God

How is it that Jehovah chose 12 houses for his people of Israel? How is it that our Lord Jesus Christ chose 12 disciples, and 12 apostles for his church? How is it that we have 12 months in a year? And how is it that the nerves exiting the skull link 12 vital organs of the upper body with 12 specific functions ? God-ordained his plan and purpose, and created our body's anatomy to mimic Heaven to keep us reminded of our connectivity to Him. The saying that an apple does not fall far from the tree applies to us human beings as well. We are his apples. We cannot fall far from him. Our life and longevity are intertwined with how we maintain our connectivity with Him How well those specific 12 vital organs function, determine our quality of life . It is no coincidence that your brain crowned in your skull sits on top of your vertebral column of 24 bones like the picture we see in Revelation 4 of Worship in Heaven. Jehovah wants you to know He made you in His image. Your body is a temple of God.

Your olfactory nerves give you the power to smell things. Optic work your sight. Oculomotor nerves move your eyeball, lens and pupils. Trochlear nerves move the superior oblique muscle of your eye. Trigeminal nerves innervate your eyes, cheeks and jaw areas, and control chewing. Abducens nerves move your eye outward. Facial nerves control the muscles of your face, scalp, ears, and salivary glands; they receive taste sensation from the anterior two-thirds of your tongue. Acoustic nerves are charged with your hearing functions and maintaining your balance. Glossopharyngeal nerves take care of your taste sensation from the back of your tongue and throat .Tagus nerves innervate your chest and abdominal organs. Spinal Accessory move your head and shoulders and Hypoglossal control your tongue muscles.

Angels in Heaven have specific functions concerning you in all of your ways.

"From the throne came flashes of lightening, rumblings, and peals of thunder." Revelation 4:5 "God is Light, and there is no darkness at al in Him."(1 John 1 : 5)

Please reflect on the Scriptures cited . Compare with your body's anatomy and its physiology. Do you see how Jehovah God made your body to reflect His Kingdom ? Your brain sits on a throne of "24 spinal bones ...Read Revelation 4: 4, 5 and 10. Dr. Stangherlin (2009) notes;

> Your brain is always lit up with electrical patterns, forming, shifting....Your nerves are

your body's telephone wires. As they exit the spinal cord, they're packed into big bundles, like electrical bundles, like electrical cables. Then, almost immediately, they start branching out. As they travel farther from the spine into ever smaller threads, weaving their way through every inch of you. They are numerous that if every part of you but your nerves disappeared, your friends could still recognize you because your nerves would form a 3-D image of incredible detail. While your nerves are like telephone wires, your body's nervous system is much more complex than any telephone network.

This complex system of nerves in your body is called "the autonomic nervous system." It divides into three sides called the enteric nervous systems, sympathetic nervous system and parasympathetic nervous system. Sympathetic and Parasympathetic Nervous Systems perform functions diametrically opposite of what the other does on the same set of organs.

God equipped your sympathetic nervous system to function as your body's security service. It sets off the body's alarms in emergencies to help you identify what your body sees as a security risk. When the body's security service is on high alert, energy is directed away from digestion. There is dilation of pupils. Your heart rate increases. There's increased breathing. There's increased sweating. An increase in salivation. Scientists say that when your body is under constant volley of hormones triggered by its sympathetic nervous mechanism, you come under stress. There is an over production of stress hormones which compromises the immune system rendering your body prone to weak eye sight, bad hearing, sinus problems, impaired heart function, impaired lungs function.

The sympathetic nervous system is your biblical equivalent of human nature which the Bible says,

> "shows itself in immoral, filthy, and indecent actions; in worship of idols and witchcraft. People become enemies and they fight; they become jealous, angry, and ambitious. They separate into parties and groups. They are envious, get drunk, have orgies, and other things like these." (Galatians 5:19-21)

Your body's parasympathetic nervous system on the other hand is analogous to the Spirit of God that indwells you from the moment you became a believer and accept the Lord as your personal Savior. Your indwelling Holy Spirit is your Comforter. He is your Counselor. He is your Advocate. He is your Helper. He helps to "fill your mind with those things that are good and that deserve praise; things that are true, noble, right, pure, lovely, and honorable." (Philippians 4:8) He gives you fruit of the Spirit --love, joy, peace, patience, kindness, goodness, faithfulness, humility and self-control are gifts the Holy Spirit gives you.(Galatians 5:22-23)) He equips you with a mindset malleable for meditation and prayer because God's divine power gives you "everything you need for life and Godliness."(2 Peter 1:3)

When your parasympathetic nervous system is at work unhindered, it summons your God-nature within to release endorphins, oxytocin hormones, nitric oxide and hosts of good bacteria - your body's equivalent of angels within - to perform the activities that medical science terms, " the body's natural self-repair." But your Creator programed your body's parasympathetic nervous system to go to work only when the sympathetic nervous system is out of the way at rest, when the parasympathetic nervous system is experiencing fruit of the Spirit: love, joy ,peace, patience, kindness, faithfulness, humility and self-control, and your mind is filled with "those things that are good and that deserve praise; things that are true, noble, right, pure, lovely, and honorable " (Phil. 4:8) your body undergoes a phenomenon that Dr. Herbert Benson (1975) and his colleague researchers call "the relaxation response" which " activates the body's natural self-repair mechanisms" (Benson,1975). Without the benefits of medical sciences and technologies, David the Prophet and king prayed: "You created every part of me; you put me together in my mother's womb....When my bones were being formed, carefully put together in my mother's womb, when I was growing there in secret you knew I was there –you saw me before I was born...(Psalm 139:13-15)

When our parasympathetic nervous system is busy, our pupils contract. Energy is diverted for food digestion. Our heart rate normalizes. 'Your body's self repair system can only function when your body is in relaxation response... Positive thoughts release feelings that activate the relaxation response." (Rankin, 2013.)

Alleviation of loneliness will depend upon the fulfillment of a combination of factors involving God, community, and the individual sufferer's willingness and dedication. To Just Say Hello, will not fix it. Dr. Lissa Rankin calls her fixes "Six Stones."

They are two, says our Lord Jesus Christ : Love your God, and your neighbor as yourself! "Love the Lord your God with all your heart with all your heart, with all your soul, and with all your mind. This is the greatest and the most important commandment. The second most important is like it: 'Love your neighbor as you love yourself. The whole Law of Moses and the teachings of the prophets depend on these two commandments." Loving your neighbor and showing him or her compassion and kindness is good for your health. Love , according to the National Institutes of Health," research shows it's good for your health. Between loving partners, between parents and children, or even between close friends, physical affection can help the brain, the heart and other body systems you might never have imagined...At the center of how our bodies respond to love and affection is a hormone called oxytocin. Most of our oxytocin is made in the area of the brain called the hypothalamus. Some is released into our bloodstream, but much of its effect is thought to reside in the brain.

Oxytocin makes us feel good when we're close to family and other loved ones, including pets. It does this by acting through what scientists call the dopamine reward system. Dopamine is a brain chemical that plays a crucial part in how we perceive pleasure. Many drugs of abuse act through this system. Problems with the system can lead to serious depression and other mental illness.

Oxytocin does more than make us feel good. It lowers the levels of stress hormones in the body, reducing blood pressure, improving mood, increasing tolerance for pain and perhaps even speeding how fast wounds heal. It also seems to play an important role in our relationships. It's been linked, for example, to how much we trust others"(NIH NEWS IN HEALTH, Feb. 2007).

DRUG FREE HEALING 11 : Medical Science Supporting Scriptures

John, in the scripture states, " Those who say 'I love Jehovah God,' and hate their brothers or sisters, are liars; for those who do not love a brother or a sister whom they have seen , cannot love God whom they have not seen" (1 John 4: 20)

The Prophet Isaiah urges, "Seek the Lord while He may be found, call upon Him while He is near" (Isaiah 55:6). The LORD is Jesus, " The Way, The Truth, and The Life!" No one goes to the Father except by Him. He came that we may have life, and have it abundantly. (John 14:6, John 10:10)

Friends, 'let us rid ourselves of everything that gets in the way . And of the sin which holds on to us tightly... Let us keep our eyes fixed on Jesus tightly." (Hebrews 12:1-2) "Lift up your tired hands, then, and strengthen your trembling knees! Keep walking on straight paths, so that the lame foot may not be disabled, but instead be healed." (Hebrews 12:12-13)

Lord Jesus, let miracles happen today... to somebody reading this book. Holy Spirit , by your power, let there be transformation in the life of somebody. Please, we ask for the salvation of somebody who is lost; for restoration, healing, love, reconciliation, provision, favor. Father we thank you.

Let us pray that the Spirit of God the Father, God the Son fill you with the knowledge of his will, with all the wisdom and understanding that his Spirit gives...May you be made strong with all the strength which comes from his glorious power so that you may be able to know his mind concerning how best to campaign to alleviate loneliness , and help the nation heal the many ills and afflictions ., for the glory of God the Father God the Son God the Holy Spirit. We praise him, honor him, thank him in Jesus name. Amen .

If you are not a Believer, know that right now, the Holy Spirit is talking to you, and calling on you to come to Jesus our Savior. Ask our LORD JESUS to come into your heart. Acknowledge that you are a sinner. Confess you believe Jesus came into this world , shed his blood to wash away your sins; he died, was buried, and rose again on the third day; he ascended to Jehovah God the Father. Thank Jesus for dying for you, and saving you. Thank Jehovah God for forgiving your sins. Amen. Now, sing with me...

Jesus Is The Answer –Andre Crouch
Jesus is the answer, for the world today.
Reflections of your past,
Seem to face you every day.
But this is one thing I do know.

Jesus is the answer, for the world today.
Above Him there's no other.
Jesus is the way.
I know you've got mountains,

DRUG FREE HEALING 11 : Medical Science Supporting Scriptures

That you think you cannot climb,
I know your skies are dark,
You think the sun won't shine,
But in case you don't know,
That the word of God is true,
Everything he's promised,.

He'll Do It Again ---Shirley Caesar

**You may be down and feel like God
Has somehow forgotten
That you are faced with circumstances
You can't get through
But now it seems that there's no way out
And you're going under
God's proven time and time again
He'll take care of you**

DRUG FREE HEALING 11 : Medical Science Supporting Scriptures

DRUG FREE HEALING 11 : Medical Science Supporting Scriptures

"Come, Children, listen to me, I will teach you the fear of the LORD. Keep your tongue from evil, and your lips from speaking deceit. Depart from evil, and do good; seek peace and pursue it." (Psalm 34:11-14)

DRUG FREE HEALING 11 : Medical Science Supporting Scriptures

References

- Zondervan NIV Study Bible. Zondervan, Grand Rapids, Michigan. 1985. ISBN 0-310-92306-9
- Merrill F. Unger . Unger's Bible Dictionary. Moody Press, Chicago, Ill. 1965
- The Holy Bible,
  The Old and New Testaments with the Apocryphal/Deuterocanonical Books,
  New Revised Standard Version. American Bible Society, NY
- The Holy Bible, Revised Standard Version. A.J.Holman Company, Philadelphia
- The Holy Bible. King James Version. A.J. Hollman Company, Philadelphia
- Henry H. Halley. Halley's Bible Handbook. Zondervan Publishing House, Grand Rapids, Michigan. 1962
- The Good News Bible Today's English Version. American Bible Society, NY. 1985
- Isadore Rosenfeld, M.D, Guide To Alternative Medicine. Random House, NY 1996

DRUG FREE HEALING 11 : Medical Science Supporting Scriptures

- Miriam Polunim. Healing Foods. DK Publishing Inc. 1997
- Michael Castleman. The New Healing Herbs.
- Christopher Hobbs. Herbal Remedies For Dummies
- Isamu Sekido. Fruits, Roots And Fungi Plants We Eat. Lerner Publication Co. 1985
- Carol Ann Rinzler. Nutrition For Dummies. Wiley Publishing
- Russell Wild. The Complete Book Of Natural Medicinal And Cures. Rodale Press Inc., Emmaus, Penn.
- Penelope Ody. The Complete Medicinal And Herbal Remedies
- Lavon J. Dunne. Nutrition Almanac. McGraw-Hill Books
- Lesley Bremness. Herbs. Dorling Kindersley Books, NY.NY, 1994
- Gillian Roberts. Trees. Eyewitness Handbook, Allen J.Coombes, Dorling Kindersley, Inc, NY. 1992.
- Judith Sumner. The Natural History Of Medicinal Plants
- Anne McIntyre. The Medicinal Garden, How to Grow and Use Your Own Medicinal Herb, Henry Holt and Company, NY 1997, ISBN 0-8050-4838-3
- Bentley, Robert and Henry Trimen. Medicinal Plants. London, Churchill, 1880. WZ 295 B556m 1880
- Ken Fern

- F. Chittendon. RHS Dictionary of Plants plus Supplement. 1956 Oxford University Press 1951
- Hedrick. U. P. Sturtevant's Edible Plants of the World. Dover Publications 1972 ISBN 0-486-20459-6
- Grieve. A Modern Herbal. Penguin 1984 ISBN 0-14-046-440-9.
- Launert. E. Edible and Medicinal Plants. Hamlyn 1981 ISBN 0-600-37216-2
- Holtom. J. and Hylton. W. Complete Guide to Herbs. Rodale Press 1979 ISBN 0-87857-262-7
- Simons. New Vegetable Growers Handbook. Penguin 1977 ISBN 0-14-046-050-0
- Philbrick H. and Gregg R. B. Companion Plants. Watkins 1979
- Riotte. L. Companion Planting for Successful Gardening. Garden Way, Vermont, USA. 1978 ISBN 0-88266-064-0
- Lust. J. The Herb Book. Bantam books 1983 ISBN 0-553-23827-2
- Thompson. B. The Gardener's Assistant. Blackie and Son. 1878
- Uphof. J. C. Th. Dictionary of Economic Plants. Weinheim 1959
- Hatfield. A. W. How to Enjoy your Weeds. Frederick Muller Ltd 1977 ISBN 0-584-10141-4
- Cooper. M. and Johnson. A. Poisonous Plants in Britain and their Effects on Animals and Man. HMSO 1984 ISBN 0112425291

- Mills. S. Y. The Dictionary of Modern Herbalism. 0
- Facciola. S. Cornucopia - A Source Book of Edible Plants. Kampong Publications 1990 ISBN 0-9628087-0-9
 Huxley. A. The New RHS Dictionary of Gardening. 1992. MacMillan Press 1992 ISBN 0-333-47494-5
- Allardice.P. A - Z of Companion Planting. Cassell Publishers Ltd. 1993 ISBN 0-304-34324-2
- Duke. J. A. and Ayensu. E. S. Medicinal Plants of Ghana Reference Publications, Inc. 1985 ISBN 0-917256-20-4
- Foster. S. & Duke. J. A. A Field Guide to Medicinal Plants. Eastern and Central N. America. Houghton Mifflin Co. 1990 ISBN 0395467225
- Thomas. G. S. Perennial Garden Plants J. M. Dent & Sons, London. 1990 ISBN 0 460 86048 8
- Bown. D. Encyclopedia of Herbs and their Uses. Dorling Kindersley, London. 1995 ISBN 0-7513-020-31
Bentley, Robert and Henry Trimen. Medicinal Plants. London, Churchill, 1880. (WZ 295 B556m 1880)
-Bikai, P. M. 1991. The Cedar of Lebanon: Archaeological and Dendrochronological Perspectives. PhD Dissertation, -
 on the religious symbolism, wood anatomy, and other aspects of the biology of the cedar is found in:-
University of California, Berkeley

Index

Almond (Amygdalus communis)	208
Balm of Gilead (Cistus incanus and perhaps other species of Cistus	174
Barley (Hordeum vulgare)	216
Cinnamon(Cinnamomum aromaticum,Czeylandica) 297	
Coriander (Coriandrum sativum)	267
Cucumber (Cucumis sativo)	275
Cypress (Cupressus sempervirens)	79
Fig (Ficus carica) Common fig	76
Flax (Linum ustitatissimum)	229
Frankincense (Boswellia species)	178
Garlic (Allium sativum)	289
God Jehovah Connecting	349
Grape (Vitis vinifera) Grape	101
Gum resin (Pistacia palaestina)Gum Resin or Mastic	
Gum tragacanth (Astragalus gummifer)	
Hyssop (Hyssopus officinalis)	239
Honey	165

Leeks (Allium porrum or A. kurrat) 288
Lentils (Lens culinaris) 127
Mandrake (Mandragora autumnalis) 143
Myrrh (Commiphora gileadensis) and other species. 185
Oak (Quercus calliprinos and Q. ithaburensis) 113
Olive (Olea europaea) 90
Onion (Allium cepa) 283
Palm (Phoenix dactylifera, Serenoa repens, Saw Palmetto, Cocos Nucifera, Coconut Palm) 247
Pistachio (Pistacia Vera) 197
Resin (Boswelia Thurifera) 178
Wheat (Triticum aestivum Bread, bricks, and beer- Wheat products and T. durum) 118
Wheatgrass 118

Glossary

Active ingredients: The ingredients contained in any formula that give the desired physiological effect i.e. The components in a moisturizing cream that improves the moisture content of the skin.

Adrenal glands: Two organs situated one upon the upper end of each kidney. Stresses of modern life can exhaust the glands.

Acidophilus: A friendly bacteria found in the digestive system which combats the activities of invading micro-organisms associated with food poisoning and other infections.

AcidoAlphaHydroxyl Ceramides: Extract from sunflowers. A lipid that strengthens the skin's capacity to retain moisture, thereby supporting and sustaining skin's youthful smoothness and softness.

Acute: A short sharp crisis of rapid onset.

Adaptogen: A substance that helps the body to "adapt" to a new stress or strain by stimulating the body's own defensive mechanism.

Aetiology: A term denoting the cause or origin of a specific disease.

Agar-agar: Gelling agent made from seaweed.

Algae: A seaweed

Alginate: Gelatinous substance obtained from seaweed and used as an emulsifier and thickening agent.

Alkalis: Substances with a pH above 7. Often used as neutralizers in cosmetics and toiletries.
Alkaloids: Basic organic substances, usually vegetable in origin and having an alkaline reaction. Like alkalis they combine with acids to form salts. Some are toxic, insoluble in water.
Aloe Vera Extract: Effective healing agent and rich emollient. Used to counteract wrinkles, it is soothing and moisturizing.
Alternative: Medicines that alter the process of nutrition, restoring in some unknown way the normal functions of an organ or system.
Allergy: Hypersensitivity to a foreign protein which produces a violent reaction e.g. hayfever, asthma, irritable bowel.
Allopathy: Conventional medicine.
Amenorrhea: Suppression or normal menstrual flow during the time of life when it should occur.
Amino acids: Group of compounds containing both the carboxyl and the amino groups. They are the building blocks of proteins and are essential for the maintenance of the body.
Amphoteric: A normaliser "improve apparently contradictory symptoms".
Analgesics: Pain relievers,
Anodynes: Herbs taken orally for relief of mild pain
Anaphrodisiac: A herb that reduces excess sexual desire.

Antacids: Remedies that correct effects of stomach acid and relieve indigestion.
Antigens: substances, usually harmful, that when entering the body stimulate the immune system to produce antibodies.
Antibacterial: Any agent or process that inhibits the growth and reproduction of bacteria.
Antibody: A substance prepared in the body for the purpose of withstanding infection by viruses, bacteria and other organisms.
Anti-catarrhals: Agents that reduce the production of mucus.
Antifungals: Herbs that destroy fungi as in the treatment of thrush, candida etc.
Antihistamines: Agents that arrest production of histamine and which are useful in allergic conditions.
Annatto: A natural colorant derived from the seeds of a tropical tree.
Anthelmintics: Anti parasite.
Anthoposophical medicine: Holistic medicine based on the work of Dr Rudolf Steiner.
Antilithics: Agents used for elimination or dissolution of stone or gravel in bladder or kidney problems.
Anti-neoplastics: Herbs that prevent formation or destroy tumor cells
Anti-pruritics: Agents to relieve intense itching.
Anti-spasmodics: Agents for relief of muscular cramps, spasm or mild pain.

Anti-tussives: Herbs that reduce cough severity, ease expectoration and clear the lungs.
Antioxidants: Substances that prevent the formation of free radicals which cause the oxidative deterioration that causes rancidity in oils or fats and also premature ageing. Natural sources include vitamins A, C and E.
Aperient: Laxative
Aqueous coating: A natural water and vegetable cellulose coating which can be used as a coating to enhance tablet disintegration and dissolution.
Ascorbic acid: The chemical name for vitamin c.
Astringents: Products that cause a tightening and contractions of the skin tissues, generally used to tone skin and close pores. Can also arrest heavy bleeding.
Barrier cream: Cream that provides a protective coating when applied to the skin e.g. hands and face.
Beeswax: A natural emulsifier and thickener.
Beta Carotene: An abundant source of Vitamin A with rich anti-oxidant properties. It is necessary for tissue repair and maintenance and accelerates the formation of healthy new skin cells. Vitamin A deters excess dryness.
Bisobolol: Main active ingredient in chamomile which has excellent skin healing properties.
Bitters: Stimulate the autonomic nervous system. Bitters increase appetite, assist assimilation.

Botanical Extract: An extract of herbs and plants. The extracting solvent can be water, oil, alcohol or any synthetic solvent such as propylene glycol.

Bronchodilators: herbs that expand the clear space within the bronchial tubes, opening up airways and relieving obstruction.

Candida albicans: A yeast that causes thrush and in more severe cases, symptoms can affect the whole body.

Capricin: A caprylic acid formulation that facilitates absorption of calcium and magnesium.

Caramel: Coloring agent derived from liquid corn syrup.

Carcinogens: Substances that bring about a malignant change in body cells.

Carmine: Natural red pigment obtained from cochineal.

Carminatives: Anti-flatulents, aromatic herbs used to expel gas from the stomach and intestines.

Catabolism: An aspect of metabolism which is concerned with the breaking down of complex substances to simpler ones, with the release of energy.

Cetyl Alcohol: Derived from coconut and palm oils. This is not a drying alcohol. Used as an emollient and to protect skin from moisture loss.

Chlorophyll: stored energy of the sun. Green coloring matter of plants.

Cholagogues: A group of agents which increases the secretion of bile and its expulsion from the gall bladder.
Choleretic: An agent which reduces cholesterol levels by excreting cholesterol.
Citric Acid: Derived from citrus fruit. A natural preservative that helps to adjust the pH of cosmetic products.
Clay: Deep-cleansing and highly absorbent. Bentonite and green clay are two types of natural clay.
Compresses: External applications to soften tissue, allay inflammation or alleviate pain.
Contra-indicated: Not indicated, against medical advice, unsuitable for use.
Cornstarch: Used as a safe base for our eye shadows, blushers and loose powders.
Coumarins: Powerful anti-coagulant plant chemicals. Used to prevent blood clotting.
Counter-irritant: An agent which produces vaso-dilation of peripheral blood vessels by stimulating nerve-endings of the skin to generate irritation intended to relieve deep-seated pain.
Cramp: Sustained contraction of a muscle.
Decoction: A preparation obtained by bringing to the boil and simmering dense herbal materials i.e. bark, root and woody parts for a plant to extract active constituents.
Decongestant: Herb which is used to loosen mucus within bronchi and lungs.

Demulcent: Anti-irritant. A herb rich in mucilage that is soothing, bland, offering protection to inflamed or irritable mucous surfaces.
Depurative: Blood purifier. Alterative.
Detoxifiers: Plant medicines that aid removal of a poison or poisonous effect, reducing toxic properties.
Diaphoretics: Herbs that induce increased perspiration.
Diuretics: Agents that increase the flow of urine from the kidneys and so excrete excess fluid from the body.
Douche: A term used to describe the cleansing of certain parts of the body eg. Washing wounds and ulcers, eye douches etc.
Eliminative: A herb to disperse and promote excretion from the body.
Emetic: A herb to induce vomiting. Given to expel poisons.
Emmenagogues: Plant substances which initiate and promote the menstrual flow.
Emollient: Any substance that prevents water loss from the skin. Most natural oils. perform this function.
Emulsifier: A substance that holds oil in water or water in oil. They are necessary in the manufacture of cream and lotions.
Emulsion: A mixture of two incompatible substances. Most creams on the cosmetic market are emulsions.
Enzyme: A biological catalyst that acts to speed up chemical reactions. Digestive enzymes are necessary

for the breakdown of proteins, carbohydrates and fats i.e. pepsin.
Enuresis: Bed wetting.
Essential Fatty Acids: A fatty acid that must be supplied in the diet as the body cannot produce it itself.
Expectorants: Herbs that increase bronchial mucous secretion by promoting liquefaction of sticky mucous and its expulsion from the body.
Fatty Acid: A monobasic acid containing only the chemicals carbon, hydrogen and oxygen. Found in vegetable and animal fats, they are important for maintaining a healthy skin and are excellent emollients.
Febrifuge: Anti-fever
Fixed Oil: A fixed oil is chemically the same as a fat, but is generally liquid i.e. Almond oil, grapeseed oil.
Flavonoids: Natural chemicals that prevent the deposit of fatty material in blood vessels.
Flaxseed Oil: Rich source of omega 3 essential fatty acids. (Also known as Linseed Oil)
Fructose: A natural sugar found in honey and fruits.
Fumigant: Herb, usually a gum, which when burnt releases mixed gases into the atmosphere to cleanse against air borne infection e.g. myrrh or frankincense.
Galactagogue: Herb to increase flow of breast milk in nursing mothers.
Glycerin (vegetable): A humectant and emollient, it absorbs moisture from the air, thereby keeping moisture in your skin.

Glycoside: An organic substance which may be broken into two parts, one of which is always sugar.
Grain Alcohol: A natural solvent that evaporates easily.
Green Tea Extract: Works towards lightening the skin by actively slowing the transport of melanin to the skin's surface. Has well known antioxidant qualities.
Guar Gum: A fiber derived from the guar plant and used as a binder in tablet manufacturing.
Haemostatics: Agents that arrest bleeding.
Hepatic: A herb that assists the liver in its function and promotes the flow of bile.
Histamine: A chemical released via the body's immune system in response to allergens.
Hypoallergenic: In the strictest sense means without fragrance, but more broadly refers to products that are unlikely to cause skin irritation.
Hyaluronic Acid: Derived from yeast cells, it is extremely hydroscopic. Binds water in the interstitial spaces between skin cells, forming a gel-like substance which holds the cells together.
Hydrogenated Palm Kernel Oil: Source of essential fatty acids.
Infusion: The liquid resulting from making a herbal tea.
Iron Oxides: Natural mineral derived color pigments.
Kaolin: Clay used to absorb oils.

Laxative: Agent used for persistent constipation to help expel faecal matter from the bowel.

Lecithin: Natural antioxidant and emollient. High in essential fatty acids. A stabilizer and emulsifier from Soya beans, corn, peanuts and egg-yolk. Cholesterol reducer.

Lymph: A straw colored fluid which circulates many tissues of the body and serves to lubricate and cleanse them.

Magnesium Carbonate: Mineral derived from dolomite, it is used in our face powders to achieve the correct shade or tone.

Mannitol: A natural sugar substitute derived from the manna plant and seaweed.

Menorrhagia: Abnormally heavy menstrual bleeding, more than normal flow and longer lasting.

Menthol: Nature constituent of peppermint oil. Used for its antiseptic properties.

Metabolism: The reactions involved in the building up and decomposition of chemical substances in living organisms.

Metrorrhagia: Bleeding from the womb between periods.

Mineral Salts: Used for color pigments in our temporary hair color.

Mucilage: A slimy product formed by the addition of gum to water. Used internally and externally to soothe irritated and inflamed membranes and surfaces.

Mucolytics: Agents that disperse or dissolve mucus.
Natural glycerine: Used to stabilize and disperse liquid nutrients inside a capsule. A clear colorless syrupy liquid with a sweet taste derived from natural fats and oil.
Nerve restoratives: Herbs used to provide support and restoration of the nervous system caused by stress, disease or faulty nutrition.
Nutrient: A non-irritating, easily digested agent which provides body nourishment and stimulates metabolic processes.
Orexigenic: A herb which increases or stimulates the appetite.
Oxytocic: A herb which hastens the process of childbirth by initiating contraction of the uterine muscle.
Parabens (parahydroxybenzoic acid esters): A family of neutral, broad-spectrum antibacterials which have been used extensively for many years in the food, cosmetic and pharmaceutical industries as mild preservatives and have not been tested on animals for a long time. They are found in nature, but the ones used in cosmetics are synthetically produced. They have a long history of relatively safe use. Like all synthetic components they are used minimally and only when necessary. Effective levels are 0.1 - 0.3% concentration in the overall product.
Peripheral: Refers to the outermost parts of the body.

Poultice: Poultices are packs of powders, dried or fresh herbs, enclosed in a muslin bag or wrapped in folds of a flannel or linen and soaked in boiling water, then applied to the affected area of the body.

Prostaglandins: Hormone like messengers in the body responsible for the control of important body functions.

Proteinuria: Presence of albumin in the urine.

Pruritus: Itching.

Purgative: An agent that encourages evacuation of matter from the bowel.

Rice Bran Wax: Derived from rice bran, used as emollient and to protect skin from moisture loss.

Reflux: A backward flow of food to the mouth from the gullet or stomach.

Refrigerant: A cooling preparation taken orally or applied externally.

Resin: A thick-solid, insoluble in water but soluble in alcohol, exude from trees or plants which are used as antiseptics.

Rubefacient: External use. An agent to draw a rich blood supply to the skin, increasing heat to the tissues to aid the body in absorption of properties from creams, lotions etc.

Rose Essential Oil: Soothing, harmonizing effect on the skin. Considered the 'queen' of all essential oils, its gentle yet powerful nature has the ability to help repair broken capillaries.

Salicylates: Salts of salicylic acid sometimes used in rheumatism, gout and acid conditions.
Saponins: Constituents of some plants that produce soap like frothing effect when agitated in water.
Sedatives: Herbs that relax the central nervous system.
Seasalt Minerals: Thickener and disinfectant in shampoos.
Sesame Oil: Rich emollient properties and provides natural sun protection.
Sialagogue: Herbs that increase production of saliva and assist digestion of starches.
Silica (hydrated): A purified mineral, used as an anti-caking agent in the production of vitamin tablets.
Sodium Laureth Sulfate: Used as a naturally derived surfactant from coconut oil to make hair care and bath care products foam.
Sorbitol: Gives a velvety feel to the skin. Derived from cherries, plums, pears, apples and seaweed.
Spasmolytic: Another name for anti-spasmodic.
Stimulants: Herbs that spur the circulation, increase energy and physical function.
Styptic: A substance that stops bleeding usually by contracting the tissue.
Sudorifics: Similar to diaphoretics but are used to stimulate more profuse abundant sweating.
Systemic: Referring to the whole of the body.

Tannins: Present in tea and coffee and many herbs. Coagulate protein and inhibit the laying down of fatty deposits. Astringent.

Urinary antiseptic: A germicidal action of a herb destructive to harmful bacteria in the urine when excreted from the body via the kidneys, bladder and ureters.

Urinary demulcent: A soothing anti-irritant used for the protection of sensitive surfaces of the kidney tubules and ureters against friction, irritation.

Urinary haemostatics: Urinary astringents that arrest bleeding from the kidneys.

Vasoconstrictors: Agents that constrict blood vessels causing an increase in blood pressure.

Vasodilators: Herbs that promote dilation of the blood vessels causing a reduction of blood pressure.

Vegetable cellulose: Substance derived from various plant fibers, used as filler, and disintegrant in the production of tablets.

Vermifuge: A substance that expels or destroys intestinal worms.

Vesicant: A blistering agent.

Vitamin A: Potent anti-oxidant, used in combination with vitamins E and C as a natural preservative. Necessary for tissue repair and maintenance and accelerates the formation of healthy new skin cells. It benefits the treatment of skin disorders and oxidant, used as a natural preservative. Anti-inflammatory properties, aids in healing.

Vitamin E: A powerful natural anti-oxidant, used in combination with vitamins A and C as a natural preservative. It slows signs of aging and the degeneration of skin cells.

Vulnerary: A plant whose external application has a cleansing and healing effect on open wounds, cuts and ulcers by promoting cell repair.

Wheatgerm Oil: Rich in vitamin E, penetrates well to prevent loss of moisture and benefit cells.

Zinc Oxide: A chemical compound, ZnO, which is nearly insoluble in water but soluble in acids or alkalis. It occurs as white hexagonal crystals or a white powder commonly known as zinc white. Zinc white is used as a pigment in paints; less opaque than lithopone, it remains white when exposed to hydrogen sulfide or ultraviolet light. It is also used as filler for rubber goods and in coatings for paper. Because it absorbs ultraviolet light, zinc oxide can be used in ointments, creams, and lotions to protect against sunburn.

DRUG FREE HEALING 11 : Medical Science Supporting Scriptures

NOTES

DRUG FREE HEALING 11 : Medical Science Supporting Scriptures

DRUG FREE HEALING 11 : Medical Science Supporting Scriptures

DRUG FREE HEALING 11 : Medical Science Supporting Scriptures

DRUG FREE HEALING 11 : Medical Science Supporting Scriptures

DRUG FREE HEALING 11 : Medical Science Supporting Scriptures

DRUG FREE HEALING 11 : Medical Science Supporting Scriptures

DRUG FREE HEALING 11 : Medical Science Supporting Scriptures

DRUG FREE HEALING 11 : Medical Science Supporting Scriptures

DRUG FREE HEALING 11 : Medical Science Supporting Scriptures

DRUG FREE HEALING 11 : Medical Science Supporting Scriptures

DRUG FREE HEALING 11 : Medical Science Supporting Scriptures

DRUG FREE HEALING 11 : Medical Science Supporting Scriptures

DRUG FREE HEALING 11 : Medical Science Supporting Scriptures

DRUG FREE HEALING 11 : Medical Science Supporting Scriptures

DRUG FREE HEALING 11 : Medical Science Supporting Scriptures

DRUG FREE HEALING 11 : Medical Science Supporting Scriptures

DRUG FREE HEALING 11 : Medical Science Supporting Scriptures

DRUG FREE HEALING 11 : Medical Science Supporting Scriptures

DRUG FREE HEALING 11 : Medical Science Supporting Scriptures

DRUG FREE HEALING 11 : Medical Science Supporting Scriptures

DRUG FREE HEALING 11 : Medical Science Supporting Scriptures

DRUG FREE HEALING 11 : Medical Science Supporting Scriptures

DRUG FREE HEALING 11 : Medical Science Supporting Scriptures

DRUG FREE HEALING 11 : Medical Science Supporting Scriptures

DRUG FREE HEALING 11 : Medical Science Supporting Scriptures

www.ingramcontent.com/pod-product-compliance
Lightning Source LLC
Chambersburg PA
CBHW020940230426
43666CB00005B/102